W9-AZZ-769

The
Greatest
Romance Stories
Ever Told

The Greatest Romance Stories Ever Told

Seventeen Unforgettable Love Stories

EDITED AND WITH AN INTRODUCTION BY
NANCY BUTLER

THE LYONS PRESS
Guilford, Connecticut
An imprint of The Globe Pequot Press

Contents

Introduction
Why Romance?

In spite of continual attacks from stuffy highbrow critics, the romance publishing industry in America is flourishing to the tune of over a billion dollars in sales each year. Currently, mass-market romances outsell all other genres put together, including westerns, mysteries, and science fiction. So what is the allure that makes love stories so compelling to the reading public? Is it the escapist desire for a happy ending as so many critics accuse? Not all romances end smoothly . . . so perhaps it is rather the exploration of love's ability to elevate us above the mundane that draws readers in and keeps them turning the pages.

True romantic fiction began evolving in the late eighteenth century, when an increasing leisure class demanded distraction at home. Writers, both men and women, turned their pens to love stories (yes, even then the critics gave a thumbs down) and a new type of popular novel was born. The nineteenth century saw the legitimizing of romantic literature, with such weighty advocates as Walter Scott, Alexandre Dumas, Colette, the Brontë sisters, Jane Austen, and Gustave Flaubert. The early twentieth century gave us a mighty romance milestone, *Gone with the Wind*, as well as memorable romances by Daphne du Maurier, Anya Seton, Rafael Sabatini, and James Hilton. More recently, a whole host of modern authors keep the romance biz booming.

While it might seem to require a full-length book to properly do justice to all the entanglements of love, a clever author can encapsulate the experience in a few thousand words. And so the romantic short story grew in popularity along with its longer, more fleshed-out sister. During the past century, magazine stories featuring romance became a mainstay of American life. Even today, romance anthologies virtually fly off the shelves.

In this collection, I have tried to represent a number of universal romance themes or conflicts: first loves, star-crossed lovers and those who fear love has eluded them, estranged spouses, and intrusive parents. The authors range from Nobel Prize winners and lauded playwrights to folklorists and authors who wrote primarily for magazines. In addition to a novella that went Hollywood, I have included a broad parody, several fairy tales and fantasies, and even a few heartwrenchers. The beauty of a romance is that even when there is not a happy ending, we come away with an enduring reassurance that love can be the greatest journey of the human heart.

Nancy Butler
September 2004

The
Greatest
Romance Stories
Ever Told

After the Theater

BY ANTON CHEKHOV

A h, young love . . . so giddy, so full of rapture, so prone to monumental disappointment. Anton Chekhov, Russia's noted playwright and man of letters, portrays a heroine torn between two objects of adolescent infatuation. As she vacillates charmingly from one to the other, the author perfectly captures the perplexities of first love: the flights of emotion, the heady expectations, and the depths of uncertainty. His heroine is skittish and willful but the reader is sure that, inevitably, she is capable of seizing great joy.

★   ★   ★   ★   ★

Nadya Zelenin had just come back with her mamma from the theatre where she had seen a performance of "Yevgeny Onyegin." As soon as she reached her own room she threw off her dress, let down her hair, and in her petticoat and white dressing-jacket hastily sat down to the table to write a letter like Tatyana's.

"I love you," she wrote, "but you do not love me, do not love me!"

She wrote it and laughed.

She was only sixteen and did not yet love anyone. She knew that an officer called Gorny and a student called Gruzdev loved her, but now after the opera she wanted to be doubtful of their love. To be unloved and unhappy—how interesting that was. There is something beautiful, touching, and poetical about it when one loves and the other is indifferent. Onyegin was interesting because he was not in love at all, and Tatyana was fascinating because she was so much in love; but if they had been equally in love with each other and had been happy, they would perhaps have seemed dull.

"Leave off declaring that you love me," Nadya went on writing, thinking of Gorny. "I cannot believe it. You are very clever, cultivated, serious, you have immense talent, and perhaps a brilliant future awaits you, while I am an uninteresting girl of no importance, and you know very well that I should be only a hindrance in your life. It is true that you were attracted by me and thought you had found your ideal in me, but that was a mistake, and now you are asking yourself in despair: 'Why did I meet that girl?' And only your goodness of heart prevents you from owning it to yourself. . . ."

Nadya felt sorry for herself, she began to cry, and went on:

"It is hard for me to leave my mother and my brother, or I should take a nun's veil and go whither chance may lead me. And you would be left free and would love another. Oh, if I were dead!"

She could not make out what she had written through her tears; little rainbows were quivering on the table, on the floor, on the ceiling, as though she were looking through a prism. She could not write, she sank back in her easy-chair and fell to thinking of Gorny.

My God! how interesting, how fascinating men were! Nadya recalled the fine expression, ingratiating, guilty, and soft, which came into the officer's face when one argued about music with him, and the effort he made to prevent his voice from betraying his passion. In a society where cold haughtiness and indifference are regarded as signs of good breeding and gentlemanly bearing, one must conceal one's passions. And he did try to conceal them, but he did not succeed, and everyone knew very well that he had a passionate love of music. The endless discussions about music and the bold criticisms of people who knew nothing about it kept him always on the strain; he was frightened, timid, and silent. He played the piano magnificently, like a professional pianist, and if he had not been in the army he would certainly have been a famous musician. The tears on her eyes dried. Nadya remembered that Gorny had declared his love at a Symphony concert, and again downstairs by the hatstand where there was a tremendous draught blowing in all directions.

"I am very glad that you have at last made the acquaintance of Gruzdev, our student friend," she went on writing. "He is a very clever man, and you will be sure to like him. He came to see us yesterday and stayed till two o'clock. We were all delighted with him, and I regretted that you had not come. He said a great deal that was remarkable."

Nadya laid her arms on the table and leaned her head on them, and her hair covered the letter. She recalled that the student, too, loved her, and that he had as much right to a letter from her as Gorny. Wouldn't it be better after all to write to Gruzdev? There was a stir of joy in her bosom for no reason whatever; at first the joy was small, and rolled in her bosom like an india-rubber ball; then it became more massive, bigger, and rushed like a wave. Nadya forgot Gorny and Gruzdev; her thoughts were in a tangle and her joy grew and grew; from her bosom it passed into her arms and legs, and it seemed as though a light, cool breeze were breathing on her head and ruffling her hair. Her shoulders quivered with subdued laughter, the table and the lamp chimney shook, too, and tears from her eyes splashed on the letter. She could not stop laughing, and to prove to herself that she was not laughing about nothing she made haste to think of something funny.

"What a funny poodle," she said, feeling as though she would choke with laughter. "What a funny poodle!"

She thought how, after tea the evening before, Gruzdev had played with Maxim the poodle, and afterwards had told them about a very intelligent poodle who had run after a crow in the yard, and the crow had looked round at him and said: "Oh, you scamp!"

The poodle, not knowing he had to do with a learned crow, was fearfully confused and retreated in perplexity, then began barking. . . .

"No, I had better love Gruzdev," Nadya decided, and she tore up the letter to Gorny.

She fell to thinking of the student, of his love, of her love; but the thoughts in her head insisted on flowing in all directions, and she thought about everything—about her mother, about the street, about the pencil, about the piano. . . . She thought of them joyfully, and felt that everything was good, splendid, and her joy told her that this was not all, that in a little while it would be better still. Soon it would be spring, summer, going with her mother to Gorbiki. Gorny would come for his furlough, would walk about the garden with her and make love to her. Gruzdev would come too. He would play croquet and skittles with her, and would tell her wonderful things. She had a passionate longing for the garden, the darkness, the pure sky, the stars. Again her shoulders shook with laughter, and it seemed to her that there was a scent of wormwood in the room and that a twig was tapping at the window.

She went to her bed, sat down, and not knowing what to do with the immense joy which filled her with yearning, she looked at the holy image hanging at the back of her bed, and said:

"Oh, Lord God! Oh, Lord God!"

The Duel

BY GEORGETTE HEYER

Britain's Georgette Heyer was well known for her charming Regency-set comedies of manners, a body of work that gave rise in the 1970s to a whole sub-genre of romance writing. The lords and ladies of early nineteenth-century England never had so adroit an interpreter. Heyer also produced a number of contemporary mysteries and several medieval histories, but it is in her short stories that her flair for characterization and her love of mining humor from the awkward situation come to life. In this story, the reader immediately suspects a critical secret about the hero that the heroine does not know, creating a delicious sense of anticipation.

★   ★   ★   ★   ★

1

IT AMUSED HIM, entering his house so unexpectedly early in the evening, to know that he had disconcerted Criddon, his porter. He suspected Criddon of having slipped out to dally with a serving-maid at the top of some area steps. The rogue was out of breath, as though, having perceived his master sauntering up the flag-way in the light of the oil street lamps, he had scurried back into the house more swiftly than befitted a man of his bulk. As he took the silk-lined cloak, the curly-brimmed beaver, and the tall cane, he wore a faint air of injury. No doubt he felt ill-used because his master, leaving the ball hours before his carriage had been ordered to call for him, had chosen to walk home, instead of looking in at Watier's, according to his more usual custom.

He told Criddon he might go to bed, and strolled to the side table, where a letter, delivered during the evening, awaited him. As he broke the wafer and spread open the sheet, his butler came up from the nether regions, but he waved him away, as irritated by his presence as he would have been angered by his absence. He threw the letter aside and opened the door into the dining-room. The room was in darkness, a circumstance which almost caused him to summon back the butler. It was his pleasure that lights should burn in every room which he might conceivably wish to enter in his great house, and well did his servants know it. But he did not call to Radstock, for his nostrils had caught the acrid smell of candles newly blown out, and he was indefinably aware that he was not alone in the room. Some of the boredom left his face: a turn-up with a housebreaker might relieve the monotony of his existence, and would certainly surprise the housebreaker, who would no doubt consider a seeming dandy in satin knee-breeches and a long-tailed coat easy game. He stepped back into the hall and picked up the heavy chandelier from the side table there. Carrying this into the dining-room, he stood for a moment on the threshold, looking keenly round. The flames of half a dozen candles flickered, and showed him only the furniture, and the wavering shadows it threw. He glanced towards the windows and it seemed to him that one of the brocade curtains bulged slightly. He set the chandelier down, trod silently to the window, and flung the curtains back.

As he did so, he sprang out of range, and brought his hands up in two purposeful fists. They dropped to his sides. No housebreaker met his astonished gaze, but a girl, shrinking back against the window, the hood of her cloak fallen away from a tangle of silken curls, her frightened face, in which two dark eyes dilated, upturned to his.

For a moment he wondered if Criddon had hidden his doxy in the dining-room; then his critical glance informed him that the girl's cloak was of velvet, and her gown of sprigged muslin the demure but expensive raiment of the débutante. His astonishment grew. He was so eligible a bachelor that he was accustomed to being pursued, and could recognize and evade every snare set in his path. But this seemed to go beyond all bounds. Anger came into his eyes; he thought he must have been mistaken in his assessment of the girl's quality, and that a fair Cyprian had invaded his house.

Then she spoke, and her words confirmed him in his first impression. 'Oh, I *beg* your pardon! P-pray forgive me, sir!' she said, in a pretty, conscience-stricken voice.

Anger gave way to amusement. 'What, ma'am, may I ask, are you doing in my house?' he demanded.

She hung her head. 'Indeed, you must think it most odd in me!'

'I do.'

'The door was open, so—so I ran in,' she explained. 'You see, there—there was a man following me!'

'If you must walk through the streets of London at this hour, I should hope your footman was following you!'

'Oh no! No one knows I am not in my bed! My mission is most secret! And I never meant to walk, but the hackney carried me to the wrong house—at least, I fear I gave the coachman the wrong direction, and he had driven away before I was made aware of my mistake. The servant told me that it was only a step, so I thought I might walk, only there was an *odious* man—! I ran as fast as I could into this street, and—and your door stood open. Indeed, I meant only to hide in the hall until that creature was gone, but then your porter came in, and I was obliged to run into this room, because how could I explain? When I told that other servant where I wished to go, he—he—' She broke off, lifting her hand to a burning cheek. 'And then you came in, so I slipped behind the curtain.'

It occurred to him, while she offered this explanation of her presence in his house, that although she was agitated she was not at all shy, and seemed not to be much afraid of him. He said: 'You intrigue me greatly. Where, in fact, *do* you wish to go?'

'I wish—I have a particular desire—to go to Lord Rotherfield's house,' she replied.

The amusement left his face. He looked frowningly at her, a hint of contempt in his rather hard eyes. He said in a dry tone: 'No doubt to call upon his lordship?'

She put up her chin. 'If you will be so obliging as to direct me to Lord Rotherfield's house, which I believe to be in this street, sir, I need no longer trespass upon your hospitality!'

'It is the last house in London to which I would direct you. I will rather escort you back to your own house, wherever that may be.'

'No, no, I must see Lord Rotherfield!' she cried.

'He is not a proper person for you to visit, my good girl. More-over, it is unlikely that you would find him at home at this hour.'

'Then I must wait for him,' she declared. 'I am persuaded he will not be so very late tonight, for he is going to fight a duel in the morning!'

He stared at her, his eyes narrowed. 'Indeed?'

'Yes!—with my brother!' she said, a catch in her voice. 'I must —I *must* prevent him!'

'Is it possible,' he demanded, 'that you imagine you can per-suade Rotherfield to draw back from an engagement? You do not know him! Who sent you on this fantastic errand? Who can have exposed you to such a risk?'

'Oh, no one, no one! I discovered what Charlie meant to do by the luckiest accident, and surely Lord Rotherfield cannot be so *very* bad? I know he is said to be heartless and excessively dangerous, but he cannot be such a monster as to shoot poor Charlie when I have explained to him how young Charlie is, and how it would utterly prostrate Mama, who is an invalid, and suffers from the most shocking palpitations!'

He moved away from the window, and pulled a chair out from the table. 'Come and sit down!' he said curtly.

'But, sir—'

'Do as I bid you!'

She came reluctantly to the chair and sat down on the edge of it, looking up at him in a little trepidation.

He drew his snuff-box from his pocket and flicked it open. 'You, I apprehend, are Miss Saltwood,' he stated.

'Well, I am Dorothea Saltwood,' she amended. 'My sister Au-gusta is Miss Saltwood, because no one has offered for her yet. And that is why I am not yet out, though I am turned nineteen! But how did you know my name is Saltwood?'

He raised a pinch of snuff to one nostril. 'I was present, ma'am, when your brother insulted Rotherfield.'

She seemed grieved. 'At that horrid gaming-hall?'

'On the contrary! At an exclusive club, to which few of us, I fancy, know how Lord Saltwood gained admission.'

She flushed. 'He prevailed upon that stupid creature, Torryburn, to take him there. I dare say he should not have done so, but Lord Rotherfield need not have given him *such* a set-down! You will own it was the unkindest thing!'

'Certainly,' he said. 'Pray do not think that I have the smallest desire to defend Rotherfield! But in justice to his lordship I must tell you that your brother offered him an insupportable insult. His lordship has many faults—indeed, I sometimes think I dislike him more than anyone of my acquaintance! —but I assure you that in all matters of play he is scrupulous. Forgive me if I venture to suggest, ma'am, that your brother will be the better for a sharp lesson, to teach him, in future, not to accuse a gentleman of using loaded dice!'

'Indeed, I know it was very bad, but if he meets Lord Rotherfield he won't have a future!'

'This is high Cheltenham tragedy with a vengeance!' he replied, amused. 'Rotherfield will scarcely proceed to such extremes as you dread, my dear child!'

'They say he never misses!' she uttered, her cheeks blanched.

'Then he will hit Saltwood precisely where he means to.'

'They must not, and they *shall* not meet!' she said earnestly. 'I am persuaded that if I can only tell Lord Rotherfield how it is with Charlie, he cannot be so cruel as to persist in this affair!'

'You would be better advised to prevail upon your brother to apologize for his conduct.'

'Yes,' she agreed mournfully. 'That is what Bernard said, but the thing is that Lord Rotherfield is so deadly a shot that Charlie would never, never do that, because everyone would think he was afraid to meet him!'

'And who, may I ask, is Bernard?'

'Mr. Wadworth. We have known him for ever, and he is one of Charlie's seconds. It was he who told me about it. I made him do so. I promised I would not disclose to Charlie that he had breathed a word to me, so what can I do but throw myself upon Lord Rotherfield's mercy?'

'Lord Rotherfield, as you are aware, has no mercy. You would, moreover, be doing Mr. Wadworth a vast disservice if you were to betray to anyone the impropriety of his conduct in speaking one word to you on this subject.'

'Oh, dear, I would not injure him for the world, poor Bernard! But I have told *you* already, sir!'

'Your confidence is quite safe in my keeping.'

She smiled engagingly up at him. 'Indeed, I know it must be! You are so very kind! But I am determined to see Lord Rotherfield.'

'And I am determined that you shall return to your home. Rotherfield's is no house for you to visit in this style. Good God, if it should become known that you had done so—!'

She got up, clasping her hands. 'Yes, but it is *desperate*! If anything were to happen to Charlie, it would kill Mama! I assure you, it is of no consequence what becomes of me! Augusta says I am bound to ruin myself, because I have no notion how I should go on, so I might as well ruin myself now as later, don't you think?'

'I do not!' he replied, laughing. 'Oh, don't look so much distressed, you absurd child! Will you trust me to see that no harm comes to your tiresome brother?'

She stared at him, sudden hope in her eyes. 'You, sir? Oh, will *you* see Lord Rotherfield, and explain to him that it was only that poor Charlie has been so sadly indulged, because my father died when he was a little boy, and Mama would not let him go to school, or permit anyone to cross him, and he has only just come to town, and he does not know how to guard his temper, or—'

He interrupted this tumbled speech, possessing himself of one agitated little hand, and kissing it lightly. 'Rest assured I will not allow Lord Rotherfield to hurt poor Charlie at all!'

'Will he listen to you?' she asked doubtfully. 'Augusta's particular friend, Miss Stanstead, says he is a very proud, disagreeable man, and cares nothing for anyone's opinion.'

'Very true, but I have it in my power to compel him to do what I wish. You may safely trust in me.'

She heaved a relieved sigh, and again the enchanting smile trembled on her lips. 'Oh yes! I do, sir! It is the oddest thing, for, to own the truth, I was a little afraid when you pulled back the curtain. You looked at me in *such* a way! But that was quite my own fault, and I saw

in a trice that there was not the smallest need for me to be afraid. You
are so very kind! I don't know how I may thank you.'

'Forget that I looked at you in *such* a way, and I shall be satisfied.
I am going to take you home now. I think you said that no one knew
you had left the house. Have you the means to enter it again without
being seen by the servants?' She nodded, a gleam of mischief in her big
eyes. The amusement in his deepened. 'Abominable girl! Lady Saltwood
has my sincere sympathy!'

'I know I have behaved shockingly,' she said contritely. 'But
what was I to do? And you must own that it has come about for the
best, sir! For I *have* saved Charlie, and I know you will never tell anyone
what a scrape I have been in. I hope—I hope you don't truthfully think
me abominable?'

'If I were to tell you what I truthfully think, *I* should be abominable. Come! I must convey you home, my little one.'

2

Never did a young gentleman embarking on his first affair of
honour receive less encouragement from his seconds than Lord Saltwood received from Sir Francis Upchurch and Mr. Wadworth. Sir Francis, being inarticulate, did little more than shake his head, but Mr.
Wadworth, presuming upon an acquaintance with his principal which
dated from the cradle, did not hesitate to speak his mind. 'Made a
dashed cake of yourself!' he said.

'Worse!' said Sir Francis, contributing his mite.

'Much worse!' corroborated Mr. Wadworth. 'Devilish bad ton,
Charlie! You were foxed, of course.'

'I wasn't. At least, not very much.'

'Drunk as a wheelbarrow. I don't say you showed it, but you
must have been!'

'Stands to reason!' said Sir Francis.

'No right to bully Torryburn into taking you to the Corinthian
Club in the first place. Above your touch, my boy! Told you so, when
you asked me to take you. No right to have stayed there after Rotherfield gave you that set-down.'

Lord Saltwood ground his teeth. 'He need not have said *that!*'

'No, I dare say he need not. Got a nasty tongue. But that don't signify. You'd no right to accuse him of using Fulhams!'

Sir Francis shuddered, and closed his eyes for an anguished moment.

'Ought to have begged his pardon then and there,' pursued Mr. Wadworth relentlessly. 'Instead of that, dashed well forced a quarrel on him!'

'If he hadn't told a waiter—a *waiter*! —to show me out—!'

'Ought to have called for the porter,' agreed Sir Francis. He then perceived that this amiable response had failed to please his fiery young friend, and begged pardon. A powerful thought assailed him. He turned his eyes towards Mr. Wadworth, and said suddenly: 'You know what, Bernie? He shouldn't have accepted Charlie's challenge. Must know he ain't been on the town above six months!'

'The point is he *did* accept it,' said Mr. Wadworth. 'But it ain't too late. Charlie dashed well ought to apologize.'

'I *will* not!' said Lord Saltwood tensely.

'You were in the wrong,' insisted Mr. Wadworth.

'I know it, and I mean to fire in the air. That will show that I acknowledge my fault, but was not afraid to meet Rotherfield!'

This noble utterance caused Sir Francis to drop with a clatter the cane whose amber knob he had been meditatively sucking, and Mr. Wadworth to stare at his principal as though he feared for his reason. 'Delope?' he gasped. 'Against Rotherfield? You must be queer in your attic! Why, man, you'd be cold meat! Now, you listen to me, Charlie! If you won't beg the fellow's pardon, you'll come up the instant you see the handkerchief drop, and shoot to kill, or I'm dashed if I'll have anything more to do with it!'

'Awkward business, if he killed him,' objected Sir Francis. 'Might have to leave the country.'

'He won't kill him,' said Mr. Wadworth shortly.

He said no more, but it was plain to Saltwood that his seconds thought poorly of his chances of being able to hit his opponent at a range of twenty-five yards. He was by no means a contemptible shot, but he suspected that it might be easier to hit a small wafer at Manton's Galleries than a large man at Paddington Green.

Mr. Wadworth called for him in a tilbury very early in the morning. He did not find it necessary to throw stones up at his lord-ship's window, for his lordship had not slept well, and was already dressed. He stole downstairs, and let himself out of the house, bidding Mr. Wadworth good morning with very creditable composure. Mr. Wadworth nodded, and cast a knowledgeable eye over him. 'No bright buttons on your coat?' he asked.

The question did nothing to allay the slightly sick feeling at the pit of Saltwood's stomach. Mr. Wadworth followed it up with a re-minder to him to turn up his collar, and to be careful to present the nar-rowest possible target to his adversary. Lord Saltwood, climbing into the tilbury, answered with spurious cheerfulness: 'I must suppose it can make little difference to such a shot as they say Rotherfield is.'

'Oh, well—! No sense in taking needless risks,' said Mr. Wad-worth awkwardly.

After that, conversation became desultory. They were the first to arrive on the ground, but they were soon joined by Sir Francis, and a man in a sober-hued coat, who chatted about the weather. Saltwood re-alized that this insensate person must be the doctor, gritted his teeth, and hoped that Rotherfield would not be late. It seemed to him that he had strayed into nightmare. He felt cold, sick, and ashamed; and it said much for the underlying steel in his spoilt and wayward nature that it did not enter his head that he might even now escape from a terrifying encounter by apologizing to Rotherfield for conduct which he knew to have been disgraceful.

Rotherfield arrived even as the church clocks were striking the hour. He was driving himself in his sporting curricle, one of his friends seated beside him, the other following him in a high-perch phaeton. He appeared to be quite nonchalant, and it was obvious that he had dressed with all his usual care. The points of his shirt stood up stiffly above an intricate neckcloth; his dark locks were arranged with casual nicety; there was not a speck upon the gleaming black leather of his Hessian boots. He sprang down from the curricle and cast his drab driving-coat into it. The seconds met, and conferred, and presently led their principals to their positions, and gave into their hands the long-barrelled duelling-pistols, primed and cocked. Across what seemed to be an immeasurable stretch of turf, Saltwood stared at Rotherfield. That cold, handsome face might have been carved in stone; it looked merciless, faintly mocking.

The doctor turned his back; Saltwood drew in his breath, and grasped his pistol firmly. One of Rotherfield's seconds was holding the handkerchief high in the air. It fell, and Saltwood jerked up his arm and fired.

He had been so sure that Rotherfield would hit him that it seemed to him that he must have been hit. He recalled having been told that the bullet had a numbing effect, and cast an instinctive glance down his person. But there did not seem to be any blood, and he was certainly still standing on his feet. Then he heard someone ejaculate: 'Good God! *Rotherfield!*' and, looking in bewilderment across the grass, he saw that Mr. Mayfield was beside Rotherfield, an arm flung round him, and that the doctor was hurrying towards them. Then Mr. Wadworth removed his own pistol from his hand, and said in a stupefied voice: 'He *missed!*'

Young Lord Saltwood, realizing that he had hit the finest pistol-shot in town and was himself untouched, was for a moment in danger of collapsing in a swoon. Recovering, he pushed Mr. Wadworth away, and strode impetuously up to the group gathered round Rotherfield. He reached it in time to hear that detested voice say: 'The cub shoots better than I bargained for! Oh, go to the devil, Ned! It's nothing—a graze!'

'My lord!' uttered Saltwood. 'I wish to offer you my apology for—'

'Not now, not now!' interrupted the doctor testily.

Saltwood found himself waved aside. He tried once more to present Rotherfield with an apology, and was then led firmly away by his seconds.

3

'Most extraordinary thing I ever saw!' Mr. Wadworth told Dorothea, when dragged by her into the small saloon, and bidden disclose the whole to her. 'Mind, now! Not a word to Charlie! Rotherfield missed!'

Her eyes widened. 'Fired in the air?'

'No, no! Couldn't expect him to do that! Dash it, Dolly, when a man does that he's owning he was at fault! Don't mind telling you I felt as sick as a horse. He was looking devilish grim. Queer smile on his face, too. I didn't like it above half. I'll swear he took careful aim. Fired a good second before Charlie did. Couldn't have missed him by more than a hair's breadth! Charlie got him in the shoulder: don't think it's serious. Thing is, shouldn't be surprised if it's done Charlie good. Tried to beg Rotherfield's pardon on the ground, and he's called once in Mount Street since then. Not admitted: butler said his lordship was not receiving visitors. Given Charlie a fright: he'll be more the thing now. But don't you breathe a word, Dolly!'

She assured him she would not mention the matter. An attempt to discover from him who, besides Lord Rotherfield, resided in Mount Street could not have been said to have advanced the object she had in mind. Mr. Wadworth was able to recite the names of several persons living in that street; but when asked to identify a gentleman who apparently resembled a demi-god rather than an ordinary mortal, he said without hesitation that he had never beheld anyone remotely corresponding to Miss Saltwood's description. He began then to show signs of suspicion, so Dorothea was obliged to abandon her enquiries and to cast round in her mind for some other means of discovering the name of her brother's unknown preserver. None presented itself; nor, when she walked down Mount Street with her maid, was she able to recognize the house in which she had taken refuge. A wistful fancy that the unknown gentleman might perhaps write to tell her that he had kept his word was never very strong, and by the end of the week had vanished entirely. She could only hope that she would one day meet him, and be able to thank him for his kind offices. In the meantime, she found herself to be sadly out of spirits, and behaved with such listless propriety that even Augusta, who had frequently expressed the wish that something should occur to tame her sister's wildness, asked her if she were feeling well. Lady Saltwood feared that she was going into a decline, and herself succumbed immediately to a severe nervous spasm.

Before any such extreme measures for the restoration to health of the younger Miss Saltwood as bringing her out that very season had been more than fleetingly contemplated by her mama and angrily vetoed by her sister, her disorder was happily arrested. Eight days after Saltwood's duel, on an afternoon in June, the butler sought out Dorothea, who was reading aloud to her afflicted parent, and contrived to get her out of the drawing-room without arousing any suspicion in Lady Salt-wood's mind that she was wanted by anyone more dangerous than the dressmaker. But once outside the drawing-room Porlock placed a sealed billet in Dorothea's hand, saying with the air of a conspirator that the gentleman was in the Red Saloon.

The billet was quite short, and it was written in the third person. *'One who had the pleasure of rendering a trifling service to Miss Dorothea Saltwood begs the honour of a few words with her.'*

'Oh!' gasped Dorothea, all her listlessness vanished. 'Porlock, pray do not tell Mama or my sister! *Pray* do not!'

'Certainly not, miss!' he responded, with a readiness not wholly due to the very handsome sum already bestowed upon him downstairs. He watched his young mistress speed down the stairs, and thought with pleasure that when Miss Augusta discovered what kind of an out-and-outer was courting her sister she would very likely go off in an apoplexy. The gentleman in the Red Saloon, to his experienced eye, was a bang-up Corinthian, a Nonpareil, a very Tulip of Fashion.

Dorothea, coming impetuously into the saloon, exclaimed on the threshold: 'Oh, I am so very glad to see you, sir! I have wished so much to thank you, and I have not known how to do so, for I never asked you your name! I don't know how I came to be such a goose!'

He came towards her, and took her outstretched hand in his left one, bowing over it. She perceived that he was quite as handsome as she had remembered, and that his right arm lay in a sling. She said in quick concern: 'How comes this about? Have you broke your arm, sir?'

'No, no!' he replied, retaining her hand. 'A slight accident to my shoulder merely! It is of no consequence. I trust that all went well that evening, and that your absence had not been discovered?'

'No, and I have not mentioned it to anyone!' she assured him. 'I am so very much obliged to you! I cannot imagine how you contrived to prevail upon that man not to hit Charlie! Bernard told me that Charlie hit *him,* and I must say I am sorry, because it was quite my fault, and although he is so odious I did not wish him to be hurt precisely!'

'To own the truth, he had little expectation of being hurt,' he said, with a smile. He released her hand, and seemed to hesitate. 'Lord

Rotherfield, Miss Saltwood, does not wish to appear odious in your eyes, believe me!'

'Is he a friend of yours?' she asked. 'Pray forgive me! I am sure he cannot be so very bad if that is so!'

'I fear he has been quite my worst friend,' he said ruefully. 'Forgive me, my child! *I* am Lord Rotherfield!'

She stood quite still, staring at him, at first pale, and then with a flush in her cheeks and tears sparkling in her eyes. '*You* are Lord Rotherfield?' she repeated. 'And I said *such* things about you, and you let me, and were so very kind, and allowed yourself to be wounded—Oh, I am sure you must be the best person in the world!'

'I am certainly not that, though I hope I am not the worst. Will you forgive me for having deceived you?'

She put out her hand, and again he took it, and held it. 'How can you talk so? I am quite ashamed! I wonder you did not turn me out of doors! How *good* you are! How truly noble!'

'Ah, how can *you* talk so?' he said quickly. 'Do not! I do not think I had ever, before that evening, wished to please anyone but myself. You came to me—enchanting and abominable child that you are! —and I wanted more than anything in life to please you. I am neither good nor noble—though I am not as black as I was painted to you. I assure you, I had never the least intention of wounding your brother mortally.'

'Oh *no*! Had I known it was you I should never have thought that!'

He raised her hand to his lips. The slight fingers seemed to tremble, and then to clasp his. He looked up, but before he could speak Lord Saltwood walked into the room.

Lord Saltwood stopped dead on the threshold, his eyes starting from their sockets. He stared in a dazed way, opened his mouth, shut it again, and swallowed convulsively.

'How do you do?' said Rotherfield, with cool civility. 'You must forgive me for having been unable to receive you when you called at my house the other day.'

'I came—I wished—I wrote you a letter!' stammered Saltwood, acutely uncomfortable.

'Certainly you did, and I have come to acknowledge it. I am much obliged to you, and beg you will think no more of the incident.'

'C-came to see *me*?' gasped Saltwood.

'Yes, for I understand you to be the head of your family, and I have a request to make of you. I trust that our late unfortunate con-tretemps may not have made the granting of it wholly repugnant to you.'

'No, no! I mean—anything in my power, of course! I shall be very happy—! If you would care to step into the book-room, my lord—?'

'Thank you.' Rotherfield turned, and smiled down into Dorothea's anxious eyes. 'I must take my leave of you now, but I trust Lady Saltwood will permit me to call on her tomorrow.'

'Yes, indeed, I am persuaded—that is, I do hope she will!' said Dorothea naïvely.

There was a laugh in his eye, but he bowed formally and went out with Saltwood, leaving her beset by a great many agitating emo-tions, foremost amongst which was a dread that Lady Saltwood would, in the failing state of her health, feel herself to be unequal to the strain of receiving his lordship. When, presently, Saltwood went up to the drawing-room, looking as though he had sustained a severe shock, Dorothea was seized by a conviction that her escapade had been dis-closed to him, and she fled to the sanctuary of her bedchamber, and in-dulged in a hearty bout of tears. From this abyss of woe she was jerked by the unmistakable sounds of Augusta in strong hysterics. Hastily dry-ing her cheeks, she ran down the stairs to render whatever assistance might be needed, and to support her parent through this ordeal. To her amazement, she found Lady Saltwood, whom she had left languishing on the sofa, not only upon her feet, but looking remarkably well. To her still greater amazement, the invalid folded her in the fondest of em-braces, and said: 'Dearest, dearest child! I declare I don't know if I am on my head or my heels! *Rotherfield!* A countess! You sly little puss, never to have told me that you had met him! And not even out yet! You must be presented at once: *that* I am determined upon! He is coming to visit me tomorrow. Thank heaven you are just Augusta's size! You must wear the pomona silk dress Celestine has just made for her: I knew how it would be, the instant I brought you out! I was never so happy in my life!'

Quite bewildered, Dorothea said: 'Presented? Wear Augusta's new dress? Mama, *why*?'

'My innocent treasure!' exclaimed Lady Saltwood. 'Tell me, my love, for you must know I am scarcely acquainted with him, do you— do you *like* Lord Rotherfield?'

'Oh, Mama!' said Dorothea impulsively. 'He is exactly like Sir Charles Grandison, and Lord Orville, only far, far better!'

'Dearest Dorothea!' sighed her ladyship ecstatically. 'Charlie, do not stand there staring! Go and throw a jug of water over Augusta this instant! This is *not* the moment for hysterics!'

Gertrude the Governess: or Simple Seventeen

S tephen Leacock, born in Hampshire in 1869, spent most of his life in Canada, where he taught modern languages in Toronto and lectured on economics at McGill University. In spite of the success of his book *Elements of Political Science* he was most known and loved as a humorist. In his lifetime, he received the Lorne Pierce Medal from the Royal Society of Canada and the Mark Twain Medal; after his death, the Stephen Leacock Medal for Humor was created in his honor. In this chuckle-out-loud story from his collection *Laugh with Leacock*, he lampoons and deftly skewers the late Victorian penchant for florid romance.

★ ★ ★ ★ ★

Synopsis of Previous Chapters:

There are no previous chapters.

It was a wild and stormy night on the West Coast of Scotland. This, however, is immaterial to the present story, as the scene is not laid in the West of Scotland. For the matter of that the weather was just as bad on the East Coast of Ireland.

But the scene of this narrative is laid in the South of England and takes place in and around Knotacentinum Towers (pronounced as if written Nosham Taws), the seat of Lord Knotacent (pronounced as if written Nosh).

But it is not necessary to pronounce either of these names in reading them.

Nosham Taws was a typical English home. The main part of the house was an Elizabethan structure of warm red brick, while the elder portion, of which the earl was inordinately proud, still showed the outlines of a Norman keep, to which had been added a Lancastrian jail and a Plantagenet orphan asylum. From the house in all directions stretched magnificent woodland and park with oaks and elms of immemorial antiquity, while nearer the house stood raspberry bushes and geranium plants which had been set out by the Crusaders.

About the grand old mansion the air was loud with the chirping of the thrushes, the cawing of partridges and the clear sweet note of the rook, while deer, antelope and other quadrupeds strutted about the lawn so tame as to eat off the sundial. In fact, the place was a regular menagerie.

From the house downwards through the park stretched a beautifully broad avenue laid out by Henry VII.

Lord Nosh stood upon the hearthrug of the library. Trained diplomat and statesman as he was, his stern aristocratic face was upside down with fury.

"Boy," he said, "you shall marry this girl or I disinherit you. You are no son of mine."

Young Lord Ronald, erect before him, flung back a glance as defiant as his own.

"I defy you," he said. "Henceforth you are no father of mine. I will get another. I will marry none but a woman I can love. This girl that we have never seen—"

"Fool," said the earl, "would you throw aside our estate and name of a thousand years? The girl, I am told, is beautiful; her aunt is willing; they are French; pah! they understand such things in France."

"But your reason—"

"I give no reason," said the earl. "Listen, Ronald, I give one month. For that time you remain here. If at the end of it you refuse me, I cut you off with a shilling."

Lord Ronald said nothing; he flung himself from the room, flung himself upon his horse and rode madly off in all directions.

As the door of the library closed upon Ronald the earl sank into a chair. His face changed. It was no longer that of the haughty nobleman, but of the hunted criminal. "He must marry the girl," he muttered. "Soon she will know all. Tutchemoff has escaped from Siberia. He knows and will tell. The whole of the mines pass to her, this property with it, and I— but enough." He rose, walked to the sideboard, drained a dipper full of gin and bitters, and became a high-bred English gentleman.

It was at this moment that a high dogcart, driven by a groom in the livery of Earl Nosh, might have been seen entering the avenue of Nosham Taws. Beside him sat a young girl, scarce more than a child, in fact, not nearly so big as the groom.

The apple-pie hat which she wore, surmounted with black willow plumes, concealed from view a face so facelike in its appearance as to be positively facial.

It was—need we say it—Gertrude the Governess, who was this day to enter upon her duties at Nosham Taws.

At the same time that the dogcart entered the avenue at one end there might have been seen riding down it from the other a tall young man, whose long, aristocratic face proclaimed his birth and who was mounted upon a horse with a face even longer than his own.

And who is this tall young man who draws nearer to Gertrude with every revolution of the horse? Ah, who, indeed? Ah, who, who? I wonder if any of my readers could guess that this was none other than Lord Ronald.

The two were destined to meet. Nearer and nearer they came. And then still nearer. Then for one brief moment they met. As they passed Gertrude raised her head and directed towards the young nobleman two eyes so eyelike in their expression as to be absolutely circular, while Lord Ronald directed towards the occupant of the dogcart a gaze so gazelike that nothing but a gazelle, or a gaspipe, could have emulated its intensity.

Was this the dawn of love? Wait and see. Do not spoil the story.

Let us speak of Gertrude. Gertrude De Mongmorenci McFiggin had known neither father nor mother. They had both died years before she was born. Of her mother she knew nothing, save that she was French, was extremely beautiful, and that all her ancestors and even her business acquaintances had perished in the Revolution.

Yet Gertrude cherished the memory of her parents. On her breast the girl wore a locket in which was enshrined a miniature of her mother, while down her neck inside at the back hung a daguerreotype of her father. She carried a portrait of her grandmother up her sleeve and had pictures of her cousins tucked inside her boot, while beneath her—but enough, quite enough.

Of her father Gertrude knew even less. That he was a high-born English gentleman who had lived as a wanderer in many lands, this was all she knew. His only legacy to Gertrude had been a Russian grammar, a Rumanian phrase book, a theodolite and a work on mining engineering.

From her earliest infancy Gertrude had been brought up by her aunt. Her aunt had carefully instructed her in Christian principles. She had also taught her Mohammedanism to make sure.

When Gertrude was seventeen her aunt had died of hydrophobia.

The circumstances were mysterious. There had called upon her that day a strange bearded man in the costume of the Russians. After he had left, Gertrude had found her aunt in a syncope from which she passed into an apostrophe and never recovered.

To avoid scandal it was called hydrophobia. Gertrude was thus thrown upon the world. What to do? That was the problem that confronted her. It was while musing one day upon her fate that Gertrude's eye was struck with an advertisement.

"Wanted a governess; must possess a knowledge of French, Italian, Russian, and Rumanian, music and mining engineering. Salary one pound, four shillings and fourpence halfpenny per annum. Apply between half-past eleven and twenty-five minutes to twelve at No. 41-A Decimal Six, Belgravia Terrace. The Countess of Nosh."

Gertrude was a girl of great natural quickness of apprehension, and she had not pondered over this announcement more than half an hour before she was struck with the extraordinary coincidence between the list of items desired and the things that she herself knew.

She duly presented herself at Belgravia Terrace before the countess, who advanced to meet her with a charm which at once placed the girl at her ease.

"You are proficient in French?" she asked.

"Oh, *oui*," said Gertrude modestly.

"And Italian?" continued the countess.

"Oh, *si*," said Gertrude.

"And German?" said the countess in delight.

"Ah, *ja*," said Gertrude.

"And Russian?"

"*Yaw.*"

"And Rumanian?"

"*Jep.*"

Amazed at the girl's extraordinary proficiency in modern languages, the countess looked at her narrowly. Where had she seen those lineaments before? She passed her hand over her brow in thought, and spit upon the floor, but no, the face baffled her.

"Enough," she said. "I engage you on the spot; tomorrow you go down to Nosham Taws and begin teaching the children. I must add that in addition you will be expected to aid the earl with his Russian correspondence. He has large mining interests at Tschminsk."

Tschminsk! Why did the simple word reverberate upon Gertrude's ears? Why? Because it was the name written in her father's hand on the title page of his book on mining. What mystery was here?

It was on the following day that Gertrude had driven up the avenue.

She descended from the dogcart, passed through a phalanx of liveried servants drawn up seven deep, to each of whom she gave a sovereign as she passed and entered Nosham Taws.

"Welcome," said the countess, as she aided Gertrude to carry her trunk upstairs.

The girl presently descended and was ushered into the library, where she was presented to the earl. As soon as the earl's eye fell upon the face of the new governess he started visibly. Where had he seen those lineaments? Where was it? At the races, or the theater—on a bus—no. Some subtler thread of memory was stirring in his mind. He strode hastily to the sideboard, drained a dipper and a half of brandy, and became again the perfect English gentleman.

While Gertrude has gone to the nursery to make the acquaintance of the two golden-haired children who are to be her charges, let us say something here of the earl and his son.

Lord Nosh was the perfect type of the English nobleman and statesman. The years that he had spent in the diplomatic service at Constantinople, St. Petersburg and Salt Lake City had given to him a peculiar finesse and noblesse, while his long residence at St. Helena, Pitcairn Island and Hamilton, Ontario, had rendered him impervious to external impressions. As deputy paymaster of the militia of the county he had seen something of the sterner side of military life, while his hereditary office of Groom of the Sunday Breeches had brought him into direct contact with royalty itself.

His passion for outdoor sports endeared him to his tenants. A keen sportsman, he excelled in fox hunting, dog hunting, pig killing, bat catching and the pastimes of his class.

In this latter respect Lord Ronald took after his father. From the start the lad had shown the greatest promise. At Eton he had made a splendid showing at battledore and shuttlecock, and at Cambridge had been first in his class at needlework. Already his name was whispered in connection with the All England ping-pong championship, a triumph which would undoubtedly carry with it a seat in Parliament.

Thus was Gertrude the Governess installed at Nosham Taws.

The days and the weeks sped past.

The simple charm of the beautiful orphan girl attracted all hearts. Her two little pupils became her slaves. "Me loves oo," the little Rasehellfrida would say, leaning her golden head in Gertrude's lap. Even the servants loved her. The head gardener would bring a bouquet of beautiful roses to her room before she was up, the second gardener a bunch of early cauliflowers, the third a spray of late asparagus, and even the tenth and the eleventh a sprig of mangelwurzel or an armful of hay. Her room was full of gardeners all the time, while at evening the aged butler, touched at the friendless girl's loneliness, would tap softly at her door to bring her a rye whisky and seltzer or a box of Pittsburg stogies.

Even the dumb creatures seemed to admire her in their own dumb way. The dumb rooks settled on her shoulder and every dumb dog around the place followed her.

And Ronald! Ah, Ronald! Yes, indeed! They had met. They had spoken.

"What a dull morning," Gertrude had said. "*Quel triste matin! Was fur ein allervendamnter Tag!*"

"Beastly," Ronald had answered.

"Beastly!!" The word rang in Gertrude's ears all day.

After that they were constantly together. They played tennis and ping-pong in the day, and in the evening, in accordance with the stiff routine of the place, they sat down with the earl and countess to 25-cent poker, and later still they sat together on the veranda and watched the moon sweeping in great circles around the horizon.

It was not long before Gertrude realized that Lord Ronald felt toward her a warmer feeling than that of mere ping-pong. At times in her presence he would fall, especially after dinner, into a fit of profound subtraction.

Once at night, when Gertrude withdrew to her chamber and before seeking her pillow, prepared to retire as a preliminary to disrobing—in other words, before going to bed, she flung wide the casement (opened the window) and perceived (saw) the face of Lord Ronald. He was sitting on a thorn bush beneath her, and his upturned face wore an expression of agonized pallor.

Meantime the days passed. Life at the Taws moved in the ordinary routine of a great English household. At seven a gong sounded for rising, at eight a horn blew for breakfast, at eight-thirty a whistle sounded for prayers, at one a flag was run up at half mast for lunch, at four a gun was fired for afternoon tea, at nine a first bell sounded for dressing, at nine-fifteen a second bell for going on dressing, while at nine-thirty a rocket was sent up to indicate that dinner was ready. At midnight dinner was over, and at 1 A.M. the tolling of a bell summoned the domestics to evening prayers.

Meanwhile the month alloted by the earl to Lord Ronald was passing away. It was already July 15, then within a day or two it was July 17, and, almost immediately afterwards, July 18.

At times, the earl, in passing Ronald in the hall, would say sternly, "Remember, boy, your consent, or I disinherit you."

And what were the earl's thoughts of Gertrude? Here was the one drop of bitterness in the girl's cup of happiness. For some reason that she could not divine the earl showed signs of marked antipathy.

Once as she passed the door of the library he threw a bootjack at her. On another occasion at lunch alone with her he struck her savagely across the face with a sausage.

It was her duty to translate to the earl his Russian correspondence. She sought in it in vain for the mystery. One day a Russian telegram was handed to the earl. Gertrude translated it to him aloud.

"Tutchemoff went to the woman. She is dead."

On hearing this the earl became livid with fury, in fact this was the day that he struck her with the sausage.

Then one day while the earl was absent on a bat hunt, Gertrude, who was turning over his correspondence, with that sweet feminine instinct of interest that rose superior to ill treatment, suddenly found the key to the mystery.

Lord Nosh was not the rightful owner of the Taws. His distant cousin of the older line, the true heir, had died in a Russian prison to which the machinations of the earl, while Ambassador of Tschminsk, had consigned him. The daughter of this cousin was the true owner of Nosham Taws.

The family story, save only that the documents before her withheld the name of the rightful heir, lay bare to Gertrude's eye.

Strange is the heart of woman. Did Gertrude turn from the earl with spurning? No. Her own sad fate had taught her sympathy.

Yet still the mystery remained! Why did the earl start perceptibly each time that he looked into her face? Sometimes he started as much as four centimeters, so that one could distinctly see him do it. On such occasions he would hastily drain a dipper of rum and vichy water and become again the correct English gentleman.

The denouement came swiftly. Gertrude never forgot it.

It was the night of the great ball at Nosham Taws. The whole neighborhood was invited. How Gertrude's heart had beat with anticipation, and with what trepidation she had overhauled her scant wardrobe in order to appear not unworthy in Lord Ronald's eyes. Her resources were poor indeed, yet the inborn genius for dress that she inherited from her French mother stood her in good stead. She twined a single rose in her hair and contrived herself a dress out of a few old newspapers and the inside of an umbrella that would have graced a court. Round her waist she bound a single braid of bag-string, while a piece of old lace that had been her mother's was suspended to her ear by a thread.

Gertrude was the cynosure of all eyes. Floating to the strains of the music she presented a picture of bright girlish innocence that no one could see undisenraptured.

The ball was at its height. It was away up!

Ronald stood with Gertrude in the shrubbery. They looked into one another's eyes.

"Gertrude," he said, "I love you."

Simple words, and yet they thrilled every fiber in the girl's costume.

"Ronald!" she said, and cast herself about his neck.

At this moment the earl appeared standing beside them in the moonlight. His stern face was distorted with indignation.

"So!" he said, turning to Ronald. "It appears that you have chosen!"

"I have," said Ronald with hauteur.

"You prefer to marry this penniless girl rather than the heiress I have selected for you?"

Gertrude looked from father to son in amazement.

"Yes," said Ronald.

"Be it so," said the earl, draining a dipper of gin which he carried, and resuming his calm. "Then I disinherit you. Leave this place, and never return to it."

"Come, Gertrude," said Ronald tenderly, "let us flee together."

Gertrude stood before them. The rose had fallen from her head. The lace had fallen from her ear and the bag-string had come undone from her waist. Her newspapers were crumpled beyond recognition. But disheveled and illegible as she was, she was still mistress of herself.

"Never," she said firmly. "Ronald, you shall never make this sacrifice for me." Then to the earl, in tones of ice, "There is a pride, sir, as great even as yours. The daughter of Metschnikoff McFiggin need crave a boon from no one."

With that she hauled from her bosom the daguerreotype of her father and pressed it to her lips.

The earl started as if shot. "That name!" he cried. "That face! That photograph! Stop!"

There! There is no need to finish; my readers have long since divined it. Gertrude was the heiress.

The lovers fell into one another's arms. The earl's proud face relaxed. "God bless you," he said. The countess and the guests came pouring out upon the lawn. The breaking day illuminated a scene of gay congratulations.

Gertrude and Ronald were wed. Their happiness was complete. Need we say more? Yes, only this. The earl was killed in the hunting field a few days later. The countess was struck by lightning. The two children fell down a well. Thus the happiness of Gertrude and Ronald was complete.

Springtime à la Carte

BY O. HENRY

T he short stories of O. Henry are noted for portraying the pithy, sometimes gritty side of life. His own life was perhaps more poignant than anything he ever set down on paper: a failed businessman charged with embezzlement, he fled to Honduras to escape prison, but returned to America to comfort his fatally ill wife. While an inmate in prison, he began his remarkable career as a short story writer, which eventually brought him the success that eluded his early years. His stories always contain a kernel of optimism; they are never wholly bleak or pessimistic. And their signature twist endings often leave readers with an ironic smile. In this light-hearted story, a young typist fretfully awaits word from her farmer lover and finds she must put him from her mind in order to get on with her work. But when spring fills the air with sparkling recollection, she inadvertently demonstrates where her heart really lies.

★　★　★　★　★

It was a day in March.

Never, never begin a story this way when you write one. No opening could possibly be worse. It is unimaginative, flat, dry and likely to consist of mere wind. But in this instance it is allowable. For the following paragraph, which should have inaugurated the narrative, is too wildly extravagant and preposterous to be flaunted in the face of the reader without preparation.

Sarah was crying over her bill of fare.

Think of a New York girl shedding tears on the menu card!

To account for this you will be allowed to guess that the lobsters were all out, or that she had sworn ice-cream off during Lent, or that she had ordered onions, or that she had just come from a Hackett matinee. And then, all these theories being wrong, you will please let the story proceed.

The gentleman who announced that the world was an oyster which he with his sword would open made a larger hit than he deserved. It is not difficult to open an oyster with a sword. But did you ever notice any one try to open the terrestrial bivalve with a typewriter? Like to wait for a dozen raw opened that way?

Sarah had managed to pry apart the shells with her unhandy weapon far enough to nibble a wee bit at the cold and clammy world within. She knew no more shorthand than if she had been a graduate in stenography just let slip upon the world by a business college. So, not being able to stenog, she could not enter that bright galaxy of office talent. She was a free-lance typewriter and canvassed for odd jobs of copying.

The most brilliant and crowning feat of Sarah's battle with the world was the deal she made with Schulenberg's Home Restaurant. The restaurant was next door to the old red brick in which she hall-roomed. One evening after dining at Schulenberg's 40-cent, five-course table d'hote (served as fast as you throw the five baseballs at the coloured gentleman's head) Sarah took away with her the bill of fare. It was written in an almost unreadable script neither English nor German, and so arranged that if you were not careful you began with a toothpick and rice pudding and ended with soup and the day of the week.

The next day Sarah showed Schulenberg a neat card on which the menu was beautifully typewritten with the viands temptingly marshalled under their right and proper heads from "hors d'oeuvre" to "not responsible for overcoats and umbrellas."

Schulenberg became a naturalised citizen on the spot. Before Sarah left him she had him willingly committed to an agreement. She was to furnish typewritten bills of fare for the twenty-one tables in the restaurant—a new bill for each day's dinner, and new ones for breakfast and lunch as often as changes occurred in the food or as neatness required.

In return for this Schulenberg was to send three meals per diem to Sarah's hall room by a waiter—an obsequious one if possible—and furnish her each afternoon with a pencil draft of what Fate had in store for Schulenberg's customers on the morrow.

Mutual satisfaction resulted from the agreement. Schulenberg's patrons now knew what the food they ate was called even if its nature sometimes puzzled them. And Sarah had food during a cold, dull winter, which was the main thing with her.

And then the almanac lied, and said that spring had come. Spring comes when it comes. The frozen snows of January still lay like adamant in the crosstown streets. The hand-organs still played "In the Good Old Summertime," with their December vivacity and expression. Men began to make thirty-day notes to buy Easter dresses. Janitors shut off steam. And when these things happen one may know that the city is still in the clutches of winter.

One afternoon Sarah shivered in her elegant hall bedroom; "house heated; scrupulously clean; conveniences; seen to be appreciated." She had no work to do except Schulenberg's menu cards. Sarah sat in her squeaky willow rocker, and looked out the window. The calendar on the wall kept crying to her: "Springtime is here, Sarah—springtime is here, I tell you. Look at me, Sarah, my figures show it. You've got a neat figure yourself, Sarah—a—nice springtime figure—why do you look out the window so sadly?"

Sarah's room was at the back of the house. Looking out the window she could see the windowless rear brick wall of the box factory on the next street. But the wall was clearest crystal; and Sarah was looking down a grassy lane shaded with cherry trees and elms and bordered with raspberry bushes and Cherokee roses.

Spring's real harbingers are too subtle for the eye and ear. Some must have the flowering crocus, the wood-starring dogwood, the voice of bluebird—even so gross a reminder as the farewell handshake of the retiring buckwheat and oyster before they can welcome the Lady in Green to their dull bosoms. But to old earth's choicest kin there come straight, sweet messages from his newest bride, telling them they shall be no stepchildren unless they choose to be.

On the previous summer Sarah had gone into the country and loved a farmer.

(In writing your story never hark back thus. It is bad art, and cripples interest. Let it march, march.)

Sarah stayed two weeks at Sunnybrook Farm. There she learned to love old Farmer Franklin's son Walter. Farmers have been loved and wedded and turned out to grass in less time. But young Walter Franklin was a modern agriculturist. He had a telephone in his cow house, and he could figure up exactly what effect next year's Canada wheat crop would have on potatoes planted in the dark of the moon.

It was in this shaded and raspberried lane that Walter had wooed and won her. And together they had sat and woven a crown of dandelions for her hair. He had immoderately praised the effect of the yellow blossoms against her brown tresses; and she had left the chaplet there, and walked back to the house swinging her straw sailor in her hands.

They were to marry in the spring—at the very first signs of spring, Walter said. And Sarah came back to the city to pound her typewriter.

A knock at the door dispelled Sarah's visions of that happy day. A waiter had brought the rough pencil draft of the Home Restaurant's next day fare in old Schulenberg's angular hand.

Sarah sat down to her typewriter and slipped a card between the rollers. She was a nimble worker. Generally in an hour and a half the twenty-one menu cards were written and ready.

To-day there were more changes on the bill of fare than usual. The soups were lighter; pork was eliminated from the entrees, figuring only with Russian turnips among the roasts. The gracious spirit of spring pervaded the entire menu. Lamb, that lately capered on the greening hillsides, was becoming exploited with the sauce that commemorated its gambols. The song of the oyster, though not silenced, was diminuendo con amore. The frying-pan seemed to be held, inactive, behind the beneficent bars of the broiler. The pie list swelled; the richer puddings had vanished; the sausage, with his drapery wrapped about him, barely lingered in a pleasant thanatopsis with the buckwheats and the sweet but doomed maple.

Sarah's fingers danced like midgets above a summer stream. Down through the courses she worked, giving each item its position according to its length with an accurate eye. Just above the desserts came the list of vegetables. Carrots and peas, asparagus on toast, the perennial tomatoes and corn and succotash, lima beans, cabbage—and then—

Sarah was crying over her bill of fare. Tears from the depths of some divine despair rose in her heart and gathered to her eyes. Down went her head on the little typewriter stand; and the keyboard rattled a dry accompaniment to her moist sobs.

For she had received no letter from Walter in two weeks, and the next item on the bill of fare was dandelions—dandelions with some kind of egg—but bother the egg!—dandelions, with whose golden blooms Walter had crowned her his queen of love and future bride—dandelions, the harbingers of spring, her sorrow's crown of sorrow—reminder of her happiest days.

Madam, I dare you to smile until you suffer this test: Let the Marechal Niel roses that Percy brought you on the night you gave him your heart be served as a salad with French dressing before your eyes at a Schulenberg table d'hote. Had Juliet so seen her love tokens dishonoured the sooner would she have sought the lethean herbs of the good apothecary.

But what a witch is Spring! Into the great cold city of stone and iron a message had to be sent. There was none to convey it but the little hardy courier of the fields with his rough green coat and modest air. He is a true soldier of fortune, this dent-de-lion—this lion's tooth, as the French chefs call him. Flowered, he will assist at love-making, wreathed in my lady's nut-brown hair; young and callow and unblossomed, he goes into the boiling pot and delivers the word of his sovereign mistress.

By and by Sarah forced back her tears. The cards must be written. But, still in a faint, golden glow from her dandeleonine dream, she fingered the typewriter keys absently for a little while, with her mind and heart in the meadow lane with her young farmer. But soon she came swiftly back to the rock-bound lanes of Manhattan, and the typewriter began to rattle and jump like a strike-breaker's motor car.

At 6 o'clock the waiter brought her dinner and carried away the typewritten bill of fare. When Sarah ate she set aside, with a sigh, the dish of dandelions with its crowning ovarious accompaniment. As this dark mass had been transformed from a bright and love-indorsed flower to be an ignominious vegetable, so had her summer hopes wilted and perished. Love may, as Shakespeare said, feed on itself: but Sarah could not bring herself to eat the dandelions that had graced, as ornaments, the first spiritual banquet of her heart's true affection.

At 7:30 the couple in the next room began to quarrel: the man in the room above sought for A on his flute; the gas went a little lower; three coal wagons started to unload—the only sound of which the phonograph is jealous; cats on the back fences slowly retreated toward Mukden. By these signs Sarah knew that it was time for her to read. She got out "The Cloister and the Hearth," the best non-selling book of the month, settled her feet on her trunk, and began to wander with Gerard.

The front door bell rang. The landlady answered it. Sarah left Gerard and Denys treed by a bear and listened. Oh, yes; you would, just as she did!

And then a strong voice was heard in the hall below, and Sarah jumped for her door, leaving the book on the floor and the first round easily the bear's. You have guessed it. She reached the top of the stairs just as her farmer came up, three at a jump, and reaped and garnered her, with nothing left for the gleaners.

"Why haven't you written—oh, why?" cried Sarah.

"New York is a pretty large town," said Walter Franklin. "I came in a week ago to your old address. I found that you went away on a Thursday. That consoled some; it eliminated the possible Friday bad luck. But it didn't prevent my hunting for you with police and otherwise ever since!

"I wrote!" said Sarah, vehemently.

"Never got it!"

"Then how did you find me?"

The young farmer smiled a springtime smile. "I dropped into that Home Restaurant next door this evening," said he. "I don't care who knows it; I like a dish of some kind of greens at this time of the year. I ran my eye down that nice typewritten bill of fare looking for something in that line. When I got below cabbage I turned my chair over and hollered for the proprietor. He told me where you lived."

"I remember," sighed Sarah, happily. "That was dandelions below cabbage."

"I'd know that cranky capital W 'way above the line that your typewriter makes anywhere in the world," said Franklin.

"Why, there's no W in dandelions," said Sarah, in surprise.

The young man drew the bill of fare from his pocket, and pointed to a line.

Sarah recognised the first card she had typewritten that afternoon. There was still the rayed splotch in the upper right-hand corner where a tear had fallen. But over the spot where one should have read the name of the meadow plant, the clinging memory of their golden blossoms had allowed her fingers to strike strange keys.

Between the red cabbage and the stuffed green peppers was the item:

"DEAREST WALTER, WITH HARD-BOILED EGG."

Mrs. Bullfrog

BY NATHANIEL HAWTHORNE

Nathaniel Hawthorne, one of America's first great masters of narrative fiction, was born in Salem, Massachusetts in 1804. The bleaker aspects of Puritan New England matched his own gloomy inner nature, which craved solitude. Yet he was not a man without sly humor, as this short story proves. Mr. Bullfrog thinks he has found the ideal woman to marry, she of the glossy ringlets and pearly white teeth. But when his "perfect" new wife begins to show her true (rather nasty) colors, he soon discovers that there is something a woman can offer a man that is even more compelling than physical beauty.

*   *   *   *   *

It makes me melancholy to see how like fools some very sensible people act in the matter of choosing wives. They perplex their judgments by a most undue attention to little niceties of personal appearance, habits, disposition, and other trifles which concern nobody but the lady herself. An unhappy gentleman, resolving to wed nothing short of perfection, keeps his heart and hand till both get so old and withered that no tolerable woman will accept them. Now this is the very height of absurdity. A kind Providence has so skillfully adapted sex to sex and the mass of individuals to each other, that, with certain obvious exceptions, any male and female may be moderately happy in the married state. The true rule is to ascertain that the match is fundamentally a good one, and then to take it for granted that all minor objections, should there be such, will vanish, if you let them alone. Only put yourself beyond hazard as to the real basis of matrimonial bliss, and it is scarcely to be imagined what miracles, in the way of recognizing smaller incongruities, connubial love will effect.

For my own part I freely confess that, in my bachelorship, I was precisely such an over-curious simpleton as I now advise the reader not to be. My early habits had gifted me with a feminine sensibility and too exquisite refinement. I was the accomplished graduate of a dry goods store, where, by dint of ministering to the whims of fine ladies, and suiting silken hose to delicate limbs, and handling satins, ribbons, chintzes, calicoes, tapes, gauze, and cambric needles, I grew up a very ladylike sort of a gentleman. It is not assuming too much to affirm that the ladies themselves were hardly so ladylike as Thomas Bullfrog. So painfully acute was my sense of female imperfection, and such varied excellence did I require in the woman whom I could love, that there was an awful risk of my getting no wife at all, or of being driven to perpetrate matrimony with my own image in the looking-glass. Besides the fundamental principle already hinted at, I demanded the fresh bloom of youth, pearly teeth, glossy ringlets, and the whole list of lovely items, with the utmost delicacy of habits and sentiments, a silken texture of mind, and, above all, a virgin heart. In a word, if a young angel just from paradise, yet dressed in earthly fashion, had come and offered me her hand, it is by no means certain that I should have taken it. There was every chance of my becoming a most miserable old bachelor, when, by the best luck in the world, I made a journey into another state, and was smitten by, and smote again, and wooed, won, and married, the present Mrs. Bullfrog, all in the space of a fortnight. Owing to these extempore measures, I not only gave my bride credit for certain perfections which have not as yet come to light, but also overlooked a few trifling defects, which, however, glimmered on my perception long before the close of the honeymoon. Yet, as there was no mistake about the fundamental principle aforesaid, I soon learned, as will be seen, to estimate Mrs. Bullfrog's deficiencies and superfluities at exactly their proper value.

The same morning that Mrs. Bullfrog and I came together as a unit, we took two seats in the stagecoach and began our journey towards my place of business. There being no other passengers, we were as much alone and as free to give vent to our raptures as if I had hired a hack for the matrimonial jaunt. My bride looked charmingly in a green silk calash and riding habit of pelisse cloth; and whenever her red lips parted with a smile, each tooth appeared like an inestimable pearl. Such was my passionate warmth that—we had rattled out of the village, gentle reader, and were lonely as Adam and Eve in paradise—I plead guilty to no less freedom than a kiss. The gentle eye of Mrs. Bullfrog scarcely rebuked me for the profanation. Emboldened by her indulgence, I threw back the calash from her polished brow, and suffered my fingers, white and delicate as her own, to stray among those dark and glossy curls which realized my daydreams of rich hair.

"My love," said Mrs. Bullfrog tenderly, "you will disarrange my curls."

"Oh, no, my sweet Laura!" replied I, still playing with the glossy ringlet. "Even your fair hand could not manage a curl more delicately than mine. I propose myself the pleasure of doing up your hair in papers every evening at the same time with my own."

"Mr. Bullfrog," repeated she, "you must not disarrange my curls."

This was spoken in a more decided tone than I had happened to hear, until then, from my gentlest of all gentle brides. At the same time she put up her hand and took mine prisoner; but merely drew it away from the forbidden ringlet, and then immediately released it. Now, I am a fidgety little man, and always love to have something in my fingers; so that, being debarred from my wife's curls, I looked about me for any other plaything. On the front seat of the coach there was one of those small baskets in which traveling ladies who are too delicate to appear at a public table generally carry a supply of gingerbread, biscuits and cheese, cold ham, and other light refreshments, merely to sustain nature to the journey's end. Such airy diet will sometimes keep them in pretty good flesh for a week together. Laying hold of this same little basket, I thrust my hand under the newspaper with which it was carefully covered.

"What's this, my dear?" cried I; for the black neck of a bottle had popped out of the basket.

"A bottle of Kalydor, Mr. Bullfrog," said my wife, coolly taking the basket from my hands and replacing it on the front seat.

There was no possibility of doubting my wife's word; but I never knew genuine Kalydor, such as I use for my own complexion, to smell so much like cherry brandy. I was about to express my fears that the lotion would injure her skin, when an accident occurred which threatened more than a skin-deep injury. Our Jehu had carelessly driven over a heap of gravel and fairly capsized the coach, with the wheels in the air and our heels where our heads should have been. What became of my wits I cannot imagine; they have always had a perverse trick of deserting me just when they were most needed; but so it chanced, that in the confusion of our overthrow I quite forgot that there was a Mrs. Bullfrog in the world. Like many men's wives, the good lady served her husband as a steppingstone. I had scrambled out of the coach and was instinctively settling my cravat, when somebody brushed roughly by me, and I heard a smart thwack upon the coachman's ear.

"Take that, you villain!" cried a strange, hoarse voice. "You have ruined me, you blackguard! I shall never be the woman I have been!"

And then came a second thwack, aimed at the driver's other ear; but which missed it, and hit him on the nose, causing a terrible effusion of blood. Now, who or what fearful apparition was inflicting this punishment on the poor fellow remained an impenetrable mystery to me. The blows were given by a person of grisly aspect, with a head almost bald, and sunken cheeks, apparently of the feminine gender, though hardly to be classed in the gentler sex. There being no teeth to modulate the voice, it had a mumbled fierceness, not passionate, but stern, which absolutely made me quiver like calf's-foot jelly. Who could the phantom be? The most awful circumstance of the affair is yet to be told: for this ogre, or whatever it was, had a riding habit like Mrs. Bullfrog's, and also a green silk calash dangling down her back by the strings. In my terror and turmoil of mind I could imagine nothing less than that the Old Nick, at the moment of our overturn, had annihilated my wife and jumped into her petticoats. This idea seemed the most probable, since I could nowhere perceive Mrs. Bullfrog alive, nor, though I looked very sharply about the coach, could I detect any traces of that beloved woman's dead body. There would have been a comfort in giving her Christian burial.

"Come, sir, bestir yourself! Help this rascal to set up the coach," said the hobgoblin to me; then, with a terrific screech at three country-men at a distance, "Here, you fellows, ain't you ashamed to stand off when a poor woman is in distress?"

The countrymen, instead of fleeing for their lives, came run-ning at full speed, and laid hold of the topsy-turvy coach. I, also, though a small-sized man, went to work like a son of Anak. The coachman, too, with the blood still streaming from his nose, tugged and toiled most manfully, dreading, doubtless, that the next blow might break his head. And yet, bemauled as the poor fellow had been, he seemed to glance at me with an eye of pity, as if my case were more deplorable than his. But I cherished a hope that all would turn out a dream, and seized the op-portunity, as we raised the coach, to jam two of my fingers under the wheel, trusting that the pain would awaken me.

"Why, here we are, all to rights again!" exclaimed a sweet voice behind. "Thank you for your assistance, gentlemen. My dear Mr. Bull-frog, how you perspire! Do let me wipe your face. Don't take this little accident too much to heart, good driver. We ought to be thankful that none of our necks are broken."

"We might have spared one neck out of the three," muttered the driver, rubbing his ear and pulling his nose, to ascertain whether he had been cuffed or not. "Why, the woman's a witch!"

I fear that the reader will not believe, yet it is positively a fact, that there stood Mrs. Bullfrog, with her glossy ringlets curling on her brow, and two rows of orient pearls gleaming between her parted lips, which wore a most angelic smile. She had regained her riding habit and calash from the grisly phantom, and was, in all respects, the lovely woman who had been sitting by my side at the instant of our overturn. How she had happened to disappear, and who had supplied her place, and whence she did now return, were problems too knotty for me to solve. There stood my wife. That was the one thing certain among a heap of mysteries. Nothing remained but to help her into the coach, and plod on, through the journey of the day and the journey of life, as comfortably as we could. As the driver closed the door upon us, I heard him whisper to the three countrymen, "How do you suppose a fellow feels shut up in the cage with a she tiger?"

Of course this query could have no reference to my situation. Yet, unreasonable as it may appear, I confess that my feelings were not altogether so ecstatic as when I first called Mrs. Bullfrog mine. True, she was a sweet woman and an angel of a wife; but what if a Gorgon should return, amid the transports of our connubial bliss, and take the angel's place. I recollected the tale of a fairy, who half the time was a beautiful woman and half the time a hideous monster. Had I taken that very fairy to be the wife of my bosom? While such whims and chimeras were flitting across my fancy I began to look askance at Mrs. Bullfrog, almost expecting that the transformation would be wrought before my eyes.

To divert my mind, I took up the newspaper which had covered the little basket of refreshments, and which now lay at the bottom of the coach, blushing with a deep-red stain and emitting a potent spirituous fume from the contents of the broken bottle of Kalydor. The paper was two or three years old, but contained an article of several columns, in which I soon grew wonderfully interested. It was the report of a trial for breach of promise of marriage, giving the testimony in full, with fervid extracts from both the gentleman's and lady's amatory correspondence. The deserted damsel had personally appeared in court, and had borne energetic evidence to her lover's perfidy and the strength of her blighted affections. On the defendant's part there had been an attempt, though insufficiently sustained, to blast the plaintiff's character, and a plea, in mitigation of damages, on account of her unamiable temper. A horrible idea was suggested by the lady's name.

"Madam," said I, holding the newspaper before Mrs. Bullfrog's eyes—and, though a small, delicate, and thin-visaged man, I feel assured that I looked very terrific,—"madam," repeated I, through my shut teeth, "were you the plaintiff in this cause?"

"Oh, my dear Mr. Bullfrog," replied my wife, sweetly, "I thought all the world knew that!"

"Horror! horror!" exclaimed I, sinking back on the seat.

Covering my face with both hands, I emitted a deep and death-like groan, as if my tormented soul were rending me asunder—I, the most exquisitely fastidious of men, and whose wife was to have been the most delicate and refined of women, with all the fresh dew-drops glittering on her virgin rosebud of a heart!

I thought of the glossy ringlets and pearly teeth; I thought of the Kalydor; I thought of the coachman's bruised ear and bloody nose; I thought of the tender love secrets which she had whispered to the judge and jury and a thousand tittering auditors,—and gave another groan!

"Mr. Bullfrog," said my wife.

As I made no reply, she gently took my hands within her own, removed them from my face, and fixed her eyes steadfastly on mine.

"Mr. Bullfrog," said she, not unkindly, yet with all the decision of her strong character, "let me advise you to overcome this foolish weakness, and prove yourself, to the best of your ability, as good a husband as I will be a wife. You have discovered, perhaps, some little imperfections in your bride. Well, what did you expect? Women are not angels. If they were, they would go to heaven for husbands; or, at least, be more difficult in their choice on earth."

"But why conceal those imperfections?" interposed I, tremulously.

"Now, my love, are not you a most unreasonable little man?" said Mrs. Bullfrog, patting me on the cheek. "Ought a woman to disclose her frailties earlier than the wedding day? Few husbands, I assure you, make the discovery in such good season, and still fewer complain that these trifles are concealed too long. Well, what a strange man you are! Poh! you are joking."

"But the suit for breach of promise!" groaned I.

"Ah, and is that the rub?" exclaimed my wife. "Is it possible that you view that affair in an objectionable light? Mr. Bullfrog, I never could have dreamed it! Is it an objection that I have triumphantly defended myself against slander and vindicated my purity in a court of justice? Or do you complain because your wife has shown the proper spirit of a woman, and punished the villain who trifled with her affections?"

"But," persisted I, shrinking into a corner of the coach, however,—for I did not know precisely how much contradiction the proper spirit of a woman would endure,—"but, my love, would it not have been more dignified to treat the villain with the silent contempt he merited?"

"That is all very well, Mr. Bullfrog," said my wife, slyly; "but, in that case, where would have been the five thousand dollars which are to stock your dry goods store?"

"Mrs. Bullfrog, upon your honor," demanded I, as if my life hung upon her words, "is there no mistake about those five thousand dollars?"

"Upon my word and honor there is none," replied she. "The jury gave me every cent the rascal had; and I have kept it all for my dear Bullfrog."

"Then, thou dear woman," cried I, with an overwhelming gush of tenderness, "let me fold thee to my heart. The basis of matrimonial bliss is secure, and all thy little defects and frailties are forgiven. Nay, since the result has been so fortunate, I rejoice at the wrongs which drove thee to this blessed lawsuit. Happy Bullfrog that I am!"

The Lad with the Goatskin

BY JOSEPH JACOBS

ustralian-born folklorist and editor Joseph Jacobs later lived in England and America, where he taught at the Jewish Theological Seminary in New York. In addition to collecting Jewish and Irish folklore, he also compiled and edited versions of *Aesop's Fables* and the *Thousand and One Nights*. In this Irish fairy tale, a stalwart youth starts out with very little and ends up, through his own clever devices, with all a man could want, including the hand of a princess.

★　★　★　★　★

Long ago, a poor widow woman lived down near the iron forge, by Enniscorth, and she was so poor she had no clothes to put on her son; so she used to fix him in the ash-hole, near the fire, and pile the warm ashes about him; and according as he grew up, she sunk the pit deeper. At last, by hook or by crook, she got a goat-skin, and fastened it round his waist, and he felt quite grand, and took a walk down the street. So says she to him next morning, "Tom, you thief, you never done any good yet, and you six foot high, and past nineteen;—take that rope and bring me a faggot from the wood."

"Never say't twice, mother," says Tom—"here goes."

When he had it gathered and tied, what should come up but a big giant, nine foot high, and made a lick of a club at him. Well become Tom, he jumped a-one side, and picked up a ram-pike; and the first crack he gave the big fellow, he made him kiss the clod.

47

"If you have e'er a prayer," says Tom, "now's the time to say it, before I make fragments of you."

"I have no prayers," says the giant; "but if you spare my life I'll give you that club; and as long as you keep from sin, you'll win every battle you ever fight with it."

Tom made no bones about letting him off; and as soon as he got the club in his hands, he sat down on the bresna, and gave it a tap with the kippeen, and says, "Faggot, I had great trouble gathering you, and run the risk of my life for you, the least you can do is to carry me home." And sure enough, the wind o' the word was all it wanted. It went off through the wood, groaning and crackling, till it came to the widow's door.

Well, when the sticks were all burned, Tom was sent off again to pick more; and this time he had to fight with a giant that had two heads on him. Tom had a little more trouble with him—that's all; and the prayers he said, was to give Tom a fife; that nobody could help dancing when he was playing it. Begonies, he made the big faggot dance home, with himself sitting on it. The next giant was a beautiful boy with three heads on him. He had neither prayers nor catechism no more nor the others; and so he gave Tom a bottle of green ointment, that wouldn't let you be burned, nor scalded, nor wounded. "And now," says he, "there's no more of us. You may come and gather sticks here till little Lunacy Day in Harvest, without giant or fairyman to disturb you."

Well, now, Tom was prouder nor ten paycocks, and used to take a walk down street in the heel of the evening; but some o' the little boys had no more manners than if they were Dublin jackeens, and put out their tongues at Tom's club and Tom's goat-skin. He didn't like that at all, and it would be mean to give one of them a clout. At last, what should come through the town but a kind of a bellman, only it's a big bugle he had, and a huntsman's cap on his head, and a kind of a painted shirt. So this—he wasn't a bellman, and I don't know what to call him—bugleman, maybe, proclaimed that the King of Dublin's daughter was so melancholy that she didn't give a laugh for seven years, and that her father would grant her in marriage to whoever could make her laugh three times.

"That's the very thing for me to try," says Tom; and so, without burning any more daylight, he kissed his mother, curled his club at the little boys, and off he set along the yalla highroad to the town of Dublin.

At last Tom came to one of the city gates, and the guards laughed and cursed at him instead of letting him in. Tom stood it all for a little time, but at last one of them—out of fun, as he said—drove his bayonet half an inch or so into his side. Tom done nothing but take the fellow by the scruff o' the neck and the waistband of his corduroys, and fling him into the canal. Some run to pull the fellow out, and others to let manners into the vulgarian with their swords and daggers; but a tap from his club sent them headlong into the moat or down on the stones, and they were soon begging him to stay his hands.

So at last one of them was glad enough to show Tom the way to the palace-yard; and there was the king, and the queen, and the princess, in a gallery, looking at all sorts of wrestling, and sword-playing, and long-dances, and mumming, all to please the princess; but not a smile came over her handsome face.

Well, they all stopped when they seen the young giant, with his boy's face, and long black hair, and his short curly beard—for his poor mother couldn't afford to buy razors—and his great strong arms, and bare legs, and no covering but the goat-skin that reached from his waist to his knees. But an envious wizened bit of a fellow, with a red head, that wished to be married to the princess, and didn't like how she opened her eyes at Tom, came forward, and asked his business very snappishly.

"My business," says Tom, says he, "is to make the beautiful princess, God bless her, laugh three times."

"Do you see all them merry fellows and skilful swordsmen," says the other, "that could eat you up with a grain of salt, and not a mother's soul of 'em ever got a laugh from her these seven years?"

So the fellows gathered round Tom, and the bad man aggravated him till he told them he didn't care a pinch o' snuff for the whole bilin' of 'em; let 'em come on, six at a time, and try what they could do.

The king, who was too far off to hear what they were saying, asked what did the stranger want.

"He wants," says the red-headed fellow, "to make hares of your best men."

"Oh!" says the king, "if that's the way, let one of 'em turn out and try his mettle."

So one stood forward, with sword and pot-lid, and made a cut at Tom. He struck the fellow's elbow with the club, and up over their heads flew the sword, and down went the owner of it on the gravel from a thump he got on the helmet. Another took his place, and another, and another, and then half a dozen at once, and Tom sent swords, helmets, shields, and bodies, rolling over and over, and themselves bawling out that they were kilt, and disabled, and damaged, and rubbing their poor elbows and hips, and limping away. Tom contrived not to kill any one; and the princess was so amused, that she let a great sweet laugh out of her that was heard over all the yard.

"King of Dublin," says Tom, "I've quarter your daughter."

And the king didn't know whether he was glad or sorry, and all the blood in the princess's heart run into her cheeks.

So there was no more fighting that day, and Tom was invited to dine with the royal family. Next day, Redhead told Tom of a wolf, the size of a yearling heifer, that used to be serenading about the walls, and eating people and cattle; and said what a pleasure it would give the king to have it killed.

"With all my heart," says Tom; "send a jackeen to show me where he lives, and we'll see how he behaves to a stranger."

The princess was not well pleased, for Tom looked a different person with fine clothes and a nice green birredh over his long curly hair; and besides, he'd got one laugh out of her. However, the king gave his consent; and in an hour and a half the horrible wolf was walking into the palace-yard, and Tom a step or two behind, with his club on his shoulder, just as a shepherd would be walking after a pet lamb.

The king and queen and princess were safe up in their gallery, but the officers and people of the court that wor padrowling about the great bawn, when they saw the big baste coming in, gave themselves up, and began to make for doors and gates; and the wolf licked his chops, as if he was saying, "Wouldn't I enjoy a breakfast off a couple of yez!"

The king shouted out, "O Tom with the Goat-skin, take away that terrible wolf, and you must have all my daughter."

But Tom didn't mind him a bit. He pulled out his flute and began to play like vengeance; and dickens a man or boy in the yard but began shovelling away heel and toe, and the wolf himself was obliged to get on his hind legs and dance "Tatther Jack Walsh," along with the rest. A good deal of the people got inside, and shut the doors, the way the hairy fellow wouldn't pin them; but Tom kept playing, and the outsiders kept dancing and shouting, and the wolf kept dancing and roaring with the pain his legs were giving him; and all the time he had his eyes on Redhead, who was shut out along with the rest. Wherever Redhead went, the wolf followed, and kept one eye on him and the other on Tom, to see if he would give him leave to eat him. But Tom shook his head, and never stopped the tune, and Redhead never stopped dancing and bawling, and the wolf dancing and roaring, one leg up and the other down, and he ready to drop out of his standing from fair tiresomeness.

When the princess seen that there was no fear of any one being kilt, she was so divarted by the stew that Redhead was in, that she gave another great laugh; and well become Tom, out he cried, "King of Dublin, I have two halves of your daughter."

"Oh, halves or alls," says the king, "put away that divel of a wolf, and we'll see about it."

So Tom put his flute in his pocket, and says he to the baste that was sittin' on his currabingo ready to faint, "Walk off to your mountain, my fine fellow, and live like a respectable baste; and if ever I find you come within seven miles of any town, I'll—"

He said no more, but spit in his fist, and gave a flourish of his club. It was all the poor divel of a wolf wanted: he put his tail between his legs, and took to his pumps without looking at man or mortal, and neither sun, moon, or stars ever saw him in sight of Dublin again.

At dinner every one laughed but the foxy fellow; and sure enough he was laying out how he'd settle poor Tom next day.

"Well, to be sure!" says he, "King of Dublin, you are in luck. There's the Danes moidhering us to no end. Deuce run to Lusk wid 'em! and if any one can save us from 'em, it is this gentleman with the goatskin. There is a flail hangin' on the collar-beam, in hell, and neither Dane nor devil can stand before it."

"So," says Tom to the king, "will you let me have the other half of the princess if I bring you the flail?"

"No, no," says the princess; "I'd rather never be your wife than see you in that danger."

But Redhead whispered and nudged Tom about how shabby it would look to reneague the adventure. So he asked which way he was to go, and Redhead directed him.

Well, he travelled and travelled, till he came in sight of the walls of hell; and, bedad, before he knocked at the gates, he rubbed himself over with the greenish ointment. When he knocked, a hundred little imps popped their heads out through the bars, and axed him what he wanted.

"I want to speak to the big divel of all," says Tom: "open the gate."

It wasn't long till the gate was thrune open, and the Ould Boy received Tom with bows and scrapes, and axed his business.

"My business isn't much," says Tom. "I only came for the loan of that flail that I see hanging on the collar-beam, for the king of Dublin to give a thrashing to the Danes."

"Well," says the other, "the Danes is much better customers to me; but since you walked so far I won't refuse. Hand that flail," says he to a young imp; and he winked the far-off eye at the same time. So, while some were barring the gates, the young devil climbed up, and took down the flail that had the handstaff and booltheen both made out of red-hot iron. The little vagabond was grinning to think how it would burn the hands o' Tom, but the dickens a burn it made on him, no more nor if it was a good oak sapling.

"Thankee," says Tom. "Now would you open the gate for a body, and I'll give you no more trouble."

"Oh, tramp!" says Ould Nick; "is that the way? It is easier getting inside them gates than getting out again. Take that tool from him, and give him a dose of the oil of stirrup."

So one fellow put out his claws to seize on the flail, but Tom gave him such a welt of it on the side of the head that he broke off one of his horns, and made him roar like a devil as he was. Well, they rushed at Tom, but he gave them, little and big, such a thrashing as they didn't forget for a while. At last says the ould thief of all, rubbing his elbow, "Let the fool out; and woe to whoever lets him in again, great or small."

So out marched Tom, and away with him, without minding the shouting and cursing they kept up at him from the tops of the walls; and when he got home to the big bawn of the palace, there never was such running and racing as to see himself and the flail. When he had his story told, he laid down the flail on the stone steps, and bid no one for their lives to touch it. If the king, and queen, and princess, made much of him before, they made ten times more of him now; but Redhead, the mean scruff-hound, stole over, and thought to catch hold of the flail to make an end of him. His fingers hardly touched it, when he let a roar out of him as if heaven and earth were coming together, and kept flinging his arms about and dancing, that it was pitiful to look at him. Tom run at him as soon as he could rise, caught his hands in his own two, and rubbed them this way and that, and the burning pain left them before you could reckon one. Well the poor fellow, between the pain that was only just gone, and the comfort he was in, had the comicalest face that you ever see, it was such a mixtherum-gatherum of laughing and crying. Everybody burst out a laughing—the princess could not stop no more than the rest; and then says Tom, "Now, ma'am, if there were fifty halves of you, I hope you'll give me them all."

Well, the princess looked at her father, and by my word, she came over to Tom, and put her two delicate hands into his two rough ones, and I wish it was myself was in his shoes that day!

Tom would not bring the flail into the palace. You may be sure no other body went near it; and when the early risers were passing next morning, they found two long clefts in the stone, where it was after burning itself an opening downwards, nobody could tell how far. But a messenger came in at noon, and said that the Danes were so frightened when they heard of the flail coming into Dublin, that they got into their ships, and sailed away.

Well, I suppose, before they were married, Tom got some man, like Pat Mara of Tomenine, to learn him the "principles of politeness," fluxion, gunnery, and fortification, decimal fractions, practice, and the rule of three direct, the way he'd be able to keep up a conversation with the royal family. Whether he ever lost his time learning them sciences, I'm not sure, but it's as sure as fate that his mother never more saw any want till the end of her days.

The Scapulary

RAFAEL SABATINI

Perhaps second only to Dumas as a purveyor of swashbuckling yarns, Rafael Sabatini was born in Italy but grew up in the north of England, where as a novelist he ultimately combined the British love of heroics and seafaring adventure with Mediterranean romance and richness of plot. His stories have entertained readers and entranced moviegoers for generations, and his masterwork, *Captain Blood*, was called by one critic, "arguably the great undiscovered epic of the twentieth century." Here, he gives us a vivid recounting of the St. Bartholomew's Day massacre in Paris, the very night an estranged husband and wife must make a decision that will affect whether they live or die.

★   ★   ★   ★   ★

The uneasiness that had been disturbing Gaspard de Putanges ever since the King had visited the wounded Admiral de Coligny reached a climax that night when he found his way barred by armed men at the Porte St. Denis, and a password was demanded of him.

'Password!' cried that Huguenot gentleman in amazement. 'Is a password necessary before a man can leave Paris? And why, if you please? Are we suddenly at war?'

'Those are the orders,' the officer stiffly answered.

'Whose orders?' M. de Putanges was impatient.

'I owe you no account, sir. You will give me the word of the night, or you may return home and wait until morning.'

Perforce he must turn his horse about, and, with his groom at his heels, ride back by the way that he had come. The vexation which at any time he must have felt at this unwarranted interference with his movements was now swollen by misgivings.

He was one of the host of Huguenot gentlemen brought to Paris for the nuptials of the King of Navarre with the sister of the King of France, a marriage which the pacifists of both parties had hoped would heal the feud between the Catholic and Protestant factions. But the Guisard attempt upon the life of Coligny, the great Huguenot leader, had now rudely dashed this hope. M. de Putanges had been one of that flock of Huguenot gentlemen who that day had thronged the wounded Admiral's antechamber, when the epileptic king and the sleepy-eyed Queen Mother came to pay their visit of sympathy. He had listened with misgivings to the braggart threats of his co-religionists; with increased misgivings he had observed the open hostility of their bearing towards Catherine de' Medici what time she stood amongst them with Anjou, whilst the king her son was closeted with his dear gossip, M. de Coligny. These hot-headed fools, he felt, were fanning a fire that might presently blaze out to consume them all. Already the Hotel de Guise was in a state of fortification, filled with armed men ripe for any mischief, whilst others of the Guisard faction were abroad exciting public feeling with fantastic stories of the Huguenot peril, stories which gathered colour from the turbulent, thrasonical bearing of these Huguenots, enraged by the attempt upon their leader's life.

And now, finding the gates of Paris barred for no apparent reason, it seemed to M. de Putanges that the danger he had been apprehending was close upon them, though in what form he could not yet discern.

It was therefore as well that he should be forced to postpone his journey into the country, however necessary, and that he should remain to watch over his wife.

Now this was a consideration in which M. de Putanges discovered a certain humour. He was a thoughtful gentleman with a lively sense of irony, and it amused him after a certain bitter fashion to observe his own mechanical obedience to his sense of duty towards the cold, arrogant, discontented lady who bore his name. You know, of course, of the beautiful Madame de Putanges and of the profound impression which her beauty and wit had made upon the Court of France upon this her first appearance there. It is even rumoured—and not at all difficult to believe—that amongst those who prostrated themselves in worship before her was the very bridegroom Henri of Navarre himself. But at least the lady was virtuous—her one saving grace in her husband's eyes—and of a mind that was not to be discomposed by the flattery of even a royal wooing. It is not without humour that the only quality M. de Putanges could find to commend in her was that same cold aloofness which so embittered him. It was a paradox upon which he had found occasion to comment to his friend and cousin Stanislas de la Vauvraye.

'The gods who cast her in a mould so fair have given her for heart a stone.'

That was the formula in which habitually he expressed it to Stanislas, conscious that it sounded like a line from a play.

'I curse her for the very quality that makes my honour safe; because this quality that in another woman would be a virtue, is almost a vice in her.'

And Stanislas, the gay trifler who turned all things to cynical jest, had merely laughed. 'Be content, Gaspard, with a blessing denied most husbands.'

Yet however little M. de Putanges might count himself blessed as a husband, he was fully conscious of a husband's duty, and his first thought now that he suspected trouble was for his wife.

He made his way to the *Veau qui Tète,* where his horses were stabled and his grooms were housed, and, having dismounted there, set out for the small house he temporarily occupied close by, in the Rue Bellerose. The summer night had closed down by then, but there was a fair moon that rendered the use of flambeaux unnecessary. As he stepped out into the street he came upon a man bent double under a load of pikes. It was an odd sight and M. de Putanges stood arrested by it, watching the fellow as he staggered down the narrow street until he was absorbed by the shadows of the night. Yet even as he vanished a second man similarly laden came stumbling past. M. de Putanges fell into step beside the fellow.

'Whither are you carrying that arsenal?' he demanded.

The perspiring hind looked up from under his sinister load, to answer this brisk authoritative questioner.

'It is for the entertainment at the Louvre, Monsieur.'

As a gentleman in the train of the King of Navarre, M. de Putanges was bidden to all court functions. Yet here was one of which he had not so much as heard, and well might he ask himself what entertainment was this that was being kept so secret and in which pikes were to be employed. It was difficult to suppose that their purpose could be festive.

With ever-mounting uneasiness M. de Putanges lengthened his stride for home. But at the corner, where the Rue Bellerose cuts across the more important Rue St. Antoine, he ran into a group of men on the threshold of an imposing house that was all in darkness. At a glance he perceived that all were armed beyond the habit of peaceful citizens. Headpiece and corselet glinted lividly in the moonlight, and as he approached he caught from one on a note of sinister laughter the word '*Parpaillots*'—the nickname bestowed on members of the Huguenot party.

That was enough for M. de Putanges. Boldly—he was a man who never lacked for boldness—he mingled with the little throng. Others were joining it at every moment and already some were passing into the house, so that his coming was hardly observed; it would be assumed that he was one of themselves, bidden like them to this assembly. Perceiving this, and overhearing from one of those beside him the boast that by morning there would not be a whole heretic skin in Paris, M. de Putanges determined to push on and obtain more complete knowledge of what might be preparing. Heedless, then, of risks, he thrust forward to the threshold and attaching himself to a little knot of gentlemen in the act of entering, he went in with them, and up a broad, scantily-lighted staircase. At the stairhead the foremost of the company knocked upon a double door. One of its leaves was half opened and there ensued between someone within and each of those who sought admittance a preliminary exchange of confused murmurs. M. de Putanges pushed nearer, straining his ears, and at last from one whose mutter was louder than the others he caught the words: 'France and the Faith.' A moment later he was giving the same countersign.

He won through into a spacious gallery that was tolerably lighted by four great girandoles, and already thronged by men from every walk of life. All were armed and all were excited. From what he observed, from what was said to him even—for there was none here to recognize this gentleman of Béarn, or to suppose him other than one of themselves—he quickly came to understand that the thing preparing was no less than a massacre of the Huguenots in Paris.

Anon, when the room was filled almost to the extent of its capacity and the doors were closed, a lean, fiery-eyed preaching friar, in the black and white habit of St. Dominic, mounted a table and delivered thence at length what might be called a 'sermon of the faith', a fierce denunciation of heresy.

'Hack it down, branch by branch, tear it up by the roots; extirpate from the land this pestilential growth, this upas tree that poisons the very air we breathe. About it, my children! Be stern and diligent and unsparing in this holy work!'

Those terrible final words of incitement were ringing in his ears when M. de Putanges quitted at last that chamber, with its physically and morally mephitic atmosphere, and was borne out upon a brawling, seething human torrent, into the clean air of early dawn. The human mass broke into packs which turned away in one direction and another to the cry—fierce and menacing as the baying of hounds upon a scent—of 'Parpaillots! Parpaillots! Kill! Kill!'

He won free of them at length, forearmed at least by knowledge of what to expect—by knowledge and something more. In that chamber, whilst the sermon had been preaching, someone had tied a strip of white calico to his left arm and set in his hat a cross made of two short pieces of white ribbon. These were the insignia of the slayers and in themselves would have afforded him immunity in the open streets, but that upon an impulse of unreasoning disgust he tore one and the other from him and flung them in the kennel. This as he plunged at last down the Rue Bellerose towards home.

In a measure as the sounds of his late companions receded from him, ahead of him grew an ominous rumble, coming from the quays and the neighbourhood of the river; and then, a crackling volley of musketry rang out abruptly from the direction of the Louvre.

M. de Putanges stood still and wondered a moment whether the faint flush in the sky was a herald of the early summer dawn or the reflection of fire. He became suddenly aware that the Rue Bellerose was astir with flitting shadows. He came upon a man setting a mark in chalk upon a door, and, peering, beheld another similarly engaged on the opposite side of the street. He understood the meaning of it, and doubting if he would be alive by morning, he considered almost dispassionately—for he was a dispassionate man despite his southern blood—that it but remained him to seek his wife and await his fate beside her. If they had never known how to conduct their joint life becomingly, at least he hoped they would know how to die becomingly together.

In this frame of mind he reached his own threshold to find one of the doorposts bearing the chalk sign that marked the inmates down for slaughter. How well informed were these cursed *papegots,* he thought; how well considered and well organized was their bloody work! With his sleeve he rubbed out the sign of doom. So much, at least, he could do in self-defence. And then he stood arrested, with pulses faintly quickening. Within the shadows of the deep porch something stirred, and at the same moment upon the deep-set inner door fell a triple knock three times repeated.

M. de Putanges stepped forward. Instantly the thing within the porch swung about and sprang to meet him, taking definite shape. It was a tall cowled figure in the white habit and black scapulary of a brother of St. Dominic. M. de Putanges realized that he came no more than in time, if, indeed, he did not already come too late. He felt his heart tightening at the thought, tightening with icy dread for the cold termagant he loved. And then, to increase his fears, the friar pronounced his name and so proclaimed that he was not there by chance nor attracted by the mark of doom upon the doorpost, but with sure knowledge of the house's inmates.

'Monsieur de Putanges . . .' the man exclaimed, and got no further, for utterance and breath were abruptly choked by the iron fingers that locked themselves about his throat.

The fellow writhed and struggled, thrusting out a leg to trip his aggressor, clawing fiercely at the hands that were crushing out his life, and tearing them with his nails. But tear as he might, those hands would not relax their deadly grip. Soon his struggles weakened; soon they became mere twitchings. His body sagged together like an empty sack. He went down in a heap, dragging his assailant with him, and lay still at last.

M. de Putanges stood over the fallen friar, breathing hard; the beads of sweat upon his brow resulted partly from the exertion, partly from horror of a thing done in such a cold, relentless fashion. Mastering himself at last, he went forward towards the door. To his surprise he found it open, and remembered then that the friar had knocked upon it a moment ago. The latch was worked by a cord from the floor above and must have been so worked in answer to that knock.

M. de Putanges paused in the act of entering. It was not well—particularly considering that his house had been marked—to leave that thing in the porch where it might be discovered. He went back and, taking the limp body by the arms, he dragged it across the threshold into the hall. And then the instinct of self-preservation that had guided him so far urged yet another step. In that *papegot* livery it was possible that he might find safety for himself and his wife from the perils that were so obviously closing round them. The faintly reflected radiance of the moon afforded sufficient light for the simple task. In a moment he had unknotted the man's girdle and relieved him of habit and scapulary. Over his own clothes he donned the Dominican's loose white habit, and drew the cowl over his head. Then he closed the door, and set foot upon the narrow stairs, even as from the street outside a sudden shrieking of women was silenced by a fusillade. The massacre, he perceived, was in full swing already.

Overhead a light gleamed faintly; looking up from the darkness that encompassed him, he beheld in the feeble aureole of a candle, which she was holding, the face of Madame de Putanges. She was peering down, seeking with her glance to pierce the darkness of the staircase. He must speak at once, lest the sight of his monkish figure should alarm her. But even as he conceived the thought her silvery voice, strained now on an anxious note, forestalled him.

'How late you are, Stanislas!' she said.

In the gloom of the staircase, Gaspard de Putanges stood petrified, whilst through his mind that welcome meant for another echoed and re-echoed:

'How late you are, *Stanislas!*'

After a moment our gentleman's wits resumed their wonted function, sharpened now perhaps beyond their usual keenness. He scarcely needed to ask himself who could be this Stanislas for whom she mistook him. It could be none other than his dear friend and cousin, that gay trifler and libertine Stanislas de la Vauvraye. And she was expecting him at a time when she must suppose M. de Putanges already far from Paris. Was it possible, he asked himself, that he had thus by chance stumbled upon the explanation of her cold aloofness towards himself? Was Stanislas the Judas who simulated friendship in order that he might the more conveniently betray? In a flash a score of trifling incidents were suddenly remembered and connected to flood the mind of M. de Putanges with the light of revelation.

'Stanislas! Why don't you answer?' rang the impatient voice he knew so well.

Whence this absolute assurance of hers that he was the man she expected? He bethought him of that curious triple knock thrice repeated with which the friar had sought admittance, and in response to which the door-latch had been so promptly lifted from above. It was a signal, of course. But, then, the friar . . .

On a sudden suspicion amounting almost to certainty, M. de Putanges stepped back.

'Stanislas!' came again Madame de Putanges' call.

'A moment,' he answered to quiet her. 'I am coming.'

He ran his fingers swiftly over the face and head of the man he had choked. Here was no tonsure; no shaven cheeks. The hair of the head was full and crisp; moustachios bristled on the lip, and a little peaked beard sprouted from the chin: there was a jewel in the left ear which, like the rest, was as it should be with Stanislas de la Vauvraye. The garments were soft and silken—a slashed doublet and the rest. No doubt remained. All that remained was the mystery of how Stanislas should have come to be muffled in that monkish robe. That, however, could wait. It mattered little in comparison with all the rest. In his cursory examination of the body, M. de Putanges had ascertained that the man still breathed. He had not quite choked out his life. It was perhaps as well.

He locked the street-door and pocketed the key; then he went up the stairs with a step that was as firm and steady as his purpose.

When at last his cowled monkish figure came within the circle of light of the waiting woman's candle, she started back.

'Why, what is this? Who are you, sir?' Then remembering the covenanted knock to which she had opened, she partly explained the monkish travesty. 'Why do you come thus, Stanislas?'

'That,' was the quiet answer, 'we may ask presently of Stanislas himself.'

She staggered at the sound of her husband's voice, and a deathly pallor overspread her face. Her dark eyes opened wide in terror: her lips parted, but instead of speech they uttered a mere inarticulate sound of fear and horror, almost piteous to hear. Than she recovered, as he flung back his cowl and smiled upon her, grim, and white-faced as herself.

'You!' she gasped.

He observed that she was dressed for travelling, cloaked and hatted, and that a valise stood beside her at the stairhead.

'I thought you were gone to Poldarnes,' she said stupidly, a mere uncontrolled utterance of her mind.

'I am sorry, madame, to discompose you by so inopportune a return. Circumstances compelled it, as I will presently explain.'

Then at last the termagant in her recovered the sway momentarily extinguished by surprise.

'It needs no explanation, sir,' she answered with angry scorn, and angry unreason. 'You returned to spy upon me.'

'O fie, madame! To accuse me of that! But how unjust, how foolishly unjust! Had you but honoured me with your confidence, had you but informed me of your intent to elope with my dear friend and kinsman, I should have left you a clear field. I am too fond of you both to attempt against you so cruel a frustration of your designs.'

'You mean that you would have been glad to be rid of me!' was her fierce reproach.

M. de Putanges laughed his bitter amusement that even in such a situation she must make her own the grievance.

'Not glad, perhaps: but fortunate, madame,' said he. 'Once the hurt and humiliation of it were overcome, I might have seen in my dear kinsman Stanislas my best of friends.'

She fastened swiftly upon this admission. 'That is why I am leaving you.'

'But, of course. Do I not perceive it? I have, madame, a more sympathetic understanding than you have ever done me the justice to suppose.'

She answered by no more than an inarticulate expression of contempt.

'I shall hope to prove it to you tonight, madame,' he insisted. 'You may come to account it as fortunate for yourself as it is unfortunate for me that I returned. If you will be so good as to step into the salon, I will fetch my dear cousin Stanislas.'

This was to arouse her alarms afresh. 'You will fetch him!' she gasped. 'Where . . . where is he?'

'He is below.'

She was suddenly suspicious, glaring, fierce as a tigress. 'What have you done to him?'

'Oh, be reassured!—no permanent injury. He is a little . . . out of breath, shall we say? But that will pass.'

'Let me go to him.'

He barred her way. 'It is not necessary. He shall come to you. In no case can you depart just now. The streets are not safe. Listen!' Vague, hideous sounds of the foul business that was afoot penetrated the silence in which they stood, and filled her with wonder and some dread. He enlightened her. 'They are murdering the Huguenots in Paris tonight. That is what brought me back, supposing you would need protection, never dreaming that you would have the dear, brave Stanislas so near at hand.'

He took advantage of her amazement to add: 'If you will forgive the impertinence of the question, how long has M. de la Vauvraye been your lover, madame?'

She flushed to her eyes. 'Why must you insult me?'

'You are susceptible then to insult?'

Her anger, goaded by his cold mockery, raced on. 'Should I have stayed a single moment under your roof after taking a lover?' she demanded passionately. 'Do you think me capable of that?'

'I see,' said M. de Putanges, and sighed. 'You possess a casuist's mind, madame. You swallow camels yet strain at gnats.'

'Maybe. But I am honest, monsieur.'

'After your own fashion, madame; strictly after your own fashion.'

'After my own fashion, if you will. You have a great gift for mockery, monsieur.'

'Be thankful, madame. The man who does not know how and when to laugh, sometimes does very foolish and very painful things. And so, you were saying that you are honest . . .'

'I think I prove it. Having taken my resolve, I am leaving your house tonight. I am going away with M. de la Vauvraye.'

She was defiant. He bowed to her will.

'Why, so you shall, for me. It remains to take measures for your safety, considering what is happening in the street. Be so good as to wait in the salon, whilst I fetch this dear Stanislas.'

He took the candle from her limp hand and went down the stairs again. He found his kinsman sitting up, in bewilderment—a bewilderment which the sight of M. de Putanges transmuted into stark fear.

But M. de Putanges was of a reassuring urbanity. 'Be good enough to step up to the salon with me, my dear cousin. Henriette desires a word with you, whereafter you may carry out or not your fond intentions. That will depend. Meanwhile, be thankful that I have returned in time, as I gather from what madame tells me. If the harm were already beyond repair I should for my honour's sake be compelled to renew, and this time to complete, the strangling of you. That would be a painful matter for us both, for I have a horror of violence, as you know, my dear Stanislas. Fortunately the affair may still be amicably decided. The circumstances of the night are particularly propitious. Be so good, then, as to come up with me.'

M. de la Vauvraye, his mind benumbed by this extraordinary turn of what should have been so simple and delightful an adventure, followed his kinsman up the stairs with an obedience of such utter helplessness as to be almost entirely mechanical.

In the salon they found Madame awaiting them. She stood by the heavy, carved table of dark oak well in the light of the dozen tapers that burned in a gilded candlebranch. Her beautiful face was pale and haggard, yet neither so pale nor so haggard as that of the lover she now confronted in circumstances so vastly different from all that she had expected of this night.

She had declared to him but yesterday that it was to be the most fateful night of her life, and in that, indeed, she appeared to have been a true prophet.

Of the three, the only one at ease—outwardly at least—was M. de Putanges. Tall, erect, virilely handsome, a man in the very flower of his age, bronzed, intrepid and aquiline of countenance, he made the golden-headed trifler la Vauvraye seem so sickly and effeminate by contrast that it was difficult to discern how any woman could have come to prefer him.

'Be seated, pray.' Suavity itself, M. de Putanges waved each in turn to a chair. 'I shall not keep you long.'

La Vauvraye, under the woman's eyes, realizing that he was in danger of cutting a poor, unheroic figure, summoned impudence to his aid. 'You relieve my fears, monsieur.' With a shrug and a half-laugh he sank to an armchair. He was not as successful as he thought, for his crumpled ruff and dishevelled hair lent him an appearance which dignity but made the more ridiculous.

'Your fears?' quoth M. de Putanges.

'Of being wearied by futile recriminations. Weariness is the thing in life that I most dread.'

'Reassure yourself. You are in no danger of it. Indeed, the night should bring a surfeit of excitement even to such a glutton for high adventure.'

La Vauvraye stifled a yawn. 'If you will but explain,' he begged on a half plaintive note.

'Of course. But first a question: How came you by this Dominican frock in which I found you?'

'Oh, that!' M. de la Vauvraye was casual. 'You will know by now what is afoot tonight. I, too, discovered it as I was coming here. At the end of the Rue Bellerose I came upon a shaveling I had met once or twice at Court. Unfortunately for him, he knew me too, and calling me by name threatened me with a heretic's doom. It was rash. I had a dagger . . . I silenced that too garrulous friar, and left him in a doorway.'

'Possessing yourself of his habit?'

'Why, yes. I realized that on such a night his scapulary would possess the virtues that are claimed for scapularies, would be a panoply against all perils. You would seem to have been of the same mind yourself when, taking me unawares, you became possessed of it and donned it in your turn.'

'And then, dear cousin? Continue, pray.'

'What more is there to tell?'

'Why, that you counted upon the frock to shield not only yourself but this Huguenot lady with whom you had planned an elopement for tonight.'

'Oh, that, of course.' The nonchalance was almost overdone.

'It was my notion, too. Since we are both agreed as to its excellence, there is no reason not to act upon it.'

The affected languor passed from M. de la Vauvraye's eyes. They became alert and keen to the point almost of anxiety. M. de Putanges proceeded to explain himself.

'Madame de Putanges must be saved,' he said quietly. 'That, you will realize, is the paramount consideration. She must be carried out of reach of this bloodshed before it is too late. Escorted by a brother of St. Dominic the thing is easy. We have but to determine which of us shall assume the frock and take her hence, which shall remain behind to die nobly for her sake. Since we both love her, the decision should be easy, for neither of us should hesitate to remain. Rather do I fear a generous emulation as to which shall go.' He dealt so delicately in irony that neither of his listeners could be certain that he was ironical.

With blanched cheeks and bulging eyes, M. de la Vauvraye stared at his cousin, waiting. The handsome woman seated in the high-backed chair looked on with parted lips, her breathing quickened, and waited, too.

M. de Putanges resumed: 'But for what is taking place in Paris tonight, my dear cousin, it might be necessary to choose some other way of resolving this painful situation. As it is, our common concern for Madame de Putanges points the way clearly. One of us goes. The other stays behind to die. Ideal and complete solution. It but remains to determine our respective parts.' He paused and the silence within that room was tense and heavy. Outside was uproar—the baying of the fanatical mob, the crash of shivered timbers and the screams of luckless victims.

M. de la Vauvraye moistened his parched lips with his tongue.

'And how . . . how is that to be determined?' he asked in a quavering, high-pitched voice that cracked on the last word.

'What way but one could gallantry conceive? It is for Madame de Putanges to choose.' He bowed deferentially, as he consigned into her hands that monstrous decision.

M. de la Vauvraye expressed in a gasp his immense relief, never doubting Madame's choice, never observing the stark horror that distorted her lovely face, nor how that horror deepened at the sound he made.

But M. de Putanges had something yet to add. He was being extremely subtle, where neither of his listeners suspected subtlety.

'Thus, madame, you shall have at last the choice that should have been yours at first. It is in your power tonight to repair the injustice that was done you three years ago when, unconsulted, you were driven into a wedlock of arrangement.' He sighed. 'Perhaps had I wooed you first and wed you afterwards all might have been well with us. I realize tonight the profound mistake of reversing that natural course of things, and I am almost glad of the opportunity to correct it, by giving you now, late though it be, the choice that is a woman's right. So pronounce, madame. Determine of your own free will which of us shall assume the frock and bear you hence, which shall remain to die.'

On that he ended, looking with solemn inscrutable glance deep into the eyes that stared at him out of his wife's white, horror-stricken face. He knew—unless he knew nothing of human nature—that the woman did not live who could take upon her conscience the responsibility of such a choice: and upon that knowledge he was boldly trading.

To help him to his deep end, came the bleating voice of his foolish rival, urgent with an obvious meaning that he dared not actually express in words. 'Henriette! Henriette!'

M. de Putanges observed her shrink and cringe before that appeal, as if conscious only of the meanness and cowardice that inspired it. Upon something of that kind, too, had he counted. He intended to compel her tonight to look, as she had never yet troubled to look, into his soul. And he intended no less to lay bare the little soul of the trifler for whom she would have left him. She should have the free choice he offered her; but first there should be full revelation to guide her in her choice.

'Well, madame?' He loosened the girdle of his monkish habit, as if to stress his readiness for renunciation at her bidding. 'Which of us shall wear the frock, the scapulary of salvation—more potently protecting tonight than any consecrated prophylactic?'

And again from M. de la Vauvraye—now half risen—came the appeal—'Henriette!'

Madame de Putanges looked with the glance of a hunted creature from one to the other of those men. Then a shudder ran through her; she twisted and untwisted the fingers of her interlocked hands, and faintly moaned.

'I cannot! I cannot!' she cried out at last. 'No—no! I cannot have the blood of either of you on my soul.'

M. de la Vauvraye flung himself back in his chair, his lip in his teeth, his hands clenched, whilst M. de Putanges smiled with wistful understanding.

'Yet consider, madame,' he urged her, 'that unless you choose we are likely all three of us to perish here together.'

'I can't! I can't! I will not choose. It is monstrous to demand it of me,' she cried.

'Demand?' echoed M. de Putanges. 'Oh, madame, I do not demand; I invite. But to spare your feelings, since you prove so tender in this matter, it shall be determined otherwise; and that I must deplore, because in no other way could your future happiness be assured. Still . . .' He broke off, and flung the Dominican frock and scapulary, of which he had now divested himself, upon the table; then he turned to a tall press that stood against the wall, and took from one of its drawers a dice-box. Rattling the cubes in their leathern container, he looked across at his kinsman.

'Come, cousin. You love a hazard. Here is one in which the stakes are something rare: love and life are here for one of us.'

M. de la Vauvraye, who had risen, shrank back in fear. If he loved hazards, he loved them not quite so hazardous.

'No, no,' he cried, thrusting out his hands in a violent gesture of denial. 'This is a horror.'

'What else remains?' asked M. de Putanges. 'Come, man. I'll lead the way.'

He threw recklessly as he spoke, thereby committing the other to the adventure. The three cubes scattered and rattled to a standstill on the polished oaken board. Madame's glittering eyes followed them and remained expressionless when the throw was revealed—two aces and a deuce.

M. de Putanges laughed softly, bitterly. 'That is my luck,' said he. 'You should have known that I was not to be feared, Stanislas. You'll scarce hesitate now to throw against me.'

Yet he was pleased enough in the heart of him. Fortune could not have served him better. Now that no risk remained M. de la Vauvraye would be as eager as before he had been hesitant, and so should make yet further self-revelation. And eager he was. It was his turn to laugh as with trembling fingers he gathered up the dice; a hectic flush tinged his cheek-bones as he threw—two fives and a four.

'Mine!' he cried, and snatched up the frock in exultation.

M. de Putanges bowed with quiet dignity.

'My congratulations, cousin; and to you, madame, since surely Fortune must have determined as you wish, yet dared not pronounce out of a generous thought for me. For that thought I thank you. What now remains for me will be the easier in the knowledge that it comes not from you, but from Fortune.' He became matter-of-fact and brisk. 'You had best make haste away. There is danger in delaying.'

'Indeed, indeed—he is right,' M. de la Vauvraye now urged her, as he shook out the folds of the frock and with trembling fingers knotted the girdle about his middle.

But Madame made no answer to either of them. With eyes of wonder she looked from one to the other, contrasting the noble calm in adversity of this husband she had never known, with the meanly selfish eagerness of the shallow courtier whom she had imagined that she loved. M. de Putanges had promised himself to afford her full revelation; and he had succeeded beyond his hopes.

M. de la Vauvraye took a step towards her. 'Come, Henriette,' he was beginning, when suddenly she laughed so oddly that he checked. She looked at him with shining eyes and oddly smiling lips.

'Do not wait for me, monsieur. All that it was yours to stake upon the throw was the scapulary that will shield your life. You have won that, and so you may win to safety. But I do not go with the scapulary. Goodnight and good fortune to you, M. de la Vauvraye.'

He stared at her, dumbfounded, stricken in his scanty wits and in his monstrous vanity.

'What?' he cried. 'You will remain?'

'With my husband, if you please, monsieur.'

Quiet and self-contained in the background beyond the table M. de Putanges looked on and wondered. M. de la Vauvraye rapped out an oath. Then anger bubbled to the surface of his shallow nature. His tone became vicious.

'Goodnight, madame.'

He turned on his heel; but as he reached the door her voice arrested him.

'M. de la Vauvraye!'

He turned again.

'A man in your place would have acted perhaps more generously. A man would have remembered all that is involved. A man would account that my final decision overrides the decision of the dice. He would have proffered the scapulary to the true winner. A man would have done that. But you, it seems, are something less. Since it has been tested, I am the more content to stay.'

He looked at her from the depths of the cowl which he had already pulled over his head, so that his face was no longer visible. Without answering her he went out, closing the door with expressive violence. They heard his steps go pattering down the stairs, and then the sound of them was drowned in the uproar from without.

They looked at each other across the table. M. de Putanges sighed as he spoke.

'Did I conceive him worthy of you, madame, I should not have suffered you to have had your way. Even now I doubt—'

'Gaspard,' she interrupted him, 'I am content. I have chosen, even though I have chosen too late.' She held out a hand to him, and he saw that she was weeping. He took the hand and very tenderly stooped to kiss it.

'My dear,' he said, 'it but remains for us to forgive each other.'

As he spoke the air was shaken by a sudden roar, deeper, fiercer, nearer than any that had gone before. She sank against him shuddering in sudden fear. 'What is that?'

'Wait.' Swiftly he quenched the lights. Then in the darkness he groped to the shutters, opened them and flung the window wide. Screened by the gloom above, they looked down into the seething, furious mob revealed by torchlight and the breaking day.

In the clutches of a knot of frenzied men, a Dominican friar was struggling wildly.

'Let us look at your face,' they were howling. 'Let us make sure that you are what you seem—that you are not the villain who murdered Father Gerbier and stole his frock.'

The cowl was suddenly torn back, and the livid, distorted face of Stanislas de la Vauvraye was revealed.

'We have found you at last, you murthering heretic!' cried a voice and a pike was swung above the Huguenot's luckless head. A roar arose:

'Kill! Kill! Death to the Parpaillot!'

M. de Putanges pulled his wife back and closed the window, and the shutters. She clung to him in the dark.

'My God!' she moaned. 'Had he been generous: had I been mad . . .' She said no more; she fell on her knees to pray.

Through the remainder of that night of St. Bartholomew they waited hand in hand for death. It was, they said thereafter, their true nuptial night. But death did not seek them. M. de Putanges, you will remember, had rubbed the sign of doom from the doorpost with his sleeve, and the house was not molested. Three days later, when the reaction had set in, they quietly slipped out of Paris unchallenged, and made their way back to Béarn having found each other.

A Husband's Confession

BY "TRISTIS"

This short anonymous piece, purportedly sent to an editor at *Good Housekeeping,* rings with a universal truth: love dies when imagination and spontaneity are suppressed. The author is no monster, but simply an "everyman" who has not trusted his instincts: after all, what man or woman in love has not unwittingly said or done something to damage a relationship and longed to take it back? Although the narrator finds himself facing a lonely old age, the result of his own misguided actions, there is such heartfelt remorse in his words, the reader can't help hoping he was at last able to express his true feelings and make things right.

★   ★   ★   ★   ★

Sometimes it seems to me as if there were no more lonely lot in this world than mine. No one who knows me would think so. I do not carry my heart on my sleeve, as the saying is, and the world judges by appearances. To its eye I am a prosperous, contented business man, in easy financial circumstances, with health and means to permit of any desired rational enjoyment.

That is all the world knows about it. I doubt if a more miserable human lives than myself, and often the refrain of an old poem or hymn I have heard some time and somewhere rises, unbidden but apropos, in my mind: " 'Twas mine own hand that built the cross I bear up Calvary."

Let's see. I was only twenty-four when I married, and my wife was barely eighteen. My people had dubbed me the "old bach"—not because of my age, but because I had never shown any inclination for the society of the other sex. This was not from shyness, but from indifference. My older and my younger brothers were both married, but I felt sure I should never marry, and often said so to my mother, with whom I lived. But "the best-laid plans o' mice and men gang aft agley."

So, when I came home one evening in that long-ago time and found Katherine, sweet, brown-eyed Katherine, sitting shyly in the big armchair near the fireplace, I fell in love at once. The affection was returned. Katie was a citybred girl and she had come out into our little village to teach school. All the boys laughed at me, I remember, because I was going to marry a city girl and a teacher. I had often expressed an adverse opinion of the merits of such girls.

My mother was nearly heartbroken. When, finally, she gave a reluctant consent, it was coupled with advice, kindly and wisely meant I am sure.

"Walter," she said, "I did hope, if you ever married, you would have found some nice girl whom I'd known all my life. Katie is sweet and pretty, but—well, you know, Walter, you must remember poor Cousin Henry. He married a city girl and a teacher, too, and we all know what a shiftless wife she made and what a comfortless home, if one could call it a home, his was.

"I've seen Florilla poking around the flower garden when there wasn't a clean dish in the house, and if his people hadn't kept sending clothes for the children, they'd have been half naked most of the time.

"Oh, she was sweet, too, and pretty, but those don't keep house, and I've seen Henry's children running around with yards of soiled lace on their frocks and their stockings as full of holes as a sieve. And yet, Walter," she said ruminatively, "I sometimes believe if Henry had put his foot down and insisted on order and sensible doings when he was first married, all would have been well. I do hope, my dear son, you will profit by his example."

And so mother went on, earnestly and eagerly, meaning, beyond a doubt, just to warn me against a social shipwreck and with no other purpose in her mind, I, poor blind bat that I was, listening uneasily, to be sure, for I knew my Katherine would never degenerate into a slattern, but still with, as time showed, a respect for mother's opinions.

Naturally I pooh-poohed mother's remarks and loyally defended the woman I loved with all my heart and mind; but, looking backward, I can but feel that some small seed of suspicion might have been sown in those conversations. I don't know as it is so. We are all prone to lay the beginning of disagreeable results to other souls rather than to shoulder the responsibility for them ourselves.

I remember our first meal together in the little house on the old farm where we began our wedded life. We drove over one June afternoon and Katie bustled around, gay as a lark and busy as a bee, getting ready our first meal in our own little home.

It was a pretty tea table. But when I saw it, suddenly there came into my foolish head a remembrance of mother's warning and Henry's miserable home. At Katie's plate and mine stood little vases of violets, and a glass dish full of the dainty flowers ornamented the center of the table. The board looked pretty, and I was always a lover of flowers; but, in my blindness and fear, I conceived a swift, mad idea that here and now I must make my stand against idle sentiment, which might, if catered to, reach too great a proportion.

Gracious! Before I knew it I might be in the same plight as my unfortunate and easy-going cousin.

So, stifling the first eager note of admiration and praise that rose spontaneously to my lips, I, instead, kept silence, and pushed, somewhat ostentatiously, the little vase away from my plate and paid no heed to the other pretty decorations.

"Don't you like the flowers, Walter?" asked my wife, with an anxious look. "I thought they made the table look pretty. There is a large bed of them in the front yard."

I wanted to jump up and hug her and tell her they were lovely, but I remembered my duty in time.

"The table is a place for food, not flowers," I said coldly.

The light died from her eyes. She never said a word, either of expostulation or criticism, but silently removed the despised vases to a side table and began helping me to tea. That was thirty-seven years ago, and never from that day to this has Katherine ever placed a flower to beautify our table. I felt both elated and chagrined at the result of my remark. I was glad that what I believed right should have been done without any quarrel, and sorry that I had achieved my desire at the expense of even five minutes of unhappiness, for my dear one.

That was the first of my efforts to train Katie in the ways I, in my conceit and complacency, honestly believed it best good housewives should go.

All of them had one and the same result: without a murmur Katie yielded. Perhaps she was different in nature from most women. I am sure if she had cried or coaxed I should have capitulated at once. She never did. And so I kept on, frustrating all her sweet efforts at sentiment with sternness. I was self-complacent enough to congratulate myself on possessing a wife of such docility, one who so readily recognized the superior good judgment of her husband.

I know better now. I know it was pride which prevented her from rebelling and self-respect which made her seek, at first involuntarily, for other ways in which to still the hunger of her heart and soothe her lacerated feelings.

I especially remember the Christmas following our marriage. I had noted how, when I entered the room suddenly, Katie would jump and cover some bundle on which she was working, and I naturally conjectured she was preparing some surprise as a gift for me.

About that time I went over to mother's. I boasted to her of my wife's skill and neatness, and with an asininity I now recognize as colossal, I mentioned the floral incident. "Ah," said my mother, wishing, I suppose, to justify her early assertions and to explain the failure of her prophecies, "that helps explain it! If Henry had only suppressed Florilla's foolish sentiment as soon as it cropped out, his home would have been different."

I loved my mother. I had always deferred to and respected her judgment, and I could not but be impressed with her words, even though I realized that I was being disloyal to Katie in listening to them, or tacitly permitting her view of the case.

Don't imagine, either, that I'm trying to lay the blame of my misfortune on my dear mother's shoulders. She and Katie became the best of friends; and my mother, in after years, often congratulated me on my good fortune in obtaining such a good wife. It was my own fatuous conceit and blindness that lost me the dearest treasure life offers or can give any man—his wife's love.

I thought as I rode home how much wiser a man I was than that bugaboo of a relative of mine. I actually imagined it was my training which made Katie the little jewel of a housewife that she was, and would have been had she never seen me.

I recall that Christmas with remorse. I recollect that as I entered the sitting room Katie started with a delicious little gurgle of a scream and threw her apron over a little bundle in her lap. I said, thinking, hapless idiot that I was, that I was being just kindly assertive: "Now, Katie, if you're fixing up any kind of fancy foolishness for a Christmas present for me, let me say right here that I don't object to a kind of celebration on a good common-sense basis, but don't waste your time on claptraps. If you're going to give me something, let it be something I need or something needed in the house. Don't waste your time on gewgaws."

A fleeting panorama of my cousin's home, with its torn tidies and tumbled lambrequins, passed mentally before my vision as I spoke and perhaps caused me to use more acerbity than I really felt, for—I recall it as plainly as if it were yesterday—I saw a shadow pass over her face, as a cloud obscures the light of the sun, and she looked at me a moment in uncertain silence, and from the corner of my eye, I saw a mist in hers, and for just a second her lips quivered. Then they tightened, as I have seen them do so many times since, and she answered, "Well, Walter, just as you say." Though pleased with her submissiveness, I longed to take her in my arms and retract all I'd said and tell her to do anything she pleased, Christmas or any other time; but my evil genius kept me from it. There was an end then to all the little mysteries and secrets of the holiday season so far as I was concerned; and I missed them, though I would not have acknowledged my inconsistency for worlds. At Christmas I received articles of necessary clothing, as I had suggested.

Last summer Katie and I went up to the attic to look through an old secretary. In one drawer she ran across a box, which she opened with curiosity.

"Why, Walter," she said, her voice, I noted, being absolutely free from any cadence of sentiment or sorrow, "if here isn't that pair of silk suspenders I started to knit for you the first Christmas after we were married. Wasn't I the silly lass in those days? I wanted to make something for you with my own hands. But you cured me, Walter, of all my sentimental ideas. Here, catch them. I'll give them to you now."

Thinking of the long, unbroken succession of sensible presents, presented prosaically, which I had received ever since, I turned to the window, pretending to examine the little bundle of faded silk, but, in reality, to hide the emotion this tangible evidence of my mistakes caused me.

Yes, I had cured her of sentiment, and of love also. I have that unfinished tangle of silk hidden away as a memory of a time when I was loved as I did not deserve.

Perhaps if we had been blessed earlier with children my defections and arbitrary ways would not have carried so much weight with her. She would have found comfort in her little ones and they would have softened me. But we had been married eight years when our first born came, and it was about this time I began to notice that I was not as necessary to my wife's happiness as she to mine, and that our interests were varied and lay apart. I was somewhat startled as I realized that she was largely self-sufficient as far as my society was concerned. I know now that, disappointed in me, she had been forced to seek sources in which to find relief.

I considered the matter. Katie never met me now at the door when I came home. She did not consult me on personal matters. She seldom kissed me. She had lost a certain buoyancy of manner which had been a great charm. At twenty-seven years she was a serious, rather silent, self-contained woman. Her calmness was becoming, too, but it was not at all flattering to me, who had deemed her happiness dependent on mine.

As the years passed little occurrences showed me that we were really living separate lives and that hers was full and complete without my being a factor of much consequence in it. She had her children, her church, her social societies and duties, a circle of friends, her relief corps, and, indeed, many more ways in which I was not considered. This was to me a poignant grief, which manifested itself in futile remonstrances and arbitrary acts. My remonstrances were disregarded and my injustice quietly borne. The latter, too, begun, as I imagined, as a necessity, had now developed into a habit against which, because of its consequences, I struggled, more or less hopelessly, for I saw that my wrong course was alienating my wife's affection. Yet, because, I suppose, my own affection was so deep and unalterable, and perhaps because I possessed a good opinion of myself, I did not realize, fully realize, until some years later that my wife's love for me was absolutely dead.

All my vanity and desire to blind my eyes to the truth could not conceal, finally, from me the fact that my presence often bored her, that my caresses were tolerated and that my absence was not a sorrow to her.

Katie was kind. She dutifully consulted me on all household matters and on all that pertained to the children. She exacted respect from the children toward me and included me in all their plans. As far as duty was concerned she fulfilled it to the last letter of the law.

Now that our last child is married and my business does not exact much care, now that we are alone, as in the beginning of our wedded life, the full measure of my loss comes upon me and seems unbearable. We might be all in all to each other and we yet live separate lives, mine solitary, burdened with unavailing regret, hers full and seemingly satisfying with her many interests.

I feel that to her I am only a familiar object, somewhat dearer than old Bose, a companion whose absence is little noted and whose demise would awaken a mild emotion of regret, but no overwhelming sense of loss.

And I—why, I love her with my whole heart and soul! I have entirely renounced my theory of superiority. I am even abject in my acceptance of her smallest wish, but all in vain.

My methods were successful beyond my wildest comprehension. I am a lonely old man. It wouldn't matter so much if I, too, were indifferent. I see couples in whose hearts passionate love has died and who jog comfortably along, cheerful comrades, having substituted friendship for the higher emotion. I cannot follow their example.

I love my wife as tenderly, as truly, as deeply, as on the day we sealed our troth, and I shall never do otherwise. Sometimes I pray that I may lose this love, and then again I feel thankful my prayer remains unanswered. Sometimes I stifle it and have a season's peace, as one suffering from an incurable disease enjoys respites from the gnawing pain at times; but always, always, the uneasiness, unrestfulness, the vain longing, return and rise into almost unbearable life and action.

I know there is no hope of resurrecting or reviving my wife's love for me. The breach between us is irreparable. It cannot be built over nor mended. I saw to it that the chasm was made deep and wide. Smile at me if you will, but be warned and remember this truth, that there is no tragedy in unrequited love of any kind which equals that of the man or woman, past the Indian summer of their life, entering the Valley of the Shadow, and entering it alone, knowing the desolation is of their own encompassing.

The Lesson

BY PEARL BUCK

As the child of missionaries, Pearl Buck grew up in China and was steeped in the lore of her adopted country. She won the Nobel Prize in 1938 for a body of work that opened readers' eyes to the culture and humanity of the Far East. In this story, a simple country girl of China is tutored in reading and Christianity by a married couple who have not put off their American trappings. When at last she leaves their school to marry, they lament that she was such a poor student who retained little of what they'd tried to teach her. But she proves wiser than they could have imagined; from observing them she has learned one very important lesson: the secret to a happy marriage.

★   ★   ★   ★   ★

"I hate to let Ru-lan go like this," said little Mrs. Stanley to her husband. "I don't believe she knows anything at all—she's not fit to be married."

She had just come in from the garden and her arms were full of roses, the swift-blooming, vivid roses of a Chinese May. Wyn Stanley looked at her, smiling, his heart caught in his throat at her loveliness. He and Mollie had been married five years but he never grew used to her. He saw her every day—how lucky he was that his work at the mission was to run the schools and not to be an itinerant evangelist! If he had had to go off on long preaching tours as Dr. Martin did, and be weeks away from Mollie, he could not have borne it. Sometimes in the night he woke to trouble and shivering, fearful lest God call him to such work, lest something happen that he and Mollie might have to be separated—suppose one of the children were to fall ill and have to be taken home across the sea to America like the Burgess child, and Mrs. Burgess away for nearly two years, or—he would put out his hand to touch Mollie's round little body lying deeply and healthfully asleep beside him. He would not wake her— but somehow she always woke and somehow he always told her his fears, and then waited to hear her laugh her sweet, contented laughter. "Oh, Wyn, as if—Anyway, God hasn't called you to evangelistic work, has he? And if I had to go home you'd come too. We'd find another job. You suppose I'd let you stay here by yourself?" He was asleep before he knew it then.

Now he looked up at her from his desk, adoring her. She dimpled and put her hand on his cheek and pretended to pout. "You haven't heard a thing I've been saying. You never listen to me."

He caught her hand and held it to his lips, a little firm hand, scratched with rose thorns. "It's because I can't keep from looking at you. What's going to happen to me if I keep loving you more all the time?" He drew her to him and leaned his face against her breast. Under his cheek he could feel the steady pounding of her heart. "True heart—true heart—" he murmured to the rhythm of her heart. She bent over his dark head, pressing it against her. They both forgot the girl Ru-lan. They were swept back into the summer morning five years ago in the little old churchyard behind the red brick church where her father had preached so many years, and where Wyn had come as substitute for a month of vacation. She and her mother had sent her father off for the trip to Palestine he had planned for a lifetime. What destiny it had been, that on the summer when the family did not all go away together Wyn had been the supply—just before he was to sail as a missionary to China!

They had fallen in love at once. The first moment she saw his tall, young figure mounting the steps of the pulpit she knew him and loved him. And he, when he looked over the congregation, saw her and thereafter her only. And then in just a few weeks, that July morning after church, when she was running home to the manse by the short cut through the churchyard, he came striding after her, still with his surplice on. He had, he said, meant only to ask her to—to walk with him, perhaps, in the evening. But when she turned and looked at him, under the deep shadows of the old elms and hidden by the lilacs along the path, he had taken her into his arms and enfolded her. There was no question asked and no answer given, simply meeting. Whenever they came together it was the same thing, the same deep union again—like this.

There was a small sound, and they jumped apart. The older missionaries always said, "The Chinese are not used to demonstration between the sexes." Mrs. Burgess had taken her aside very soon and said, "Try not to take your—Mr. Stanley's—hand in front of the Chinese, dear. It is—they would consider it indelicate." So she and Wyn had tried very hard to learn to wait until they were alone. But hand went so instinctively to hand, his arm was around her so naturally. Now they looked guiltily toward the door.

There she stood, Ru-lan, the girl she had come in to see Wyn about, the poor stupid girl. She was standing there in the doorway, dressed in a clean, blue cotton coat and trousers, with a blue and white print handkerchief tied full of the books she never could learn. Her father had come for her to take her home to be married, and she was ready to go.

"Come in, Ru-lan," Mollie said. She smiled, her heart full of compassion. The girl's round, placid face responded at once with a childlike pleasure. Above the large full cheeks her black eyes shone faintly. Mollie Stanley looked down at the roses and went over and took the girl's plump hand.

"I'm sorry you must go," she said in Chinese. "But your father will not consent to your staying longer. Sit down, child, and let me talk with you a little."

The girl sat down obediently, in silence. The smile had gone from her face now and she sat staring quietly at these two, observing all they did.

Mollie looked at her and was discouraged. She had so often in the schoolroom faced that dense placidity.

"Wyn, what shall we do?" she asked, turning to him. "She's seventeen and she's been here ever since we came, and I don't believe she will ever learn much. She's been through all the classes—Bible and arithmetic and hygiene—she reads a few hundred characters and that's all you can say. She just isn't fit for marriage—such a good, faithful, kind, *stupid* girl! You know she came up for baptism twice, and she just can't remember enough to answer Dr. Martin's questions, however hard I coach her. I'm sometimes afraid she's still heathen."

"No, I know," answered Wyn. "It's no good her staying here. If she had any promise at all I'd try to persuade her father to let her finish at least the grades. But I haven't the heart to let him think she ever could finish. Maybe she'd better go on and be married."

"Wyn Stanley!" his wife cried out at him, "as if it weren't serious that a girl like that is to be married and have a lot of children! Of course she will have a lot of children!"

They both looked, troubled, at Ru-lan, who meeting their eyes instantly broke into her great, beaming smile, not understanding a word of their English. They were baffled by her smile.

"Do you know whom you are going to marry, Ru-lan?" asked Mollie gently in Chinese. The girl shook her head. "It is a landowner's son," she answered simply. "My father is a landowner, too. The son of another village landlord, it is."

She seemed to put the matter aside and continued to watch them intently. Mollie Stanley sighed. She put down the roses on the desk and went over to the girl and sat down on a chair next to her and took her hand again. "Try to remember," she said, "some of the things you have been taught. Remember about keeping things clean and remember how dangerous the flies and mosquitoes are, especially to little children—and how little children should not be given cucumbers and green melons to eat, and—remember about your prayers, and about the kind Christ, who came to save our souls—remember all the things we have tried to teach about being clean and good."

"Yes, teacher," the girl replied. She was looking closely at Mollie Stanley's wedding ring. Now she asked suddenly, "Did the other teacher give you the ring?"

Mollie dropped the hand she was holding and turned to her husband, "Oh dear—" she said.

"Don't worry, dear," said Wyn instantly, "I can't bear that look in your eyes. You mustn't, mustn't try to bear on your dear self all the troubles of everyone else. We've done the best we can for this child. Now she must go home. Come—" he stood and took up the roses. "Here are your roses, darling. Run along now. I'll see that Ru-lan gets away. Where *is* her father? In the school hall? I'll go, then."

"No, but, Wyn, I can't go so lightly. Tell her—tell him we'll come to see her sometime, anyway—Ru-lan"—she turned to the girl and changed her tongue quickly—"we shall come to see you sometime—I'm coming to see if you remember everything—you must try—do not let yourself be like all the others who have never come to mission school."

"No, teacher," the girl said. She was staring at Wyn's hand resting unconsciously upon Mollie's shoulder, and he took it abruptly away.

Crossing the school lawn ahead of her, he thought to himself that Ru-lan was really a very tiresome girl. It was not only that she was so stupid, it was also that one could not be sure of what she was thinking. He would have said, for instance, that she was stolid and unfeeling; yet just now when she was about to follow him out of his study she had made one of her great, broad smiles that seemed to enwrap him and Mollie, and she had taken Mollie's hand and held it, and had said with simple, utter gratitude, "You have both taught me. Together you have taught me."

He remembered now how often they would find her staring at them in her silent persevering way, that time at supper, for instance, when he had sat holding Mollie's hand as he ate—they always sat side by side—and Ru-lan had come in with a note from one of the teachers. She always contrived, he did believe, now that he thought of it, to be the one to carry notes. He'd supposed it was because she was such a faithful sort of person that they had sent her. But perhaps it was because she wanted to come. There she had stood, staring at them with that silent, beaming look—slightly feebleminded, undoubtedly. He sighed. Well, it was sad when years went into teaching someone like that, someone who could never learn, when there were so many who could, and had no chance. But she had been there when he and Mollie came, and her father had come twice a year with her fees, and so she had stayed. There were not many fathers who paid full fees for a daughter.

He entered the hall, and there the father was, a plain brown-faced countryman in a blue cotton gown cut a little too long and too broad for him, but of good stout homewoven stuff. He was not a poor man, it was evident, from his bearing. He rose politely as the white man entered.

"Sit down, please, Mr. Yang. Do not be polite," said Wyn, seating himself also. The girl stood a little to one side, waiting.

"This girl," said the father nodding his head toward her, "I might have left her with you to become a teacher for you out of gratitude for all your efforts, but unfortunately she was early betrothed to the son of a friend whom I do not care to offend, and now the family demand the marriage. Otherwise I would give her to you to help you in your school."

"I thank you certainly," said Wyn. He wondered uncomfortably if in honesty he should tell the father that they could never have used Ru-lan as a teacher because she was too stupid. He thrust an apologetic thought toward God—it was difficult to be honest if it hurt someone else. Mr. Yang was obviously so proud of his daughter. He turned toward Wyn now saying, "She has had, you will remember, sir, eight years of schooling. It is not every man's son who has such a wife. But I have treated her as though she were to be my own daughter-in-law and to remain in my family. I value my friend as myself."

"It is very honorable of you," murmured Wyn. At least he would not tell lies and say he was sorry that Ru-lan must go. He waited in courteous silence until the father rose, briskly dusting cake crumbs from his lap. "There—it is pleasant to sit drinking your tea and eating your cakes, but I have miles of country road to put beneath my beast's feet before night comes. Say good-bye and give your gratitude to your teacher, Ru-lan."

"I thank you, teacher," murmured the girl. "I thank you for all I have learned."

They bowed to him together, father and daughter, and Wyn bowed, waiting at the door while they turned and bowed again.

He watched them while they went out of the compound gate. "I suppose," he thought a little sadly, "that measured by any standard it must be said that we have wasted the church's substance upon that girl. Mollie's hours and mine, too! I wonder why they do not seem so important as dollars in the mission budget? Anyway, all waste! She's not even a church member."

He walked back, a little discouraged. It was so difficult to know what was worth while in the work. One was conscientious, did each day what it seemed should be done, should be taught, and then realized suddenly, as he and Mollie had today, that no fruit was possible. He sighed a little grimly. Well, Ru-lan was gone.

In the village of Long Peace the people were all very well content. They had just finished three days of great feasting entirely at the elder Liu's expense, since he was marrying his eldest son to Ru-lan, the daughter of his brother-friend Yang in the village of The Fighting Cocks. Everybody had eaten. First the tables were set for Mr. Liu's friends among the gentry, and the common people had waited their time, patiently and decently. Then the tables were set again and again, with pork and with fish, broiled with sugar and wine and vinegar, with beef and pork ground and stewed with cabbage and greens, with noodles and with sweet rice. In fact, nothing had been left undone, and everyone had drunk all the wine he could and had eaten far more than he should, and mothers had prudently tied into large blue and white handkerchiefs such tidbits as they could not eat or force their children to eat at table. Servants had been tipped, gifts had been given, and firecrackers exploded in immense volleys. The bride, moreover, had been exhibited and commented upon, and though after all she seemed to be nothing extraordinary, no one liked Elder Liu and Mr. Yang any the less for it.

There had been a great deal of curiosity to see her, because everybody knew Mr. Yang had sent his eldest daughter to a foreign school for eight years, and anything might have happened. She might even have changed the color of her eyes and hair, or the white women might have taught her how to bleach her skin, since it is well known the white people have magic. But she was nothing at all out of the ordinary. She was, in fact, a little more common than otherwise, a large, lumpish girl with very plump round cheeks and small mild eyes. In addition her feet were large. Country wives nudged each other and whispered, "Look at her feet—big feet!" "Yes, but the foreigners do not allow their pupils to bind their feet!" "Ah, indeed! How lucky that the Elder Yang betrothed her in babyhood and to his best friend's son!" Young men glanced at the bride and made jokes concerning the width of her nose and the size of her mouth, and went home in high good humor because they need not be envious of the Elder Liu's son. Indeed, everybody was happy because for once the Elder Liu did not seem to be so very lucky, and one or two fathers whose daughters had been teasing to be allowed to go to a foreign school went home resolute for refusal. What—to waste eight years of fees and then have a daughter at the end who looked exactly as though she had never left the village! So everyone was happy. They went home by moonlight the night of the third day, full of cheerful vilifying talk.

In the house of the Elder Liu, in the court belonging to his eldest son, Ru-lan sat upon the edge of the large nuptial bed, hung with pictures of babies and pomegranates and mandarin ducks and every lucky sign for marriage, and waited for her husband. She had enjoyed everything very much, so much that she often forgot to keep her eyes downcast as she should. But this did not greatly trouble her. She had remembered enough, she thought comfortably, and tonight they had given her a good dinner. The more tedious part of the wedding was over. She had now come to the part which was her own affair.

This was the time, she knew, when maidens should feel shy and uncomfortable and even afraid. She knew because as a very small girl in the women's courts of her father's house she had squatted on her heels listening as all the little girls did to the women's talk. They listened while the women whispered loudly to each other, "I tell you, he was like a tiger—his great eyes—" "I tell you, nothing told is so terrible as—" "I tell you, I was like a chicken before a wolf—"

They all enjoyed telling each other of this hour when their unknown bridegrooms first appeared. She thought now, staring reflectively through the old-fashioned veil of beads that hung over her face, that it was natural they should be afraid of marriage. What they had seen of the thing between men and women was not comfortable. But she had been to school for eight years with the foreigners. There was the difference. Not that the first years she had been there were of any use to her at all. She could not see much use, for instance, in reading books. In the first place books told nothing interesting. If they were about God, there was no understanding them—how could humans understand gods? She had listened politely to Mrs. Burgess and been glad when Mrs. Burgess had been compelled to go to America. For then the dear little Stanley teacher had come, that little pretty round-faced teacher, whose eyes were also brown so that one liked to look at her. The Stanley teacher had worked so hard to teach her that sometimes she almost felt she should try to listen perhaps to what the Stanley teacher was saying, but when she did it had seemed not valuable.

No, she had learned nothing until that day when she had observed the man Stanley place his arms about the woman Stanley. At first she thought with consternation that these were two wicked and unmannered people. But they were not punished if they were. In rapid succession they had two small sons, both healthy, both dark-eyed. Evidently their God was pleased with them. After that she had watched them many times. When they did not know it she had stolen in the night across the school campus, and had gazed steadily between the curtains of the room where they sat after the children were put to bed and, watching them, had come to learn something from them. To this learning she applied her mind. So now she was not at all afraid. She waited peacefully for Yung-en, sitting at ease upon the bed, her hands folded in her red satin lap.

Everywhere through the courts quiet was descending after the noisy days of feasting. Children who had eaten too well ceased their crying and fell asleep, and servants yawned and barred the doors of courtyards and went to their own beds. Her own serving woman was only waiting until the master came in to spread her pallet down across the door to sleep. When everyone was still, when the young men had all gone home, wearied at last with their baiting and teasing of the bridegroom, then through the silent empty courts he would come. She had stolen her glances at him and she was pleased with his looks. He was an honest, sturdy young man, with a square, dark face, not too smiling. He was shy, she could see, not quick to speak. A woman could live with such a man. She was not afraid, having learned so much about a man and a woman.

Then suddenly the door creaked upon its wooden hinges and there he was, still in his bright blue wedding robes. He did not speak, nor did he look at her at once. He came in and sat down beside the table and began to crack watermelon seeds. She rose and poured out a cup of tea for him and he nodded and she sat down again. She was not impatient. He could not go on cracking watermelon seeds all night. Outside the door she heard a loud yawn and soon a muffled snore. Her serving woman was asleep. Now everyone slept except these two.

She waited, smiling a little, watching him through the beads of her veil, but he did not look at her. She waited and at last she caught his eyes, stealing toward her. She answered instantly, frankly, smiling her beam of a smile. He stared at her and coughed and after a second of surprise he grew very red and made haste to return to his watermelon seeds.

She suddenly perceived that he was afraid of her.

"And why are you afraid of me?" she asked, making her voice soft as she had heard the little Stanley teacher's voice soft.

He turned his head from her's. "I am so ignorant," he said at last in a low voice. "You have been away to a foreign school and I have always lived in this village. You will laugh at me."

She watched him. How now would the Stanley teacher speak if the man Stanley had spoken like this? Once the man Stanley had put his head down upon the woman's shoulder and for some trouble had wept as a little boy weeps, and the woman had not laughed. She had taken him into her arms and pressed his head down and murmured to him as a mother murmurs to a suffering child, and soon he was quieted. Rulan had not understood the woman Stanley's words, but the sounds she understood, and the way she understood. It had made the man Stanley feel strong again and cease his weeping.

She looked demurely down at her hands and spoke in a small plaintive voice. "I have to confess to you," she said, "although I was so long in that school I have remained ignorant. You cannot be as ignorant as I am. I do believe there are a thousand things you know I do not know. There I remained for eight years shut behind walls, but my brain is too stupid to learn from books. So I am very ignorant. I have everything to learn from you."

He gazed at her now, forgetting that she was his bride and that he was afraid of her. "Did you not learn to read?" he demanded.

"Only a very little," she replied.

"Did you read to the end of the Four Books?" he asked again.

"Alas, I never read any of the Four Books," she answered.

"Then what did you do in all that time?" he inquired, astonished.

"I sat on benches in schoolrooms," she replied humbly, "and there were those who talked to me, but I could not understand them, being stupid from birth. They told me of gods and of magic, and of small insects that cause disease if eaten, but then who eats insects? At least we do not. So I learned nothing."

"Nothing at all?" he asked severely.

"Nothing at all," she answered sadly.

He was silent, but now he looked at her quite easily and he had stopped cracking watermelon seeds. She could see the shyness leaving him as he thought over what she had told him.

"I only learned one thing," she said after a long time. Now she leaned forward and looked at him and he looked at her.

"What is that one thing?" he asked.

"There was a white woman who was my teacher," she said, "and she was married to a white man, and they were very lucky, for one after the other they had two strong dark-eyed sons, and this when the other children of white people all have blue or green eyes. I learned from them something."

"What was the thing you learned?" he asked. "Certainly two dark-eyed sons are very lucky."

"I learned," she said considering, choosing some one thing among all she had learned, "that it is lucky when a man and his wife speak together freely and always with kind voices, as though they were friends speaking easily together and not as they do in our houses, where it seems shameful so to speak."

"Do you mean speak together anywhere?"

"Yes, I mean that."

He gazed at her steadily. "What then?"

"And then it is lucky if the husband helps the wife if there is a thing to be done, such as to carry a basket or a bundle, if there is not a servant near."

"What does the wife do?" he asked, astonished.

"She also wishes to carry the things, and so they try mutually to help each other."

"And who wins?" he asked.

"They share the thing," she replied simply.

She waited a little, thinking, remembering. . . . Once she had seen the man Stanley lift his wife over a pool of mud in the road, and carry her through and set her down on the other side, one afternoon, when they thought none saw them. But before he set her down he had held her hard and placed his cheek against hers, and then they had gone on hand in hand until they saw her. But she had seen them long since. She had wanted to say, "Do not drop your hands apart. I know it is your pleasure to walk thus." But she had not spoken. . . .

"What else have you learned?" he asked.

"It is lucky," she said slowly, "for a man and his wife to clasp their hands together sometimes—it is not shameful."

He coughed and looked away and she went on quickly. "There are many things not shameful that we have thought shameful—they are lucky between man and wife. But I cannot speak them—they are things to be done rather than to be spoken."

He looked down and did not answer. He did not answer for quite a long time. Then he said a little gruffly, "Then do them—do what you have learned."

She rose slowly and went over to him. She knelt down on the floor before him as often she had seen the woman Stanley do. But she could not go on, although she knew quite well what came next. Next was to put her head down upon his knees and clasp her arms about his waist. But she could not do it. Now it was she who was shy. It had looked so easy when the woman Stanley did it.

"I cannot do it all at once," she faltered. "A little every day. But perhaps—at least take my hands."

He sat quite still and then he lifted her hands in his own. Something rushed between them through their hands, and suddenly her heart began to pound. Did the woman Stanley's heart pound like this also? What was the matter with her?

"What next did you learn?" he asked.

She could not answer. She drew their hands together and laid her head down upon their knotted hands. She should have asked the woman Stanley about this pounding heart.

"Lift up your head," he said. How gentle his voice was, as gentle as the man Stanley's voice was! "Lift up your head and let me take away your veil that I may see you."

She lifted up her head, and he drew his hands away and took off the headdress and the veil and set them on the table and then he looked at her. And then he went on speaking in that same gentle voice, "And did you learn it was lucky for a man to like very well the woman chosen for him?" He had taken her hands again. He was gazing at her, smiling, happy, as the man Stanley gazed at that woman who knelt to him. The man Stanley had also asked something of the woman in that strange tongue of theirs and she had answered. Oh, what was the answer to the gentle question? There must be an answer—she should have learned the answer. Then suddenly it came to her. It came to her, not out of her brain which was so slow and stupid and never quick to speak. It came from her pounding heart. "Yes, it is a lucky thing, I know, and the luck is perfect if the woman likes also very well the man to whom she is given."

She felt his cheek against hers, even as she had learned.

If Ru-lan had been able to write she would long ago have written to her teacher Stanley to ask her why, when she had said she would come to see her, she had not yet come, although it had been now nearly five years since Ru-lan had left the school. In the five years she had grown heavier, as what woman would not who had given birth to three large, strong sons and now a small, pretty daughter, so pretty that the child's father went against all nature and loved her twice as well, apparently, as even he loved his sons.

But then there was of course no man on the earth's surface like Yung-en. The man Stanley was never better to his wife than Yung-en was to Ru-lan. Bit by bit, through the five years, she had told him what she had seen those two white ones do, how they looked at each other, how they spoke, and with the telling new comprehension had come to them of what those looks and words meant. She was now sure that when those two spoke to each other in that strong, soft fashion they said in their own tongue what came welling up from her own heart and Yung-en's. It was wonderful to think how alike were hearts. She knew this because it was so soon an instinct to move freely with Yung-en, walking beside him freely, moving toward him freely and fully when they were alone. She knew that the women in the courts were often disapproving. She knew they said, "It is the boldness she learned in the foreign school—it is the freedom of the modern ways." She smiled, knowing there was truth in what they said.

She pondered a good deal on her own ease. It did not occur to her, for instance, to share the anxiety of the other women lest their husbands take concubines. Did she not know Yung-en's heart? That was what she had learned, how to know his heart. They talked together sometimes about it, and how their life was different from those about them, and Yung-en said gratefully always, "If the man and woman Stanley should ever come to see us, there would not be enough I could do for them to thank them for what you learned from them. If you had not seen and learned, my life would not have been above any other man's. As it is, you have contented me so that all other women in the world might die and I should not know it." She smiled, knowing she had never been beautiful and now was less so than ever, if one should measure her by a beautiful woman. But she feared none of them.

So when suddenly one August morning a letter came from the school she could hardly wait for Yung-en to come home to read it. She had long given up any pretense at reading. The characters she had once known had quite slipped out of her memory. If some woman asked her in curiosity sometimes what a character was on a bit of paper found, she laughed comfortably and said, "If once I knew, that once is long gone. I have so little use for letters these days." Or if her elder son, now beginning to learn, ran to ask her the meaning of a word she would say, always laughing, "You must go ignorant if you ask learning of me, my son!"

She put the letter by until she heard Yung-en come and then she went to him and waited while he opened it, her hand upon his arm. After these five years it was more than ever necessary to her to put her hand upon his arm, and he moved toward her when he felt her touch, understanding.

"It is a letter from the man Stanley," he said after murmuring the letters aloud awhile. "They wish to open a chapel here in our village and preach their religion, and there will be also a school, and he is coming and with him the woman Stanley."

"Of course they would not be separated," she said gently.

"No," he said, folding the letter. He was planning rapidly. "We shall have them here in our own house. There is the south room upon the old peony terrace where I have my few books and where I never go. Prepare it with the best bed and with the blackwood furniture my father gave us from the south. And I shall invite guests—all my friends. I do not care to invite guests for the religion, but it is a way to repay these two if I show myself a friend. Now I can thank them for all they taught you."

"Yes," she said. "And we can show them our sons—"

"And we can send our daughter to their school," he cried, smiling. They sat down together in simple pleasure, holding each other's hands, laughing a little. "Everything is lucky in our life," he said.

"Everything," she echoed fervently.

So it was that on a certain morning in August, nearly at the end of summer, she welcomed those two. There they were at the door, standing together, a little thinner than she remembered them, a little gray in their hair. "You are tired," she cried, her heart rushing out to them. "Come in—rest and eat. Oh, how welcome you are!"

Yung-en gave up his work when they came and stayed at home, running hither and thither, himself carrying trays of sweetmeats and keeping plates full and pouring tea and going to see what quilts were rolled upon the bed and if the mosquito net was properly drawn. "I can never do enough for them," he said to her in passing.

Well, there it was. The two Stanleys stayed three days and into the days Yung-en and Ru-lan heaped all that they had, all the years of their happy life together, all their luck in the three sons and the little girl. Ru-lan had meant to dress the children in their best, but then it was so hot that she let it go. It was better that they be comfortable. Besides, they were so beautiful and so healthy it must be a pleasure for anyone to see their little brown bodies bare to the waist. She had meant, too, to clean the house a little more, to wipe the dust from the table legs and from the gilt crevices of the family gods. But the summer days passed so quickly until the guests came, and once they were come there was no time for anything except urging them to eat, to talk, to rest themselves, to enjoy the huge feast and the lanterns hung to welcome them, to see the fireworks Yung-en bought and bade the servants fire for their amusement.

She had planned to try to tell the dear teachers Stanley a little about her own life and how much she owed them. She had planned to say at least that she had been very happy. But there was no time for anything. They were busy about the new school, planning, working hard as they always did.

But they were still happy. She knew that. They still paused as they used to pause, to look at each other deeply. When they went away, so soon, so far too soon, she loved them more than ever. She stood beside Yung-en at the gate waving to them, crying to them to go slowly, to return quickly. And then when Yung-en shouted after them, "Our daughter shall be your first girl pupil!" her heart overflowed toward them and she cried after them, "Yes—teach her, for you taught me so much!" That was all she had the time to say. But she did not worry— they would understand. She went back into her house with Yung-en. His hand sought hers comfortably, and they sauntered across their courtyard, well content.

Rocking down the road in their rickety mission Ford, Mollie leaned back against Wyn, grateful to be alone again with him. Now, as always, when she sat beside Wyn she began to feel warm, deep peace welling up in her. They were going home, they were together. They were going back to the children. She crept more closely to him, and he put his arm about her. He drove very expertly one-armed.

"Sweetheart!" he said gently. "It was wonderful of you to leave the children and make this trip with me. I shouldn't have blamed you, you know, if you hadn't."

"I can't be away from you, Wyn."

"No, I know." They fell into intimate, peaceful silence.

Over the Chinese landscape twilight was beginning to fall, creeping up in small mists from the ponds and the canals, darkening over the hills from the sky. From the thatched roofs the blue lines of smoke of fires kindled for the evening meal rose straightly into the still air. How strange, how different the scene was from the rough hills of her own home country, from the sharp angular American towns! And yet how little strange, how little different! These were homes, too, and these were people living together in their families. And here was her home. Wherever Wyn was, was her home. She was instantly deeply content, content with everything, with everybody.

Then suddenly she thought of Ru-lan.

"Wyn!" she said. "What did you really think of Ru-lan?"

"Well?" asked Wyn, twinkling at her a little. "What did you really think?"

"It was just exactly as I was afraid it would be," she answered dolefully. "She's lost even the little she had. Wyn, you wouldn't have known, now would you honestly, that Ru-lan had ever been outside that village? Did you see the slightest difference between her house and any other ignorant village woman's house?"

"No," said Wyn thoughtfully. He guided the car skillfully between two deep wheelbarrow ruts.

Mollie stared mournfully over the landscape, the valleys tawny with ripening rice, the hills browning with ending summer, the willow-encircled villages. "No," she continued, "the house was dusty and not very clean, and the children were eating just anything. I saw that little girl chewing on a cucumber, skin and all."

"So did I," he said briefly.

"And Ru-lan is just like an amiable cow. She just sits and smiles and smiles. She doesn't read, she doesn't seem to do anything in the village, she's just an ordinary woman—after all those years away. I don't believe she does one thing different in her home for all the hours I tried to teach her."

"Mollie, did you see those idols?" Wyn said gravely.

"Yes," said Mollie reluctantly.

They rolled along in silence for a moment, remembering the row of gilt figures with the guttered candles before them. They had taught Ru-lan so patiently to say over and over again, "Thou shall have no other gods before Me. . . ." "Ru-lan, what are gods?" she used to ask. Ru-lan had smiled apologetically. "Teacher, tell me, for I do not know."

"They are idols, Ru-lan. You must not worship them, Ru-lan."

"Yes, Teacher, it is what I thought."

And then when Dr. Martin had once asked her in the catechism class what God was, she had said, "Sir, God is an idol." Poor stupid Ru-lan! There was no telling how she would learn a thing. . . .

She thought over the two crowded days, days full of too much food and too much noise and many children and curious neighbors coming in and out to see the newcomers. But Ru-lan had not seemed to mind anything. She had sat tranquil in the midst of the confusion, smiling and smiling. And everybody had seemed fond of her—her children ran to her often, and the neighbors called to her cheerfully, and Yung-en . . . She was struck now, remembering Yung-en.

"Wyn!" she said suddenly, looking up at him.

"Yes, darling?"

He turned and smiled down at her. There she was snuggled down by him like a kitten, looking not a day older . . .

"There was one thing about Ru-lan—her husband really seemed to like her."

"I believe he does," he said slowly. "Yes—I don't know why exactly—she certainly doesn't remember anything we ever taught her!"

The Packed Suitcase

Born in 1890, native New Yorker Manuel Komroff was once the editor of the Russian *Daily News* in Petrograd (now St. Petersburg) before the Bolsheviks seized power. An author, editor, and journalist, Komroff was a versatile writer whose small gem of a short story offers a parable on marriage, demonstrating how a symbolic guarantee of freedom is sometimes all that is required to effect a permanent commitment.

★   ★   ★   ★   ★

They were happy. The happiest couple you ever knew. And the great secret of this happiness was the packed suitcase.

For twenty years the suitcase stood in the hall closet, packed and ready. Never once did it leave the house. But the feeling that it was there was very important to John. The suitcase symbolized freedom. With such a symbol, no marriage could fail.

Or, as John himself often put it: "Mary and I are happy, and the reason is very simple. We are not tied to each other. We feel free. She knows that economically she is provided for, and if we ever decide to disagree, I can walk out. In fact, my suitcase is packed and has been packed since the first day of our marriage. It stands in the hall closet and is ready at any time of the day or night."

At other times he would say: "Do you want to be happy? Pack a suitcase and keep it ready. The chances are a hundred to one that you never will use it. But to know it is there at any time—ah, that gives you a good feeling! After all, happiness is only a good feeling."

Often people asked Mary if it were true that her husband had his suitcase packed and always ready.

"Yes, it is true," she would reply with a smile.

Then some woman was certain to say: "Oh, my! It would feel like a dagger over my head."

"Not at all," Mary would reply. "What is good for the goose is good for the gander. The sword of freedom cuts two ways. In fact, I myself packed the suitcase for him. He was terribly afraid for his independence and freedom when we married, and he spoke a good deal about losing them. Finally he hit on the device of a packed suitcase, and I agreed that it was a good idea. For certainly I did not wish to hold my husband against his will. An unwilling husband is just about the worst pest in the world. So I made this my first duty, the very first duty of our married life. I myself packed the suitcase. When he came home that first evening, I told him about it. 'Complete,' I said. 'Extra suit, extra shoes, three shirts, underwear, socks, shaving kit, brush, comb, six ties, handkerchiefs, nail file—in fact, everything a foot-free man could wish.' That pleased him. It made him feel good. He said I was the best sport in the world. 'It is the kind of thing one might never need,' he explained. 'Yet it is good to know it is there. Something like a fire extinguisher.' We laughed."

During the twenty years of their married life—twenty-one and a half, to be exact—they moved several times. But the packed suitcase always went with them; always it was placed immediately in the hall closet.

In time the tan leather of the suitcase grew brown and the brass locks became tarnished to an inky black. But the handle seemed fresh and good, for never once had the suitcase been used.

One day—this was about eight years after they were married—John happened to remark, "I don't suppose that old suit would fit me."

"What old suit?" Mary asked.

"The one in the suitcase."

Mary laughed. "Why, no, of course not. But that need not matter. A suit never made the man. And a free man always could buy himself a new suit. It's not the suit, it's the symbol that is important."

"That's right," he agreed. "It's the symbol."

"The suitcase is your badge of freedom. You know it is there, waiting for you, any time you want it."

"Yes, Mary. It's the symbol. The symbol is important. We all live by symbols."

To this she agreed.

And then once again, when they had been married fourteen years, the suitcase was mentioned.

"I say, Mary," called John from the hallway, "why don't you throw that thing out?"

"What thing?"

"The old suitcase."

"Don't you touch that old suitcase," she called back. "It's supposed to stand there. It's a symbol—a badge of freedom."

"Now, you know, Mary, that I never will walk out on you."

"But it's supposed to be there, so you always can feel free. It's a wonderful thing to feel free."

"Yes, I guess it is," he agreed.

That is how the packed suitcase remained in the hall closet.

And during all those many years, whenever anyone mentioned a "skeleton in the closet," John and Mary would burst out laughing.

"Why, we've got one!" they would exclaim.

And to those who did not know, they would explain all about the packed suitcase and what it symbolized.

But never once in all their married years did that suitcase have the slightest chance of a solo flight. Never were there any angry words between John and Mary. And never once was there a serious quarrel or misunderstanding. Never once.

The secret of this great companionship was attributed to the packed suitcase standing ever ready in the hall closet.

That is how they lived together for twenty years—twenty-one and a half, to be exact. But last month, alas! after a long illness, the happy companionship ended. Mary died.

And yesterday John's eyes fell on the suitcase in the hall closet. All those years it had stood guard, a sentinel of freedom. But now it had no reason or purpose. He pulled it out and opened the tarnished locks.

Lo and behold! The suitcase was full. It was full of Mary's clothes.

Love Comes to Miss Kissinger

BY WINFRED VAN ATTA

Winfred Van Atta was best known as a writer of mysteries, but here she tackles a mainstay of romantic fiction: the older single woman who believes she has grown beyond the point of passionate love. In spite of its mid-twentieth-century setting, the story has a contemporary feel. Miss Kissinger is a career woman with a position of authority in a bank. She fears the encroachment of younger employees, has to fend off the advances of senior bank staff, and is bored by the one man who is courting her. It's all beginning to wear her down . . . so that when love finally does enter the scene, Miss Kissinger is almost too angry to see that what she's been longing for is right under her nose.

★   ★   ★   ★   ★

The Rockdale National Bank & Trust Company held its annual employes' meeting on the first Monday in June. As usual, the meeting convened at 7 A.M., disrupting the sleeping habits of fifty-seven employes, including Miss Muriel Kissinger of the checking department.

President Stone, running true to form, opened the meeting by stating unequivocally that National's greatest assets were the loyalty, honesty, and industry of its employes. There followed a lengthy summary of business progress, which, it was carefully pointed out, had been reflected in the Christmas bonus and in salary increases for the deserving. New goals for the coming fiscal year were properly identified by charts and graphs, but they could be realized, of course, only if each employe added his own extra bit of effort and courtesy. Two vice-presidents confirmed all that Mr. Stone had said, interspersing compliments for a job well done with appeals for recognition of the greater job ahead.

Miss Kissinger, wearing a new linen ensemble from Block & Kubal's spring sale, sat on a folding chair near the front of the lobby, anxious to be done with the meeting, which offered nothing new over previous years. Her new pumps were beginning to hurt, and she wanted to get to her desk upstairs, since this was the day statements went in the mail. Besides, Mr. Saddler was staring at her again from his place at the officers' table. Mr. Saddler was vice-president and manager of industrial loans. His wife had been dead for almost two years now, and his only son had recently married. For years Mr. Saddler had treated Miss Kissinger as impersonally as a piece of office furniture. Recently he had been going out of his way to be friendly. One of these days soon, she thought, she'd have to put Mr. Saddler in his place, even though he was Herbert Martin's immediate superior.

President Stone's voice suddenly penetrated Miss Kissinger's thoughts, causing her to tense.

"And so this year we decided to award gold watches to the ladies in our organization who have given twenty continuous years of loyal service. We have two such ladies. First, of course, is our lovely Miss Kissinger, whom I personally hired just twenty years ago this month, shortly after her graduation from West High. Will Miss Kissinger please step forward?"

Miss Kissinger's face was white, and she was raging inwardly. How could they be so cruel, so thoughtless? A forced smile came to her lips as she walked to the officers' table.

She listened to the presentation speech, still smiling, determined that no one should guess her true feelings. She accepted the watch, mumbled thanks, then walked back to her chair, less aware of the applause than of the knowing looks on the faces of most of the women, who could not possibly understand that circumstances rather than personal desires sometimes determined a girl's fate.

As the meeting broke up, many employes rushed up to shake Miss Kissinger's hand and offer congratulations. She thanked them politely, never once letting resentment show on her face or in her speech. Suddenly Mr. Saddler was holding her hand, looking directly into her eyes. Other employes moved discreetly away.

"You—you look lovely this morning, Miss Kissinger," he said. "I doubt whether there is anything the bank could award you that would be a true token of our affection and appreciation. Only the other Sunday I was telling my son and his wife about—"

"Thank you. Thank you very much," Miss Kissinger said, feeling the color rushing to her cheeks. She pulled free and literally ran up the marble stairway.

She turned on the lights as she entered her office, then went to her desk and sat down, putting her purse and gloves in the bottom drawer. She wanted to cry. It didn't seem possible that she could have been working here twenty years, that her thirty-eighth birthday would be coming up in another week. Where had the years gone? And the dreams?

Miss Huddleston, her assistant, came into the room humming "I'm in the Mood for Love."

"Statements today, Louise," said Miss Kissinger. "We'll have to hurry to get out on time tonight."

Still humming, Miss Huddleston removed the cover from the big accounting machine, then began entering final checks on the yellow statement forms. When she brought the first stack to Miss Kissinger's desk, she laid them down awkwardly with her left hand, displaying a diamond on her ring finger.

Miss Kissinger made a mental note that she would soon have to break in a new assistant, but she looked up and smiled. "How exciting, Louise."

"It happened last night," said Miss Huddleston. "Honestly, I was never so surprised in my life. I still can't imagine where Joe raised the money, but isn't the ring lovely?"

Miss Kissinger wanted to say that having met Joe several times, she was sure he would be making payments to Acme Credit Jewelers for the next fifty-two weeks. Instead she said, "It's beautiful, Louise. When?"

"Oh, not right away. Joe and I are both so young, and the folks think we should wait at least a year." Miss Huddleston hesitated, then added slyly, "I bet Mr. Martin will be giving you a ring one of these days soon, Miss Kissinger."

Miss Kissinger stiffened in her chair. So young, my eye! Louise Huddleston was twenty-five if she was a day. And just because a person happened to be friends with Herbert Martin and went out to dinner and a movie with him once a week was no reason for anyone to assume that she was waiting for him to buy her a ring.

"We must hurry now, Louise," Miss Kissinger said. "I want to get through the *R's* by lunch."

When she settled down to the job at hand, starting with the *A* accounts, Miss Kissinger's anger passed. A smile came to her face as she checked the account of Mr. Harold Abrams, 223 Magnolia Avenue, Rolling Greens. As usual, there were five checks for the month—mortgage payment, utilities, telephone, insurance, and the regular $20 check to Dr. Oliver. Miss Kissinger had checked too many family accounts not to know what regular $20 payments to Rockdale's leading obstetrician signified.

In many ways, thought Miss Kissinger, hers was a fascinating job. It was remarkable how much one could learn about a person simply by checking his bank statement each month. She had been following Harold Abrams' account for nine years, since his high-school days when he was a part-time clerk at the big supermarket on State Street. Now he managed a branch store, was buying a new home in the Rolling Greens development, and would soon become a father.

Miss Kissinger sighed wistfully, wondering what her own life would be like if she could have met and fallen in love with a steady boy like Harold Abrams shortly after graduation from high school. There had been opportunities, of course, plenty of them; but her mother had died that year, a sister was still in high school, and her father had been out of work because of the Depression. One could not harbor personal ambitions in those days and still remain breadwinner for a family one loved. Now her father too was dead, her sister married and living in California, and she was alone. If the years could be erased and she again be faced with the same decision, what would she do? The answer came sharp and clear. She would do exactly as before. A person of character always faced his responsibilities with dignity and courage, holding on to his values, whatever the price. She sighed again, putting melancholy behind her, working rapidly through the *B, C*, and *D* accounts. A deep frown came to her face as she started on the *F*'s and came to the account of Mr. Jed Fraim, c/o The Belmont Hotel. She wondered what new cause for indignation she would find among his checks this month.

She found it immediately. The last of some sixty-odd checks drawn by Jed Fraim during the month of May was for $52.50, made out to the Individual Finance Company. Now he had taken out one of those $300 personal loans, paying heaven only knew how much interest—and him with a salary of well over $1,000 a month after withholding! It was unbelievable that any man could be so irresponsible about money. Twice each month $546.84 was deposited in his account; then a week later he was overdrawn. Most disgusting of all, thought Miss Kissinger, was the bank's attitude toward this client. A red star adorned the Fraim account card. This meant that no check could be refused without approval by an officer of the bank. During the eight-month history of this account, not a single check had been returned marked "Nonsufficient Funds."

Miss Kissinger's lips curled scornfully as she hurried through the checks. Whom did he think he was fooling by drawing them for "Cash" when they were endorsed by such places as Joe's Bar & Grill, The Highway Inn, and other equally disreputable establishments? There was one check to Main Street Florists for $46.85. Imagine anyone spending that much money for flowers in a single month! The women who received them should know the full truth about Mr. Jed Fraim— the $50 check, for instance, that went to Dr. T. L. Dorrence each month. Miss Kissinger did not know a Dr. Dorrence in Rockdale, but she felt sure in her own mind that he must be treating Jed Fraim for dope addiction, alcoholism, or some other horrible disease. Noting that Jed Fraim had ended the month with a red debit figure of $157.60, and thinking of all the bills she had to pay out of her own meager salary each week, Miss Kissinger's teeth snapped together, and she rose from her chair. It was again time to call this account to the attention of an officer of the bank.

Mr. Saddler was the only vice-president at his desk back of the brass rail in the lobby. He looked up and smiled, catching Miss Kissinger's eye before she could turn away. He came forward with a springy step.

"Why, Miss Kissinger, how nice to see you again," he said. "I do say that is a becoming dress you are wearing."

She handed him the account card and statement. "Someone," she said, "should do something about this man. He has been consistently overdrawn for the past eight months."

Mr. Saddler looked at the account card, then smiled and handed it back with the statement. "It's quite all right, my dear," he said. "Mr. Stone is personally interested in this account. You can be absolutely sure that Mr. Fraim is responsible."

"Why?" Miss Kissinger cried. "Someone please tell me why! Mr. Stone refused to honor the overdrawn checks of his own son when the boy was in college."

"Ours not to question why, Miss Kissinger," Mr. Saddler said.

Miss Kissinger's lips came together in a straight line as she turned on her heel and pounded out her indignation on the terra-cotta floor and marble stairs.

Herbert Martin came into Miss Kissinger's office shortly before lunch. He was a short little man with a bland pink face and gentle brown eyes that blinked frequently back of thick bifocals.

"Muriel," he said excitedly, "you know that new plant The Hobart Company is building on River Street—the one the bank put up the big loan for? Well, it's being completed this morning, and they are having a party out there this evening to show it off. It's mostly for the workmen, who completed the job two months ahead of schedule, but a lot of important business people about town have been invited too. There'll be an orchestra, food, cocktails, all the trimmings. I've been given two tickets. Will you go with me?"

"But your mother, Herbert! This is her night to—"

"I've already talked to her on the telephone," he interrupted. "She understands that this is important bank business. Sister is coming over to drive her to the doctor's. We'll have fun. And it won't cost a penny. What do you say?"

At that moment Mr. Saddler came into the office and glared at Herbert Martin.

Herbert seemed to shrink back against the wall. "I—I was just checking an account with Miss Kissinger, Mr. Saddler," he said obsequiously. "This man has a small welding shop on West Street and has applied for a minimum loan to—"

"Yes, Martin," Mr. Saddler said coldly. "And now that you've finished—"

Herbert edged toward the door and went out with a swish.

A smile replaced the frown on Mr. Saddler's face. He glanced around the office, noting that Miss Huddleston was out; then he walked over and closed the door and, returning, sat down in the chair beside Miss Kissinger's desk.

There was a moment of silence. Mr. Saddler gave his throat a final clearing.

"I'm a direct person, Miss Kissinger," he said. "I've been wanting to talk with you alone for some time. No, don't interrupt me, please, until I've finished. As you perhaps know, it has now been two years since Mrs. Saddler, God bless her, passed away. My son agrees that I would be foolish not to consider a second marriage. I am only fifty-seven years old. Most people usually guess me younger, but there would be no point in lying. My salary here at the bank is among the top ones, and I've made many prudent investments through the years. The woman who shares my remaining years will enjoy every luxury. Indeed, I would expect to make a property settlement as a part of any marital—"

"But, Mr. Saddler! Please. I—"

"Hear me out, my dear. I've not approached this conversation lightly. You are a mature, attractive, sensible woman. I've known and admired your fine qualities for many years. I doubt that you have any serious romantic interests, certainly not in Herbert Martin—not that I wish to belittle him, but—"

As if in answer to her prayer, the telephone rang. She answered it, then handed the receiver to Mr. Saddler.

"Hello," he said irritably. "Oh, Mr. Stone. Put him on, please."

There were long silences, punctuated by such statements as "Yes, sir. Yes, Mr. Stone. Of course, Mr. Stone."

He replaced the telephone and rose. "Mr. Stone wants me to go with him to a directors' meeting at The Hobart Company," he said. "I'll be away for the rest of the day, but I'd like to continue this conversation in the morning. In the meantime, my dear, please give serious thought to what I've already said."

Mr. Saddler went out, wearing an expression not unlike the one on Herbert Martin's face only a few minutes before.

Miss Kissinger stared blankly at the statement before her, tears swimming in her eyes. I'm old, she thought, really old. The past twenty years, each submerged in the routine of job, home, and, yes, boredom, had become realities. Always until this moment a real, if undefined, dream had made each new year bearable. Sooner or later she would meet a man worthy of her love, and they would marry. A home and children would naturally follow. But one year had slipped into the next, each with its special problem. Her father had been ill for so long. There had been college debts of her sister's. Now it was too late. She hadn't known, but Mr. Saddler knew. He never made propositions unless all conditions were favorable to himself. He knew that the time had come for her to consider comfort, position, and security as substitutes for romantic dreams. She buried her face in her hands, sobbing.

The sobbing stopped finally, and she straightened in her chair, reaching for her purse. After she had repaired her make-up, she phoned Herbert Martin to say she would go to the Hobart party.

That evening, at five to seven, Miss Kissinger stepped out of the bathtub into a white negligee. She went into the bedroom and loosened her silky black hair. For a long moment she gazed at herself in the mirror. Old, old, she said to herself; but it was absurd to suppose she spoke of the woman in the mirror, her skin faintly flushed from her bath, her gentle curves enhanced by the lines of the negligee. After a while Miss Kissinger picked up her brush. This time she did not pull her hair back in the severe style she ordinarily affected.

When she was dressed, she turned out the lights and walked downstairs. Herbert was waiting in his car at the curb.

"Muriel!" he cried, as she got in beside him. "You look so different. What—"

"Thank you, Herbert," she said coolly.

Herbert continued to glance at her out of the corner of his eye as he drove cautiously through town and across the Jefferson Street Bridge, turning south on River Street.

The new Hobart plant, consisting of four long, low buildings, was brightly lighted. Herbert pulled in and parked among the hundred or so cars in front.

As they got out and started toward the brightly lighted entrance, Miss Kissinger said, "Herbert, I presume Mr. Saddler will be here this evening. I do not intend to dance with him. I—I'd appreciate it if you would see to it that refusing him does not become necessary."

"But, Muriel!" Herbert cried. "He's a vice-president. He's my boss—"

"I do not intend to dance with him," she repeated decisively, then walked ahead of Herbert into the building. It had just occurred to her that she did not like Herbert Martin. She thought of the sixteen hundred dollars in her savings account. She would turn in her resignation at the end of the month. She had enough for a trip to Europe. When she came back, she'd go to New York and look for a new job there.

The long main building, not yet equipped with machinery, reverberated with music from a small orchestra on a platform erected in the center of the building. A large crowd stood about a cleared area, where several couples were dancing. Waiters from a catering service passed among the guests with cocktails and canapés. The music stopped just as Miss Kissinger and Herbert Martin came up to the edge of the crowd.

Mr. Hobart, Mr. Stone of the bank, and one of the ugliest men Miss Kissinger had ever seen mounted the platform and walked over to stand in front of a microphone. Apparently there would be speeches before dancing resumed.

"Friends and fellow workers," said Mr. Hobart. "You were invited here to have fun and inspect our wonderful new plant. Since Randolph Stone, of Rockdale National, put up most of the money for it, I'm going to turn the mike over to him and ask him to introduce the man chiefly responsible for getting it completed two months ahead of schedule. Randy Stone!"

Mr. Stone, who at the bank always looked as though he had just bit into a green persimmon, now was a picture of relaxed affability. "Friends," he said in a stentorian voice, "it is a real pleasure to introduce my good friend Jed Fraim, of the Pan-American Construction Company."

Miss Kissinger suddenly gasped. "Well, for goodness sake!" she said to no one in particular, staring at the man whose spending habits she had condemned for the past eight months.

"I would be remiss in my duty," said Mr. Stone, "if I did not say that this plant was finished ahead of schedule because Jed Fraim and his fine workmen knew that it was to manufacture a vitally needed instrument of war for our boys in Korea. That war has ended, to be sure, but may I remind you, my friends, that the threat to our security still exists."

"Hey, Jed, you old patriot," cried a rough character from the edge of the crowd, "why don't you wave a flag?"

Mr. Stone went on and on. Not only was Jed Fraim a great construction superintendent but a man of character and integrity. It was no secret that Jack Hobart was trying to get him to remain in Rockdale as plant manager of the new factory. Rockdale needed men like Jed Fraim.

"Character, my eye!" said Miss Kissinger to Herbert. "This is the most disgusting spectacle I have ever witnessed."

"Speech, Jed, you old patriot!" the same rough voice cried.

Silence came over the room as Jed Fraim raised his big hamlike hand and scowled in the direction of the voice. "There are a few knuckleheads present," he said, "who are not used to mixing in nice company.

To them, I have this to say: We have exactly five days to clean and repair our equipment. On Sunday a truck-and-trailer convoy heads for New Orleans, where a ship is waiting to take it to South America. I want every man of you on the job tomorrow morning. Have fun tonight, but the first tough guy who starts a fight or makes unpleasant remarks about how this party is being run will wake up in the morning with more than a hang-over. I'm not kidding!"

"Just exactly as I've always imagined him," whispered Miss Kissinger. "Vulgar, uncouth, disgusting, a bully—"

"And to the rest of you nice people," said Jed Fraim, "I want to say how much my men and I have enjoyed working and living among you. We are construction craftsmen with the special skills required to put up buildings in a world that needs them. If you want to thank my men for the job they did on this plant, why not buy another savings bond? Your government still needs to sell them."

"Oh, for goodness sake," said Miss Kissinger. "If he ever saved a penny for a bond, it would be a miracle!"

As the music started, Herbert took Miss Kissinger's arm and guided her to the dancing area. They had circled the floor only once when the orchestra leader came to the microphone. "Mr. Herbert Martin is wanted on the telephone."

As Herbert hurried away, Miss Kissinger waited at the edge of the crowd, watching the dancers, tapping time with her toe. A hand suddenly touched her shoulder. She turned, expecting Herbert, but it was Mr. Saddler, smiling happily.

"Martin's sister just called," he said. "She has a flat tire. He's gone to help her. I told him not to come back, that I would drive you home."

Mr. Stone, leading Jed Fraim by the arm, appeared suddenly. "Why, Miss Kissinger," he said, "how nice to find you here this evening! I want you to meet my good friend Jed Fraim. Jed, this is Miss Kissinger, one of the nicest people at our bank. You two have a dance while Saddler and I talk business."

Eager to get away from Mr. Saddler at whatever cost, Miss Kissinger permitted Jed Fraim to lead her out to the dance floor. She felt embarrassed as she opened her arms and started dancing with him.

He was such a huge and ugly man. But surprisingly he was an excellent dancer, light on his feet and a gentle leader.

"Thank you," he said, as they reached the far side of the floor. "I've been trying to get away from that old windbag for the past twenty minutes. I'll take you back to your husband whenever you say."

Miss Kissinger looked into his face for the first time since they had started dancing, surprised by his directness. His face was not dissipated after all; it was the fluorescent lights above the orchestra that had made him look that way. He was simply wind-burned. "I—I doubt that you heard my name correctly," she said. "I am *Miss* Kissinger."

He smiled down at her. "There must be something wrong with the men in this town," he said. "You are beautiful, and the best dancer I've ever danced with."

She knew that she should feel offended, but it seemed to be one of the nicest compliments she had ever received. Dropping her cheek against Jed Fraim's massive chest, she gave herself completely to a saxophone that was taking privileges with "Star Dust."

The music stopped just as they came alongside Mr. Saddler, who was now standing alone. He stepped out to take Miss Kissinger's arm possessively. "Just one waltz with me, my dear," he said authoritatively, "then I'll drive you home. Big day tomorrow."

Miss Kissinger looked pleadingly into Jed Fraim's eyes. He seemed to sense her feelings and deliberately moved between her and Mr. Saddler. A look of annoyance came over the vice-president's face, but he continued to smile.

"Perhaps we should go right now," said Mr. Saddler, "and we'll stop off at the Union Club for a late supper. You'll like the club, I'm sure."

"I'm sure she would, Saddler," said Jed Fraim, "but it happens that Miss Kissinger has promised to have a late supper with me. If you'll excuse us now—"

Without waiting for a reply, Jed took Miss Kissinger's arm and guided her past Mr. Saddler and toward the door that led to the parking lot. When they were outside, he said, "I don't blame you for wanting to get away from that old buzzard, but you don't have to be burdened with me either. Perhaps you'll let me drive you to wherever you want to go?"

"You are very kind, Mr. Fraim," she said, feeling grateful. "I would like a sandwich, but there's a snack bar near my apartment. If—"

"Of course," he said, guiding her toward a beat-up old convertible.

They drove slowly across the bridge and turned up Main Street. Jed Fraim suddenly pulled over to the curb, stopping in front of the Main Street Florists, where a man was working on a new window display. "I almost forgot," he said. "Will you excuse me a minute?"

The door of the store was locked, but Jed Fraim pounded on it until the man left the window and admitted him. A few minutes later he returned to the car carrying a large box of flowers and a single rose. He got into the car, placing the box on the seat between them. He remained silent for a moment, then handed her the rose. "I—I bought two dozen for a friend of mine," he said, "and there was only one left. I thought you might like it."

"Why—why thank you," she said, wondering why she should feel annoyed.

"I usually have these things delivered," he said, "but the delivery boy had gone home, so I'll have to take them myself. Maybe you'd like to ride out to the hospital with me? Visiting hours are over at nine, and it's a quarter to now."

Her annoyance vanished completely as they drove toward the hospital, and Jed Fraim explained. "Mrs. Swenson had her baby this morning," he said, then added, "I think you'd like her. Why don't you come up with me? It will take only a minute."

Mrs. Swenson beamed as they came into the room. Jed opened the box and laid it on the bed beside her. "For my favorite mamma," he said. "Swenson tells me he's a fine big boy."

Mrs. Swenson reached up suddenly and pulled Jed Fraim's face down so she could kiss his cheek. "Oh, Jed, you are the sweetest person I know." She then turned to Miss Kissinger. "This big oaf tries to act like a tough guy," she said, "but don't let him fool you, Miss—"

"Miss Kissinger," Jed said, "I'm sorry I forgot to introduce you."

"He must have a hundred men in his crew, Miss Kissinger," said Mrs. Swenson, "but there's always flowers from Jed at every wedding, birth, or funeral. He must spend a fortune on flowers every month. How such a nice guy has managed to stay single for forty years—"

"We'd better go now, Miss Kissinger," said Jed Fraim. He was blushing like a schoolboy.

"Jed," said Mrs. Swenson, as they said good-bye and started to leave, "I wonder if you'd round Swenson up and send him back to the trailer. He don't have a son every day, and you know Swenson."

"Sure," said Jed, "and don't worry about catching up with us in New Orleans. Arrangements have been made to have you and the baby flown down."

After they were in the car and driving back toward town, Jed said, "You've been very kind to me this evening, Miss Kissinger, and I'd like to buy you a nice dinner at the Starlight Room in the Coronado Hotel, but I should round my gang up first and start them for the trailer camp. Would you mind riding to a couple of places? It won't take long."

The Highway Inn was a dimly lit ginmill on Route 20. Jed parked among the cars in front of it, excused himself, and went inside, coming back shortly to get his checkbook from the glove compartment. "I've got three in there," he said, "all of them with bar bills to be squared away before we leave town."

He went back inside. In a few minutes he came out, herding three husky men ahead of him. One started to turn about and go back, but Jed gave him a shove. "That's all for tonight, Gurowski," Jed said. "You are going home now, and you, Brennan, are going to take him. As for you, Swenson, if you hit another joint tonight, I'm going to tell your wife I had to make your final payment to that finance company last month. Get going."

The three men grinned sheepishly, got into a car, and drove off toward town. Jed followed slowly behind them. "They are good boys," he said, "but they play just as hard as they work. I don't know what they'd do if they didn't have me to ride herd on them and pay their bills. You wouldn't believe it, but I've got over six thousand dollars out to my men on this job alone. I must write more checks than any man in this town."

Miss Kissinger said, "I'm sure you do. I shouldn't think you could afford to."

"Oh, I always get it back," he said, "when they receive their bonus at the end of a job. There'll be a good one on this Hobart contract. I explained my situation to old man Stone at the bank when I first opened my account there. They've been very nice about letting me overdraw. I'll bet I'm overdrawn at least a hundred dollars right now."

Miss Kissinger started to say, "It's exactly a hundred fifty-seven dollars and sixty cents," but caught herself in time. Instead she said, "I can understand why you need a special arrangement with a bank in your particular job." Inwardly she felt a warm glow, remembering the look on Mrs. Swenson's face as she kissed Jed Fraim's cheek. A woman like that seldom misjudged a man.

Additional stops were made at The Lodi Restaurant, Joe's Bar & Grill, The Moose Club, and Harry's Townhouse. A total of fourteen men, several weaving unsteadily, were started for the trailer camp at the edge of town. Jed Fraim's checkbook was needed at two places.

It was eleven thirty before Jed Fraim and Miss Kissinger arrived at the beautiful Starlight Room in the Coronado Hotel. It was almost three when they left. Jed paid their bill with a check.

Miss Kissinger could not sleep after she was home and in bed. It had been the most exciting evening of her life, and it now seemed that she had known Jed Fraim for years. His shyness had vanished after a couple of glasses of champagne in the dimly lighted room, and he talked freely about himself. He was the oldest of seven children and had started in the construction business when he was seventeen; he had since worked all over the world. He had helped three of his younger brothers through college, one of whom was now assistant chief engineer of his company. He'd often thought of marriage, he said, and the home he was missing, but what woman would want to share a trailer in the out-of-the-way places where he usually worked?

Take this job in South America, for instance. It was to be a hospital in a small city far inland from the coast. The climate would be hard, and there would be few diversions. After this job was completed, his crew would move on to Venezuela to put up an oil-processing plant, a job that might take two years. A woman would have to be out of her mind to agree to share that kind of life. Miss Kissinger, who had never been farther from Rockdale than Chicago, wanted to say that it sounded like a fascinating life; but that, she knew, would make her appear forward.

Jed Fraim had walked with her from his car to the door of her apartment building, and he held her hand for just a moment. "You've been very kind to me, Miss Kissinger," he said. "I probably bored you with all that talk, but—"

"Not at all," she interrupted. "I enjoyed every minute of it. You—you'll be leaving soon?"

"Sunday," he said, then turned quickly and walked to his car.

It was almost nine when Miss Kissinger reached the bank next morning, late for the first time in three years. She didn't care. One thought was uppermost in her mind. Would Jed Fraim call her before he left? Mr. Saddler started to approach her in the lobby as she was going out to lunch, but she looked him coldly in the eye and walked past. At three in the afternoon Herbert Martin came into her office to apologize for not returning the previous evening. She informed him that no explanation was necessary. Then she went home two hours early.

Mrs. Nelson, who lived below her, stopped her as she came into the building and handed her a large box of flowers. She hurried up to her apartment and rapidly opened the box to find two dozen American Beauty roses and a card reading "For the best dancer I know. Called to Chicago on business, but will be back Friday. Will you have dinner with me then?" The card was signed "Jed."

Wednesday and Thursday passed slowly. On Friday she called the bank to tell them she would not be at work that day. She spent the morning touring Rockdale's leading stores, settling on a beautiful evening gown of white tulle, sprinkled with rhinestones. She purchased evening sandals and a bag to match, then, throwing away all caution, paid a hundred and fifty dollars for a fur stole. It was the most extravagant shopping spree of her life.

Jed called at six that evening to say he would be held on the job until seven and might he pick her up at eight? She tried not to appear too eager. Eight would be quite satisfactory, she told him.

Dressed and waiting, she became nervous, sure that she was too conspicuous in her new clothes. Would he think her too bold in such a low-cut dress? Her buzzer sounded at exactly eight o'clock. Her heart began to pound as she opened her door and walked to the head of the stairs to tell Jed to come up.

She stepped back into her apartment to wait, wishing she had worn her plain brown suit. Then everything was quite perfect. Jed Fraim, looking awkward and ill at ease in a new tuxedo and black tie, filled her doorway, grinning shyly as he looked about the colorful room. His eyes came to rest on her suddenly, and his square jaw sagged.

"You—you are beautiful," he said. "You are beautiful."

She felt the color rushing to her cheeks but stepped forward and guided him into the room and to a chair. "I'll be ready in just a minute," she said, and went into her bedroom to wipe away the tears.

At two A.M. they sat at a table near the dance floor in the Starlight Room, flushed and warm from dancing. The orchestra started playing again. Miss Kissinger started to get up, but Jed reached over and took her hand. "Let's sit this one out," he said. "There's something I want to tell you."

She looked down at her glass, waiting, knowing that this was the happiest moment of her life, that it could not have been more beautiful or thrilling if it had happened when she was twenty. There wasn't the slightest doubt in her mind about what Jed Fraim was going to say.

"I went to Chicago," he said, "to resign my job with Pan-American."

"But why should you resign your job?" she asked. "Surely—"

"They've offered me a good thing at Hobart's," he said. "I've been knocking around too long. I liked this little city from the first day I started work here. When I met you the other night and learned that you were unmarried, I thought—well, I thought that given a year to get acquainted, you might overlook my rough spots and find me a person worth—" He faltered, groping for words.

She looked into his eyes. "I knew what kind of person you were when I went with you to visit Mrs. Swenson." She hesitated, dropping her eyes to her glass. "But you've misjudged me. I—I wouldn't mind living in a trailer. Unless you'd prefer working and living here in Rockdale, I would love to go with you to South America. I think it would be quite the most—" She stopped suddenly, aware that she had said too much; then it didn't matter.

His happiness showed in his eyes as he rose and came around the table to take her hand and guide her onto the floor. She was in his arms, tightly held, moving slowly and rhythmically to the lilting waltz. At the far side of the floor, back of an imitation palm, he kissed her, then led her toward the checkroom to get his hat.

They were silent as they drove slowly toward her apartment. As they stopped in front of the building, he said, "I can get three weeks off before the job in South America starts. We could be married here, then stop off for ten days in Bermuda. There's just one thing."

"What?" she asked breathlessly.

"Do you like dogs?"

"I love them," she said.

"I'm glad," he replied. "I forgot to tell you about Tinker, my old boxer. I've been boarding him with Doctor Dorrence, a veterinarian who has an animal hospital out on Route Twenty."

"Oh," said Miss Kissinger, her happiness complete. And again she knew that this moment could not have been more perfect if it had happened when she was twenty.

Night Bus

BY SAMUEL HOPKINS ADAMS

S amuel Hopkins Adams was a noted American journalist and author who, as a muckraking investigative reporter in the early twentieth century, exposed patent medicine frauds, leading to the passage of the first Pure Food and Drugs Act. His books include a biography of President Warren G. Harding and a fictionalized account of that scandal-plagued administration called *Revelry.* This novella, the humorous story of a runaway heiress and the young man who appoints himself her watchdog, might seem familiar to readers. It should: it was the basis for *It Happened One Night,* a film that not only put Clark Gable on the cinematic map (and drastically reduced sales of men's undershirts), but swept the Oscars in 1934.

★　★　★　★　★

Through the resonant cave of the terminal, a perfunctory voice boomed out something about Jacksonville, points north, and New York. The crowd at the rail seethed. At the rear, Mr. Peter Warne hoisted the battered weight of his carryall, resolutely declining a porter's aid. Too bad he hadn't come earlier; he'd have drawn a better seat. Asperities of travel, however, meant little to his seasoned endurance.

Moreover, he was inwardly fortified by what the advertisement vaunted as "The Best Fifteen-cent Dinner in Miami; Wholesome, Clean and Plentiful." The sign knew. Appetite sated, ticket paid for, a safe if small surplus in a secure pocket; on the whole, he was content with life.

Behind him stood and, if truth must be told, shoved a restive girl. Like him she carried her own luggage, a dressing case, small and costly. Like him she had paid for her ticket to New York. Her surplus, however, was a fat roll of high-caste bills. Her dinner at the ornate Seafoam Club had cost somebody not less than ten dollars. But care sat upon her somber brow, and her expression was a warning to all and sundry to keep their distance. She was far from being content with life.

All chairs had been filled when Peter Warne threaded the aisle, having previously tossed his burden into an overhead bracket. Only the rear bench, stretching the full width of the car, offered any space. Three passengers had already settled into it; there was accommodation for two more, but the space was piled full of baled newspapers.

"Hi!" said the late arrival cheerfully to the uniformed driver, who stood below on the pavement looking bored. "I'd like one of these seats."

The driver turned a vacant gaze upon him and turned away again.

"Have this stuff moved, won't you?" requested the passenger, with unimpaired good humor.

The official offered a fair and impartial view of a gray-clad back.

Mr. Warne reflected. "If you want a thing well done, do it yourself," he decided. Still amiable, he opened the window and tossed out four bundles in brisk succession.

Upon this, the occupant of the uniform evinced interest. "Hey! What d'you think you're doin'?" He approached, only to stagger back under the impact of another bale which bounded from his shoulder. With a grunt of rage, he ran around to the rear door, yanked it open and pushed his way in, his face red and threatening.

Having, meantime, disposed of the remainder of the papers, Mr. Warne turned, thrust his hand into his rear pocket, and waited. The driver also waited, lowering but uncertain. Out popped the hand, grasping nothing more deadly than a notebook.

"Well, come ahead," said its owner.

"Come ahead with what?"

"You were figuring to bust me in the jaw, weren't you?"

"Yes; and maybe I *am* goin' to bust you in the jor."

"Good!" He made an entry in the book. "I need the money."

The other goggled. "What money?"

"Well, say ten thousand dollars damages. Brutal and unprovoked assault upon helpless passenger. It ought to be worth that. Eh?"

The official wavered, torn between caution and vindictiveness. A supercilious young voice in the aisle behind Peter Warne said: "Do you mind moving aside?"

Peter Warne moved. The girl glided into the corner he had so laboriously cleared for himself. Peter raised his cap.

"Take my seat, madam," he invited, with empressement. She bestowed upon him a faintly speculative glance, indicating that he was of a species unknown to her, and turned to the window. He sat down in the sole remaining place.

The bus started.

Adjustment to the motion of ten tons on wheels is largely a matter of technique and experience. Toughened traveler as he was, Peter Warne sat upright, swaying from the hips as if on well-oiled hinges. Not so the girl at his side. She undertook to relax into her corner with a view to forgetting her troubles in sleep. This was a major error. She was shuttled back and forth between the wall and her neighbor until her exasperation reached the point of protest.

"Tell that man to drive slower," she directed Peter.

"It may surprise you, but I doubt if he'd do it for me."

"Oh, of course! You're afraid of him. I could see that." Leaning wearily away, she said something not so completely under her breath but that Peter caught the purport of it.

"I suspect," he observed unctuously and with intent to annoy, "that you are out of tune with the Infinite."

Unwitherable though his blithe spirit was, it felt the scorch of her glare. Only too obviously he was, at that moment, the focal point for a hatred which included the whole universe. Something must have seriously upset a disposition which, he judged, was hardly inured to accepting gracefully the contrarieties of a maladjusted world.

She looked like that. Her eyes were dark and wide beneath brows that indicated an imperious temper. The long, bold sweep of the cheek was deeply tanned and ended in a chin which obviously expected to have its own way. But the mouth was broad, soft and generous. Peter wondered what it would look like when, as, and if it smiled. He didn't think it likely that he would find out.

Beyond Fort Lauderdale the bus was resuming speed when the feminine driver of a sports roadster, disdaining the formality of a signal, took a quick turn and ran the heavier vehicle off the road. There was a bump, a light crash, a squealing of brakes, the bus lurched to a stop with a tire ripped loose. After a profane inspection, the driver announced a fifteen-minute wait.

They were opposite that sign manual of Florida's departed boom days, a pair of stone pillars leading into a sidewalked wilderness and flanked by two highly ornamental lamp-posts without glass or wiring. The girl got out for a breath of air, set her dressing case at her feet and leaned against one of the monuments to perishable optimism. As she disembarked, her neighbor, in a spirit of unappreciated helpfulness, had advised her to walk up and down; it would save her from cramps later on.

Just for that she wouldn't do it. He was too officious, that young man. Anyway, the fewer human associations she suffered, the better she would like it. She had a hate on the whole race. Especially men. With a total lack of interest, she observed the parade of her fellow wayfarers up and down the road, before shutting them out from her bored vision.

A shout startled her. The interfering stranger on the opposite side of the road had bounded into the air as if treacherously stabbed from behind, and was now racing toward her like a bull at full charge. At the same time she was aware of a shadow moving away from her elbow and dissolving into the darkness beyond the gates. Close to her, the sprinter swerved, heading down the deserted avenue. Beyond him she heard a crash of brush. His foot caught in a projecting root and he went headlong, rising to limp forward a few yards and give it up with a ruefully shaken head.

"Lost him," he said, coming opposite her.

"I don't know why that should interest me." She hoped that she sounded as disagreeable as she felt. And she did.

"All right," he replied shortly, and made as if to go on, but changed his mind. "He got your bag," he explained.

"Oh!" she ejaculated, realizing that that important equipment was indeed missing. "Who?" she added feebly.

"I don't know his name and address. The thin-faced bird who sat in front of you."

"Why didn't you catch him?" she wailed. "What'll I do now?"

"Did it have much in it?"

"All my things."

"Your money and ticket?"

"Not my ticket; I've got that."

"You can wire for money from Jacksonville, you know."

"Thank you. I can get to New York all right," she returned, with deceptive calm, making a rapid calculation based on the six or eight dollars which she figured (by a considerable overestimate) were still left her.

"Shall I report your loss at the next stop?"

"Please don't." She was unnecessarily vehement. One might almost suppose the suggestion had alarmed her.

Joining the others, she climbed aboard. The departed robber had left a chair vacant next the window. One bit of luck, anyway; now she could get away from that rear seat and her friendly neighbor. She transferred herself, only to regret the change bitterly before ten miles had been covered. For she now had the chair above the curve of the wheel, which is the least comfortable of bus seats. In that rigorously enforced distortion of the body she found her feet asleep, her legs cramped. Oh, for the lesser torments of the place she had so rashly abandoned!

Twisting her stiffening neck, she looked back. The seat was still vacant. The chatty young man seemed asleep.

Lapsing into the corner, she prepared for a night of heroism. The bus fled fast through the dark and wind. Exigencies of travel she had known before; once she had actually slept in the lower berth of a section, all the drawing-rooms and compartments being sold out. But that was less cramped than her present seat. Just the same, she would have stood worse rather than stay at home after what had happened!

If only she had brought something to read. She surveyed her fellow passengers, draped in widely diverse postures. Then the miracle began to work within her. She grew drowsy. It was not so much sleep as the reflex anaesthetic of exhaustion. Consciousness passed from her.

Sun rays struck through the window upon her blinking lids. White villas slid by. A milk cart rattled past. Stiff and dazed, she felt as if her legs had been chilled into paralysis, but all the upper part of her was swathed in mysterious warmth. What were those brown, woolly folds?

The tanned, quick-fingered hands explored, lifted a sleeve which flopped loose, discovered a neatly darned spot; another; a third. It had seen hard service, that garment which wrapped her. She thought, with vague pleasure of the senses, that it had taken on a sturdy personality of its own connected with tobacco and wood smoke and strong soap; the brisk, faintly troubling smell of clean masculinity. She liked it, that sweater.

From it, her heavy eyes moved to her neighbor who was still asleep. By no stretch of charity could he be called an ornament to the human species. His physiognomy was blunt, rough and smudgy with bristles; his hair reddish and uncompromisingly straight.

Nevertheless, a guarded approval might be granted to the setting of the eyes under a freckled forehead, and the trend of the mouth suggested strong, even teeth within. Nose and chin betokened a careless good humor. As for the capable hands, there was no blinking the stains upon them.

His clothing was rough and baggy, but neat enough except for a gaping rent along one trouser leg which he had come by in chasing her thief. For the first time in her life, she wished that she knew how to sew. This surprised her when she came to consider it later.

For the moment she only smiled. It was a pity that Peter Warne could not have waked up at the brief, warm interval before her lips drooped back to weariness.

Nearly an hour later, he roused himself at the entrance to Jacksonville where a change of lines was due, and his first look rested upon a wan and haggard face.

"Breakfast!" said he, with energy and anticipation.

The face brightened. "The Windsor is a good place," stated its owner.

"I wouldn't doubt it for a minute. So is Hungry Joe's."

"Do you expect me to eat at some horrid beanery?"

"Beans have their virtue. But oatmeal and coffee give you the most for your money."

"Oh, money! I'd forgotten about money."

"If you want to change your mind and wire for it—"

"I don't. I want to eat."

"With me?"

She speculated as to whether this might be an invitation; decided that it probably wasn't. "If the place is clean."

"It's cleaner than either of us at the present moment of speaking," he grinned.

Thus recalled to considerations of femininity, she said: "I'll bet I look simply *terrible!*"

"Well, I wouldn't go as far as that," was the cautious reply.

"Anyhow, there's one thing I've got to have right away."

"What's that?"

"If you must know, it's a bath."

"Nothing doing. Bus leaves in fifty minutes."

"We can tell the driver to wait."

"Certainly, we can tell him. But there's just a possibility that he might not do it."

This was lost upon her. "Of course he'll do it. People always wait for me," she added with sweet self-confidence. "If they didn't, I'd never get anywhere."

"This is a hard-boiled line," he explained patiently. "The man would lose his job if he held the bus, like as not."

She yawned. "He could get another, couldn't he?"

"Oh, of course! Just like that. You haven't happened to hear of a thing called unemployment, have you?"

"Oh, that's just socialistic talk. There are plenty of jobs for people who really want to work."

"Yes? Where did you get that line of wisdom?"

She was bored and showed it in her intonation. "Why, everybody knows that. Bill was saying the other day that most of these people are idle because they're just waiting for the dole or something."

"Who's Bill?"

"My oldest brother."

"Oh! And I suppose Bill works?"

"We-ell; he plays polo. Almost every day."

Mr. Warne made a noise like a trained seal.

"What did you say?"

"I said, 'here's the eatery.' Or words to that effect."

The place was speckless. Having a healthy young appetite, the girl disdained to follow the meager example of her escort, and ordered high, wide and handsome. Directing that his fifteen-cent selection be held for five minutes, Peter excused himself with a view to cleaning up. He returned to find his companion gone.

"At the Windsor, having my bath," a scrawl across the bill of fare enlightened him. "Back in half an hour."

That, he figured after consultation of his watch, would leave her just four minutes and twenty seconds to consume an extensive breakfast and get around the corner to the terminal, assuming that she lived up to her note, which struck him as, at the least, doubtful. Well, let the little fool get out of it as best she could. Why bother?

Peter ate slowly, while reading the paper provided free for patrons. At the end of twenty-five minutes, he was craning his neck out of the window. A slight figure turned the corner. Relief was in the voice which bade the waiter rush the order. The figure approached—and passed. Wrong girl. Peter cursed.

Time began to race. Less than five minutes to go now. Half of that was the minimum allowance for getting to the starting place. Peter bore his grip to the door, ready for a flying take-off, in case she appeared. In case she didn't. . . . People always waited for her, did they? Well, he'd be damned if he would! In one short minute he would be leaving. Thirty seconds; twenty; fifteen; five. Sister Ann, do you see anything moving? *Malbrouck s'en va-t'en guerre.* No dust along the road? We're off!

Such was the intention. But something interfered; an intangible something connected with the remembrance of soft contours on a young, sleeping face, of wondering eyes slowly opened. Peter dashed his valise upon the floor, kicked it, cast himself into a chair and sulked. His disposition was distinctly tainted when the truant made triumphal entrance. She was freshened and groomed and radiant, a festal apparition. Up rose then Mr. Warne, uncertain where to begin. She forestalled him.

"Why, how nice you look!" By virtue of his five minutes, the freedom of the washroom, and a pocket kit, he had contrived to shave, brush up, and make the best of a countenance which, if by strict standards unbeautiful, did not wholly lack points. "How much time have I for breakfast?"

"Plenty," barked Peter.

"Swell! I'm starving. I *did* hurry."

"Did you?" he inquired, between his teeth.

"Of course I did. Didn't you just say I had plenty of time?"

"You certainly have. All day."

She set down her coffee cup. "Why, I thought our bus—"

"Our bus is on its way to New York. The next one leaves at eight tonight."

"I do think you might have telephoned them to wait," she protested. A thought struck her impressionable mind. "Why, you missed it, too!"

"So I did. Isn't that extraordinary!"

"Because you were waiting for me?"

"Something of the sort."

"It was awfully nice of you. But why?"

"Because the poor damfool just didn't have the heart to leave a helpless little hick like you alone," he explained.

"I believe you're sore at me."

"Oh, not in the least! Only at myself for getting involved in such a mix-up."

"Nobody asked you to miss the old bus," she stated warmly. "Why did you?"

"Because you remind me of my long-lost angel mother, of course. Don't you ever go to the movies? Now, do you still want to go to New York?"

"We-ell; I've got my ticket. I suppose that's still good."

"Up to ten days. At this rate, it'll take us all of that to get there. The thing is to figure out what to do now."

"Let's go to the races," said she.

"On what?" he inquired.

"I've got some money left."

"How much?"

She examined her purse. "Why, there's only a little over four dollars," she revealed in disappointed accents.

"How far d'you think that'll take you?"

"I could bet it on the first race. Maybe I'd win."

"Maybe you'd lose, too."

"I thought you had that kind of disposition the minute I set eyes on you," she complained. "Pessimist!"

"Economist," he corrected.

"Just as bad. Anyway, we've got a whole day to kill. What's your dashing idea of the best way to do it?"

"A park bench."

"What do you do on a park bench?"

"Sit."

"It sounds dumb."

"It's cheap."

"I hate cheap things, but just to prove I'm reasonable I'll try it for a while."

He led her a block or so to the area of palms and flowers facing the Windsor where they found a bench vacant and sat down. Peter slouched restfully. His companion fidgeted.

"Maybe the band will play by and by," said he encouragingly.

"Wouldn't that be nah-ice!" murmured the girl, and Peter wondered whether a hard slap would break her beyond repair.

"How old are you, anyway?" he demanded. "Fifteen?"

"I'm twenty-one, if you want to know."

"And I suppose it cost your family a bunch of money to bring you to your present fine flower of accomplished womanhood."

"You shouldn't try to be poetic. It doesn't, somehow, go with your face."

"Never mind my face. If I take you to the station and buy you a ticket to Miami—day coach, of course," he interpolated, "will you go back, like a sensible girl?"

"No, I won't. Think how silly I'd look, sneaking back after having—"

"You'd look sillier trying to get to New York at your present rate of expenditure," he warned, as she failed to complete her objection.

"If you can put up the price of a ticket to Miami," said she, with a luminous thought, "you might better lend me the money. I'll pay you back—twice over."

"Tha-anks."

"Meaning you won't?"

"Your powers of interpretation are positively uncanny."

"I might have known you wouldn't." She turned upon him an offended back.

"My name," he said to the back, "is Peter Warne."

A shrug indicated her total indifference to this bit of information. Then she rose and walked away.

He called after her: "I'll be here at six-thirty. Try not to keep me waiting *more* than half an hour."

Just for that—thought the girl—I'll be an hour late.

But she was not. It annoyed her to find how a day could drag in a town where she knew nobody. She went to a movie. She lunched. She went to another movie. She took a walk. Still, it was not yet six o'clock.

At six-thirty-one she started for the park. At six-thirty-four she was at the spot, or what she had believed to be the spot, but which she decided couldn't be, since no Peter Warne was visible. Several other benches were in sight of the vacant band stand. She made the rounds of all. None was occupied by the object of her search. Returning to the first one, she sat down in some perturbation. Perhaps something had happened to Peter Warne. Nothing short of an accident could explain his absence.

There she sat for what seemed like the better part of an hour, until an ugly suspicion seeped into her humiliated mind that she had been left in the lurch. And by a man. A clock struck seven. She rose uncertainly.

"Oh!" she said, in a long exhalation.

Peter Warne was strolling around the corner of the stand.

"Where have you been?" she demanded, like an outraged empress.

He remained unstricken. "You were late," he observed.

"I wasn't. What if I was? Only a minute."

"Nearer five."

"How do you know? You must have been watching. You were here all the time. And you let me think you'd gone away. Oh! Oh! *Oh!*"

"You're pretty casual about keeping other people waiting, you know."

"That's different." She spoke with a profound conviction of privilege.

"I'm not going to argue that with you. Have you any money left?"

"A dollar and four cents," she announced, after counting and recounting.

Cooly he took her purse, transferred the coins to his pocket, and handed it back. "Confiscated for the common necessity," he stated, and she refrained from protest. "Come along."

She fell into step with him. "Could I please have something to eat?"

"Such is the idea. We'll try Hungry Joe's again."

This time he did the ordering for both of them: soup, hash, thick, pulpy griddle cakes and coffee. Total, sixty-five cents. Fortified by this unfamiliar but filling diet, she decided to give Mr. Peter Warne a more fitting sense of their relative status. Some degree of respect was what her soul demanded to bolster her tottering self-confidence. She had heard that a married woman was in a better position to assert herself than a girl. On that basis she would impress Peter.

"You've been treating me like a child," she complained. "You may as well understand right now that I'm not. I'm a married woman. I'm Mrs. Corcoran Andrews." She had selected this name because Corcoran, who was her third or fourth cousin, had been pestering her to marry him for a year. So he wouldn't mind. The effect was immediate.

"Huh?" jerked out the recipient of the information. "I thought Corker Andrews married a pink chorine."

"They're divorced. Do you *know* Corker?"

"Sure I know Corker."

"You're not a *friend* of his?" The implication of her surprise was unflattering.

"I didn't say that." He grinned. "The fact is, I blacked his boots once for three months."

"What did you do that for?"

"What does a man black boots for? Because I had to. So you're Cor—Mr. Andrews wife." His regard rested upon her small, strong, deeply browned left hand. She hastily pulled it away.

"My ring's in the bag that was stolen."

"Of course," he remarked. (What did he mean by that?) "Time to be moving."

They emerged into a droning pour of rain. "Can't you get a taxi?" she asked.

"We walk," was the uncompromising reply, as he tucked his hand beneath her arm. They caught the bus with little to spare, and again drew the rear seat.

Outside, someone was saying: "Since Thursday. Yep; a hundred miles up the road. There'll be bridges out."

Feeling sleepy and indifferent, she paid no heed. She lapsed into a doze which, beginning bumpily against the wall, subsided into the unrealized comfort of his shoulder.

Water splashing on the floor boards awakened her; it was followed by the whir of the wheels, spinning in reverse.

"Got out by the skin of our teeth," said Peter Warne's lips close to her ear.

"What is it?"

"Some creek or other on the rampage. We'll not make Charleston this night."

He went forward, returning with dreary news. "We're going to stay in the nearest village. It looks like a night in the bus for us."

"Oh, no! I can't stand this bus any longer. I want to go to bed," she wailed.

He fetched out his small notebook and fell to figuring. "It'll be close reckoning," he said, scowling at the estimate. "But if you feel that way about it—" To the driver he shouted: "Let us off at Dake's place."

"What's that?"

"Tourist camp."

"Aren't they awful places? They look it."

"The Dake's chain are clean and decent enough for anybody," he answered in a tone so decisive that she followed him meekly out into the night.

Leading her to a sort of waiting room, he vanished into an office, where she could hear his voice in colloquy with an unseen man. The latter emerged with a flash light and indicated that they were to follow. Her escort said to her, quick and low: "What's your name?"

"I told you," she returned, astonished. "I'm Mrs. Cor—"

"Your first name."

"Oh. Elspeth. Why? What's the matter?" She stared at him.

"I had to register as Mr. and Mrs.," he explained nervously. "It's usual for a husband to know his wife's first name."

She asked coldly: "What is the idea?"

"Do you mind," he urged, "talking it over after we get inside?"

Their guide opened the door of a snug cabin, lighted a light and gave Elspeth a shock by saying: "Good night, Mrs. Warne. Good night, Mr. Warne. I hope you find everything comfortable."

Elspeth looked around upon the bare but neat night's lodging: two bunks separated by a scant yard of space, a chair, four clothes hooks, a shelf with a mirror above it. Peter set down his carryall and sat at the head of a bunk.

"Now," said he, "you're free to come or go."

"Go where?" she asked blankly.

"Nowhere, I hope. But it's up to you. You're a lot safer here with me," he added, "than you would be by yourself."

"But why did you have to register that way? To save appearances?"

"To save two dollars," was his grim correction, "which is more to the point. That's the price of a cabin."

"But *you're* not going to stay *here.*"

"Now, let me explain this to you in words of one syllable. We've got darn little money at best. The family purse simply won't stand separate establishments. Get that into your head. And I'm not spending the night outside in this storm!"

"But I—I don't know anything about you."

"All right. Take a look." He held the lamp up in front of what developed into a wholly trustworthy grin.

"I'm looking." Her eyes were wide, exploring, steady, and—there was no doubt about it in his mind—innocent.

"Well; do I look like the villain of the third act?"

"No; you don't." She began to giggle. "You look like a plumber. A nice, honest, intelligent, high-principled plumber."

"The washroom," he stated in the manner of a guidebook, "will be found at the end of this row of shacks."

While she was gone, he extracted a utility kit from his bag, tacked two nails to the end walls, fastened a cord to them and hung a spare blanket, curtain-wise, upon it.

"The walls of Jericho," was his explanation, as she came in. "Solid porphyry and marble. Proof against any assault."

"Grand! What's this?" She recoiled a little from a gaudy splotch ornamenting the foot of her bed.

"Pajamas. My spare set. Hope you can sleep in them."

"I could sleep," she averred with conviction, "in a straitjacket." She had an impulse of irrepressible mischief.

"About those walls of Jericho, Peter. You haven't got a trumpet in that big valise of yours, have you?"

"Not even a mouth organ."

"I was just going to tell you not to blow it before eight o'clock."

"Oh, shut up and go to sleep."

So they both went to sleep.

Something light and small, falling upon her blanket, woke Elspeth.

"Wha' za'?" she murmured sleepily.

"Little present for you," answered Peter.

"Oh-h-h-h-h-h!" It was a rapturous yawn. "I never slept so hard in my *whole* life. What time is it?"

"Eight o'clock, and all's well before the walls of Jericho."

She ripped the small package open, disclosing a toothbrush. "What a snappy present! Where did it come from?"

"Village drug store. I'm just back."

"How nice of you! But can we afford it?" she asked austerely.

"Certainly not. It's a wild extravagance. But I'm afraid to cut you off from all luxuries too suddenly. Now, can you get bathed and dressed in twenty minutes?"

"Don't be silly! I'm not even up yet."

"One—two—three—four—"

"What's the count about?"

"On the stroke of ten I'm going to break down the wall, drag you out and dress you myself if neces—"

"Why, you big bum! I believe you wou—"

"—five—six—seven—"

"Wait a *minute!*"

"—eight—ni-i-i-i—"

A blanket-wrapped figure dashed past him and down to the showers. After a record bath she sprinted back to find him squatted above a tiny double grill which he had evidently extracted from that wonderbox of a valise.

"What we waste on luxuries we save on necessities," he pointed out. "Two eggs, one nickel. Two rolls, three cents. Tea from the Warne storehouse. Accelerate yourself, my child."

Odors, wafted from the cookery to her appreciative nostrils, stimulated her to speed. Her reward was a nod of approval from her companion and the best egg that had ever caressed her palate.

"Now you wash up the dishes while I pack. The bus is due in ten minutes."

"But they're greasy," she shuddered.

"That's the point. Get 'em clean. Give 'em a good scraping first."

He vanished within. Well, she would try. Setting her teeth, she scraped and scrubbed and wiped and, at the end, invited his inspection, confident of praise. When, with a pitying glance, he silently did over two plates and a cup before stacking and packing them, she was justifiably hurt. "There's no suiting some people," she reflected aloud and bitterly.

Flood news from the northward, they learned on boarding the bus, compelled a re-routing far inland. Schedules were abandoned. If they made Charleston by nightfall they'd do pretty well, the driver said. Elspeth, refreshed by her long sleep, didn't much care. Peter would bring them through, she felt. . . .

Yellow against the murk of the night sky shone the lights of Charleston. While Peter was at the terminal office making inquiries, Elspeth, on the platform, heard her name pronounced in astonishment. From a group of company chauffeurs a figure was coming toward her.

"Andy Brinkerhoff! What are you doing in that uniform?"

"Working. Hello, Elspie! How's things?"

"Working? For the bus company?"

"Right," he chirped. "This being the only job in sight and the family having gone bust, I grabbed it. What-ho!"

"How awful!"

"Oh, I dunno. I'd rather be the driver than a passenger. What brought you so low, Elspie?"

"Sh! I've beat it from home."

"Gee! Alone?"

"Yes. That is—yes. Oh, Andy! I never dreamed how awful this kind of travel could be."

"Why don't you quit it, then?"

"No money."

The lad's cherubic face became serious. "I'll raise some dough from the bunch. You could catch the night plane back."

For a moment she wavered. In the distance she sighted Peter Warne scanning the place. There was a kind of expectant brightness on his face. She couldn't quite picture him going on alone in the bus with that look still there. She flattered herself that she had something to do with its presence.

"I'll stick," she decided to herself, but aloud: "Andy, did you ever hear of a man named Peter Warne?"

"Warne? No. What about him?"

"Nothing. What's a telegram to Miami cost?"

"How much of a telegram?"

"Oh, I don't know. Give me a dollar." And then she wrote out a message:

> Mr. Corcoran D. Andrews, Bayside Place, Miami Beach, Fla.
> Who what and why is Peter Warne Stop Important I should know Stop On my way somewhere and hope to get there some time Stop This is strictly confidential so say nothing to nobody Stop Having a helluvaruff time and liking it Stop Wire Bessie Smith, Western Union, Raleigh, N. C.
>
> El

"Oh, here you are," said Peter, barely giving her time to smuggle the paper into Brinkerhoff's hand. "We're going on. Think you can stand it?"

"I s'pose I've got to," replied Elspeth.

Incertitude had discouraged about half the passengers. Consequently, the pair secured a window chair apiece. At the moment of starting there entered a spindly young male all aglow with self-satisfaction which glossed him over from his cocky green hat to his vivid spats.

By the essential law of his being it was inevitable that, after a survey of the interior, he should drop easily into a seat affording an advantageous view of the snappy-looking girl who seemed to be traveling alone. He exhumed a magazine from his grip and leaned across.

"Pardon *me*. But would you care to look at this?"

Elspeth wouldn't but she looked at Mr. Horace Shapley with attention which he mistook for interest. He transferred himself with suitable preliminaries to the vacant chair at her side and fell into confidential discourse.

His line, so Elspeth learned, was typewriter supplies and he hailed from Paterson, New Jersey. Business was punk but if you knew how to make yourself solid with the girl behind the machine (and that was his specialty, believe *him*), you could make expenses and a little bit on the side.

Elspeth glanced across at Peter to see how he regarded this development. Peter was asleep. All right, then; if he wanted to leave her unprotected against the advances of casual strangers. Unfamiliar with this particular species, she was mildly curious about its hopeful antics.

She smiled politely, asked a question or two, and Mr. Shapley proceeded to unfold romantic adventures and tales of life among the typewriters. The incidents exhibited a similarity of climax: "And did *she* fall for me! Hot momma!"

"It must be a fascinating business," commented his listener.

"And how! I'll bet," said Mr. Shapley, with arch insinuation, "you could be a naughty little girl yourself, if nobody was lookin'." He offered her a cigaret. She took it with a nod and tossed it across the aisle, catching the somnolent Peter neatly in the neck. He woke up.

"Hi!"

"Come over here, Peter." He staggered up. "I want you to know" (with a slight emphasis on the word) "Mr. Shapley."

"Pleezetomeetcha," mumbled that gentleman in self-refuting accents.

"He thinks," pursued Elspeth, "that I'm probably a naughty little girl. Am I?"

"You can't prove it by me," said Peter.

"Say, what's the idea?" protested the puzzled Mr. Shapley.

"I don't like him; he nestles," stated Elspeth.

"Aw, now, sister! I was just nicin' you along and—"

"Nicing me along!" Elspeth repeated the phrase with icy disfavor. "Peter; what are you going to do about this?"

Peter ruminated. "Change seats with you," he said brightly.

"Oh!" she choked as she rose. As she stepped across her neighbor to gain the aisle, he gave a yelp and glared savagely, though it was presumably an accident that her sharp, high heel had landed upon the most susceptible angle of his shin. After a moment's consideration, Peter followed her to her new position.

So entered discord into that peaceful community. Mr. Shapley sulked in his chair. Elspeth gloomed in hers. Discomfort invaded Peter's amiable soul. He perceived that he had fallen short in some manner.

"What did you expect me to do about that bird?" he queried.

"Nothing."

"Well, that's what I did."

"I should say you did. If it had been me, I'd have punched his nose."

"And got into a fight. I never could see any sense in fighting unless you have to," he argued. "What happens? You both get arrested. If I got arrested and fined here, how do we eat? If they jug me, what becomes of you? Be sensible."

"Oh, you're sensible enough for both of us." It was plain, however, to the recipient of this encomium, that it was not intended as a compliment. "Never mind. What are we stopping for?"

The halt was occasioned by evil reports of the road ahead, and the chauffeur's unwillingness to risk it in darkness.

"I'll do a look-see," said Peter, and came back, pleased, to announce that there was a cheap camp around the turn. Without formality, the improvised Warne family settled in for the night.

Silence had fallen upon the little community when an appealing voice floated across the wall of their seventy-five-cent Jericho. "Peter. Pe-*ter!*"

"Mmpff."

"You're not a very inquisitive person, Peter. You haven't asked me a single question about myself."

"I did. I asked you your name."

"Because you had to. In self-protection."

"Do you want me to think up some more questions?"

She sniffed. "You might show a *little* human interest. You know, I don't like you much, Peter. But I could talk to you, if you'd let me, as freely as if you were—well, I don't know how to put it."

"Another species of animal."

"No-o-o-o. You mustn't belittle yourself," said she kindly.

"I wasn't. And I didn't say an inferior species."

It took her a moment to figure this out, and then she thought she must have got it wrong. For how could his meaning possibly be that her species was the inferior? . . . Better pass that and come to her story. She began with emphasis:

"If there's one thing I can't stand, it's unfairness."

"I thought so."

"You thought *what?*"

"Somebody's been interfering with your having your own sweet way, and so you walked out on the show. What was the nature of this infringement upon the rights of American womanhood?"

"Who's making this stump speech; you or me?" she retorted. "It was about King Westley, if you want to know."

"The headline aviator?"

"Yes. He and I have been playing around together."

"How does friend husband like that?"

"Huh? Oh! Why, he's away, you see. Cruising. I'm staying with Dad."

"Then he's the one to object?"

"Yes. Dad doesn't understand me."

"Likely enough. Go ahead."

"I'll bet you're going to be dumb about this, too. Anyway, it was all right till King got the idea of finding the lost scientific expedition in South America. Venezuela, or somewhere. You know."

"Professor Schatze's? South of the Orinoco. I've read about it."

"King wants to fly down there and locate them."

" 'S all right by me. But where does he figure he'll land?"

"Why, on the prairie or the pampas."

"Pampas, my glass eye! There isn't any pampas within a thousand miles of the Orinoco."

"What do you know about it?"

"I was there myself, five years ago."

"You were! What doing?"

"Oh, just snooping around."

"Maybe it wasn't the same kind of country we were going to."

"*We?*" She could hear a rustle and judged that he was sitting upright. She had him interested at last.

"Of course. I was going with him. Why, if we'd found the expedition I'd be another Amelia Earhart."

Again the cot opposite creaked. Its occupant had relaxed. "I guess your family needn't have lost any sleep."

"Why not?" she challenged.

"Because it's all a bluff," he returned. "Westley never took a chance in his life outside of newspaper headlines."

"I think you're positively septic. The family worried, all right. They tried to keep me from seeing him. So he took to nosing down across our place and dropping notes in the swimming pool, and my father had him arrested and grounded for reckless flying. Did you ever hear anything like that?"

"Not so bad," approved Peter.

"Oh-h-h-h! I might know you'd side against me. I suppose you'd have had me sit there and let Dad get away with it."

"Mmmmm. I can't exactly see you doing it. But why take a bus?"

"All the cars were locked up. I had to sneak out. I knew they'd watch the airports and the railroad stations, but they wouldn't think of the bus. Now you've got the whole story, do you blame me?"

"Yes."

"I do think you're unbearable. You'd probably expect me to go back."

"Certainly."

"Maybe you'd like to send me back."

"You wouldn't go. I did try, you know."

"Not alive, I wouldn't! Of *course* you wouldn't think of doing anything so improper as helping me any more."

"Sure, I will," was the cheerful response. "If you've got your mind set on getting to New York, I'll do my best to deliver you there intact. And may God have mercy on your family's soul! By the way, I suppose you left some word at home so they won't worry too much."

"I did not! I hope they worry themselves into convulsions."

"You don't seem to care much about your family," he remarked.

"Oh, Dad isn't so bad. But he always wants to boss everything. I—I expect I didn't think about his worrying. D'you think he will—much?" The query terminated in a perceptible quaver.

"Hm. I wonder if you're really such a hard-boiled little egg as you make out to be. Could you manage with a bag of pecans for dinner tomorrow?"

"Ouch! Do I have to?"

"To wire your father would come to about the price of two dinners."

"Wire him? And have him waiting in New York for me when we get there? If you do, I'll jump through the bus window and you'll never see me again."

"I see. Westley is meeting you. You don't want any interference. Is that it?"

"I left him a note," she admitted.

"Uh-huh. Now that you've got everything movable off your mind, what about a little sleep?"

"I'm for it."

Silence settled down upon the Warne menage.

Sunup brought Peter out of his bunk. From beyond the gently undulant blanket he could hear the rhythm of soft breathing. Stealthily he dressed. As he opened the door, a gust of wind twitched down the swaying screen. The girl half turned in her sleep. She smiled. Peter stood, bound in enchantment.

In something like panic he bade himself listen to sense and reason. That's a spoiled child, Peter. Bad medicine. Willful, self-centered—and sweet. (How had that slipped in?) Impractical, too. Heaven pity the bird that takes her on! Too big a job for you, Peter, my lad, even if you could get the contract. So don't go fooling with ideas, you poor boob.

Breakfast necessities took him far afield before he acquired at a bargainer's price what he needed. Elspeth had already fished the cooking kit out of the bag and made ready in the shelter of the shack.

Not a word did she say about the fallen blanket. This made Peter self-conscious. They breakfasted in some restraint.

A wild sky threatened renewal of the storm. Below the hill a shallow torrent supplanted the road for a space. Nevertheless, the bus was going on. Elspeth washed the dishes—clean, this time.

"You get out and stretch your legs while I pack," advised Peter.

As she stepped from the shack, the facile Mr. Shapley confronted her.

"The cream off the milk to you, sister," said he, with a smile which indicated that he was not one to bear a grudge. "I just want to square myself with you. If I'd known you was a married lady—"

"I'm not," returned Elspeth absently.

Mr. Shapley's eyes shifted from her to the shack. Peter's voice was raised within: "Where are your pajamas, Elspeth?"

"Airing out. I forgot 'em." She plucked them from a bush and tossed them in at the door.

"*Oh*-oh!" lilted Mr. Shapley, with the tonality of cynical and amused enlightenment. He went away, cocking his hat.

Warning from the bus horn brought out Peter with his bag. They took their seats and were off.

The bus's busy morning was spent mainly in dodging stray watercourses. They made Cheraw toward the middle of the afternoon. There Peter bought two pounds of pecans; a worthy nut and one which satisfies without cloying. They were to be held in reserve, in case. In case of what? Elspeth wished to be informed. Peter shook his head and said, darkly, that you never could tell.

North of Cheraw, the habits of the bus became definitely amphibian. The main route was flowing in a northeasterly direction, and every side road was a contributory stream. A forested rise of land in the distance held out hope of better things, but when they reached it they found cars parked all over the place, waiting for a road-gang to strengthen a doubtful bridge across the swollen river.

"Let's have a look at this neck of the woods," Peter suggested.

To determine their geographical circumstances was not difficult. Rising waters had cut off from the rest of the world a ridge, thinly oval in shape, of approximately a mile in length, and hardly a quarter of a mile across. On this were herded thirty or forty travelers, including the bus passengers.

There was no settlement of any sort within reach; only a ramshackle farmhouse surrounded by a discouraged garden. Peter, however, negotiated successfully for a small box of potatoes, remarking to his companion that there was likely to be a rise in commodity prices before the show was over.

A sound of hammering and clinking interspersed with rugged profanity, led them to a side path. There they found a well-equipped housekeeping van, the engine of which was undergoing an operation by its owner while his motherly wife sat on the steps watching.

"Cussin' never done you any good with that machine, Abner," said she. "It ain't like a mule."

"It is like a mule. Only meaner." Abner sighted Peter. "Young man, know anything about this kind of critter?"

"Ran one once," answered Peter. He took off his coat, rolled up his sleeves, and set to prodding and poking in a professional manner. Presently the engine lifted up its voice and roared.

Elspeth, perched on a log, reflected that Peter seemed to be a useful sort of person to other people. Why hadn't he done better for himself in life? Maybe that was the reason. This was a new thought and gave her something to mull over while he worked. From the van she borrowed a basin of water, a bar of soap and a towel, and was standing by when he finished the job.

"What do I owe you, young man?" called Abner Braithe, from the van.

"Noth-*uh!*" Elspeth's well-directed elbow had reached its goal in time.

"Don't be an idiot!" she adjured him.

A conference took place.

"You see," said Peter at its close, "my—uh—wife doesn't sleep well outdoors. If you had an extra cot, now—"

"Why, we can fix that," put in Mrs. Braithe. "We haven't got any cot, but if you can sleep in a three-quarter bed—"

"We can't," said both hastily.

"We're used to twin beds," explained Elspeth.

"My wife's quite nervous," put in Peter, "and—and I snore."

"You don't," contradicted Elspeth indignantly, and got a dirty look from him.

It was finally arranged that, as payment for Peter's services, the Braithes were to divide the night into two watches; up to and after one A.M., Elspeth occupying the van bed for the second spell while Peter roosted in the bus.

This being settled, the young pair withdrew to cook a three-course dinner over a fire coaxed by Peter from wet brush and a newspaper; first course, thin potato soup; second course, boiled potatoes with salt; dessert, five pecans each.

"We've been Mr. and Mrs. for pretty near three days now, Peter," remarked the girl suddenly, "and I don't know the first darn thing about you."

"What d'you want to know?"

"What have you got in the line of information?"

"Not much that's exciting."

"That's too bad. I hoped you were an escaped con or something, traveling incog."

"Nothing so romantic. Just a poor but virtuous specimen of the half-employed."

"Who employs you?"

"I do. I'm a rotten employer."

"Doing what? Besides blacking boots."

"Oh, I've nothing as steady as that since. If you want to know, I've been making some experiments in the line of vegetable chemistry; pine tar, to be exact. I'm hoping to find some sucker with money to take it up and subsidize me and my process. That's what I'm going to New York to see about. Meantime," he grinned, "I'm traveling light."

"What'll the job be worth if you do get it?"

"Seven or eight thousand a year to start with," said he, with pride.

"Is *that* all?" She was scornful.

"Well, I'll be—Look here, Elspeth, I said per year."

"I heard you. My brother Bill says he can't get along on *ten* thousand. And," she added thoughtfully, "he's single."

"So am I."

"You didn't tell me that before. Not that it matters, of course. Except that your wife might misunderstand if she knew we'd been sl— traveling together."

"I haven't any wife, I tell you."

"All right; all *right!* Don't bark at me about it. It isn't my fault."

"Anything else?" he inquired with careful politeness.

"I think it's going to rain some more."

They transferred themselves to the bus and sat there until one o'clock, when he escorted her to the Braithe van. He returned to join his fellow passengers, leaving her with a sensation of lostness and desertion.

Several small streams, drunk and disorderly on spring's strong liquor, broke out of bounds in the night, came brawling down the hills and carried all before them, including the bridge whereby the marooned cars had hoped to escape.

"I don't care," said Elspeth, when the morning's news was broken to her. She was feeling gayly reckless.

"I do," returned Peter soberly.

"Oh, you're worrying about money again. What's the use of money where there's nothing to buy? We're out of the world, Peter. I like it, for a change. What's that exciting smell?"

"Fish." He pointed with pride to his fire, over which steamed a pot. Dishing up a generous portion he handed it to her on a plate. "Guaranteed fresh this morning. How do you like it?"

She tasted it. "It—it hasn't much personality. What kind of fish is it?"

"They call it mudfish, I believe. It was flopping around in a slough and I nailed it with a stick. I thought there'd be enough for dinner, too," said he, crestfallen by her lack of appreciation.

"Plenty," she agreed. "Peter, could I have four potatoes? Raw ones."

"What for?"

"I'm going marketing."

"Barter and exchange, eh? Look out that these tourists don't gyp you."

"Ma feyther's name is Alexander Bruce MacGregor Andrews," she informed him in a rich Scottish accent. "Tak' that to heart, laddie."

"I get it. You'll do."

Quenching his fire, he walked to the van. A semicircle of men and women had grouped about the door. Circulating among them, Abner Braithe was taking up a collection. Yet, it was not Sunday. The explanation was supplied when the shrewd Yankee addressed his audience.

"The morning program will begin right away. Any of you folks whose money I've missed, please raise the right hand. Other news and musical ee-vents will be on the air at five-thirty this P.M. and eight tonight. A nickel admission each, or a dime for the three performances."

Having no nickel to waste on frivolities, Peter moved on. Elspeth, triumphant, rejoined him with her booty.

Item: a small parcel of salt.

Item: a smaller parcel of pepper.

Item: a half pound of lard.

Item: two strips of fat bacon.

Item: six lumps of sugar.

"What d'ye ken about that?" she demanded. "Am I no the canny Scawtswumman?"

"You're a darn bonny one," returned Peter, admiring the flushed cheeks and brilliant eyes.

"Is this the first time you've noticed that?" she inquired impudently.

"It hadn't struck in before," he confessed.

"And now it has? Hold the thought. It can't hurt you." (He felt by no means so sure about that.) "Now Mr. Shapley"—her eyes shifted to the road up which that gentleman was approaching—"got it right away. I wonder what's his trouble."

Gratification, not trouble, signalized his expression as he sighted them. His bow to Elspeth was gravely ceremonious. He then looked at her companion.

"Could I have a minute's conversation apart with you?"

"Don't mind me," said Elspeth, and the two men withdrew a few paces.

"I don't want to butt into your and the lady's private affairs," began Mr. Shapley, "but this is business. I want to know if that lady is your wife."

"She is. Not that it's any concern of yours."

"She said this morning that she wasn't married."

"She hasn't got used to the idea yet," returned Peter, with great presence of mind. "She's only been that way a few days. Honeymoon trip."

"That's as may be," retorted the other. "Even if it's true, it wouldn't put a crimp in the reward."

"What's this?" demanded Peter, eying him in surprise. "Reward? For what?"

"Come off. You heard the raddio this morning, didn'cha?"

"No."

"Well, is that lady the daughter of Mr. A. B. M. Andrews, the yachting millionaire, or ain't she? 'Cause I know she is."

"Oh! You know that, do you! What of it?"

"Ten grand of it. That's what of it," rejoined Mr. Shapley. "For information leadin' to the dis—"

"Keep your voice down."

"Yeah. I'll keep my voice down till the time comes to let it loose. Then I'll collect on that ten thou'. They think she's kidnaped."

"What makes you so sure of your identification?"

"Full description over the air. When the specifications came across on the raddio I spotted the garments. Used to be in ladies' wear," he explained.

"If you so much as mention this to Mi—to Mrs. Warne, I'll—" began Peter.

"Don't get rough, now, brother," deprecated the reward-hunter. "I ain't lookin' for trouble. And I'm not sayin' anything to the little lady, just so long as you and me understand each other."

"What do you want me to understand?"

"That there's no use your tryin' to slip me after we get out of this place. Of course, you can make it hard or easy for me. So, if you want to play in with me and be nice, anyway—I'm ready to talk about a little cut for you . . . No? Well, suit yourself, pal. See you in the mornin'."

He chuckled himself away. Peter, weighing the situation, discovered in himself a violent distaste at the thought of Mr. Horace Shapley collecting Elspeth's family's money for the delivering up of Elspeth. In fact, it afflicted him with mingled nausea and desire for manslaughter. Out of this unpromising combination emerged an idea. If he, Peter, could reach a wire before the pestilent Shapley, he could get in his information first and block the reward.

Should he tell Elspeth about the radio? Better not, he concluded.

It was characteristic of her and a big credit mark in his estimate of her, that she put no questions as to the interview with Shapley. She did not like that person; therefore, practically speaking, he did not exist. But the mudfish did. With a captivating furrow of doubt between her eyes, she laid the problem before her partner: could it be trusted to remain edible overnight?

"Never mind the fish. Can you swim?"

She looked out across the brown turbulence of the river, more than two hundred yards now to the northern bank. "Not across that."

"But you're used to water?"

"Oh, yes!"

"I've located an old boat in the slough where I killed the fish. I think I can patch her up enough to make it."

"Okay by me; I wouldn't care to settle here permanently. When do we start?"

"Be ready about ten."

"In the dark?"

"We-ell, I don't exactly want the public in on this. They might try to stop us. You know how people are."

"Come clean, Peter. We're running away from something. Is it that Shapley worm?"

"Yes. He thinks he's got something on me." This explanation which he had been at some pains to devise, he hoped would satisfy her. But she followed it to a conclusion which he had not foreseen.

"Is it because he knows we're not married?"

"He doesn't know ex—"

"I told him we weren't. Before I thought how it would look."

"I told him we were."

"Did he believe you?"

"Probably not."

"Then he thinks you're abducting me. Isn't that priceless!"

"Oh, absolutely. What isn't so funny is that there are laws in some states about people—er—traveling as man and wife if not married."

She stared at him, wide-eyed. "But so long as—Oh, Peter! I'd *hate* it if I got you into any trouble."

"All we have to do is slip Shapley. Nobody else is on." He sincerely hoped that was true.

The intervening time he occupied in patching up the boat as best he might. He had studied the course of various flotsam and thought that he discerned a definite set of the current toward the northern bank which was their goal. With bailing they ought to be able to keep the old tub afloat.

Through the curtain of the rushing clouds the moon was contriving to diffuse a dim light when they set out. The opposite bank was visible only as a faint, occasional blur. Smooth with treachery, the stream at their feet sped from darkness into darkness.

Peter thrust an oar into Elspeth's hand, the only one he had been able to find, to be used as a steering paddle. For himself he had fashioned a pole from a sapling. The carryall he disposed aft of amidships.

Bending over Elspeth as she took the stern seat, he put a hand on her shoulder.

"You're not afraid?"

"No." Just the same, she would have liked to be within reach of that firm grasp through what might be coming.

"Stout fella! All set? Shove!"

The river snatched at the boat, took it into its secret keeping—and held it strangely motionless. But the faintly visible shore slipped backward and away and was presently visible no more. Peter, a long way distant from her in the dimness, was active with his pole, fending to this side and that. It was her job to keep them on the course with her oar. She concentrated upon it.

The boat was leaking profusely now. "Shall I bail?" she called.

"Yes. But keep your oar by you."

They came abreast of an island. As they neared the lower end, an uprooted swamp maple was snatched outward in the movement of the river. Busy with her pan, Elspeth did not notice it until a mass of leafy branches heaved upward from the surface, hovered, descended, and she was struggling in the grasp of a hundred tentacles.

"*Peter!*" she shrieked.

They had her, those wet, clogging arms. They were dragging her out into the void, fight them as she would in her terror and desperation. Now another force was aiding her; Peter, his powerful arms tearing, thrusting, fending against this ponderous invasion. The boat careened. The water poured inboard. Then, miraculously, they were released as the tree sideslipped, turning again, freeing their craft. Elspeth fell back, bruised and battered.

"Are you all right?"

"Yes. It t–t–tried to drag me overboard!"

"I know." His voice, too, was unsteadied by that horror.

"Don't go away. Hold me. Just for a minute."

The skiff, slowly revolving like a ceremonious dancer in the performance of a solo waltz, proceeded on its unguided course. The girl sighed.

"Where's my oar?" It was gone.

"It doesn't matter now. There's the shore. We're being carried in."

They scraped and checked as Peter clutched at a small sapling, growing at the edge of a swampy forest. From trunk to trunk he guided the course until there was a solid bump.

"Land ho!" he shouted, and helped his shipmate out upon the bank.

"What do we do now?"

"Walk until we find a road and a roost."

Valise on shoulder, he set out across the miry fields, Elspeth plodding on behind. It was hard going. Her breath labored painfully after the first half-mile, and she was agonizingly sleepy.

Now Peter's arm was around her; he was murmuring some encouraging foolishness to her who was beyond courage, fear, hope, or any other emotion except the brutish lust for rest. . . . Peter's voice, angry and harsh, insisting that she throw more of her weight on him and *keep* moving. How silly! She hadn't any weight. She was a bird on a bough. She was a butterfly, swaying on a blossom. She was nothing. . . .

Broad daylight, spearing through a paneless window, played upon her lids, waking her. Where was the shawl of Jericho? In its place were boards, a raw wall. Beneath her was fragrant hay. She was actually alive and rested. She looked about her.

"Why, it's a barn!" she exclaimed. She got up and went to the door. Outside stood Peter.

"How do you like the quarters?" he greeted her. "Room"—he pointed to the barn—"and bath." He indicated a huge horse trough fed by a trickle of clear water. "I've just had mine."

She regarded him with stupefaction. "And now you're *shaving.* Where's the party?"

"Party?"

"Well, if not, why the elaborate toilet?"

"Did you ever travel on the thumb?"

She looked her incomprehension. He performed a digital gesture which enlightened her.

"The first rule of the thumb," explained Peter, "is to look as neat and decent as you can. It inspires confidence in the passing motorist's breast."

"Is that the way we're going to travel?"

"If we're lucky."

"Without eating?" she said wistfully.

"Tluck-tluck!" interposed a young chicken from a near-by hedge, the most ill-timed observation of its brief life.

A handy stick, flung deftly, checked its retreat. Peter pounced. "Breakfast!" he exulted.

"Where do we go now?" inquired his companion, half an hour later, greatly restored.

"The main highways," set forth Peter, thinking of the radio alarm and the state police, "are not for us. Verdant lanes and bosky glens are more in our line. We'll take what traffic we can."

Hitch-hiking on sandy side roads in the South means slow progress. Peter finally decided that they must risk better-traveled roads, but select their transportation cautiously. It was selected for them. They had not footed it a mile beside Route 1, when a touring car, battered but serviceable, pulled up and a ruddy face emitted welcome words.

"Well, well, well! Boys *and* girls! Bound north?"

"Yes." It was a duet, perfect in accord.

"Meet Thad Banker, the good old fatty. Throw in the old trunk."

"What's the arrangement?" queried Peter, cautious financier that he was.

"Free wheeling," burbled the fat man. "You furnish the gas and I furnish the spark." They climbed in with the valise. "Any special place?" asked the obliging chauffeur.

"Do we go through Raleigh?" asked the girl, and upon receiving an affirmative, added to Peter: "There may be a wire there for me."

Which reminded that gentleman that he had something to attend to. At the next town he got a telegraph blank and a stamped envelope.

After some cogitation, he produced this composition, addressed to Mr. A. B. M. Andrews, Miami Beach, Fla.

> Daughter taking trip for health and recreation. Advise abandonment of efforts to trace which can have no good results and may cause delay. Sends love and says not to worry. Undersigned guarantees safe arrival in New York in a few days. Pay no reward to any other claimant as this is positively first authentic information.
>
> Peter Warne

To this he pinned a dollar bill and mailed it for transmission to Western Union, New Orleans, Louisiana, by way of giving the pursuit, in case one was instituted, a pleasant place to start from. Five cents more of his thin fortune went for a newspaper. Reports from the southward were worth the money; there was no let-up in the flood. Competition from Mr. Shapley would be delayed at least another day.

Mr. Thad Banker was a card. He kept himself in roars of laughter with his witty sallies. Peter, in the rear seat, fell peacefully asleep. Elspeth had to act as audience for the conversational driver.

At Raleigh she found the expected telegram from Corcoran, which she read and thrust into her purse for future use. Shortly after, a traffic light held them up and the policeman on the corner exhibited an interest in the girl on the front seat quite disturbing to Peter.

The traffic guardian was sauntering toward them when the green flashed on. "Step on it," urged Peter.

Mr. Banker obliged. A whistle shrilled.

"Keep going!" snapped Peter.

Mr. Banker still obliged, slipping into a maze of side streets. It did not occur to Peter that their driver's distaste for police interference was instinctive. Also successful, it began to appear; when a motor cop swung around unexpectedly and headed them to the curb. The license was inspected and found in order.

"Who's the lady?" the officer began.

"My niece," said Mr. Banker, with instant candor.

"Is that right, ma'am?"

"Yes, of course it is." (Peter breathed again.)

"And this man behind?"

"Search me."

"He thumbed us and Uncle Thad stopped for him." (Peter's admiration became almost more than he could bear.)

"Have you got a traveling bag with you, ma'am?" (So the radio must have laid weight on the traveling bag, now probably in some Florida swamp.)

"No. Just my purse."

The cop consulted a notebook. "The dress looks like it," he muttered. "And the description sort of fits. Got anything on you to prove who you are, ma'am?"

"No; I'm afraid—Yes; of course I have." She drew out the yellow envelope. "Is that enough?"

"Miss Bessie Smith," he read. "I reckon that settles it. Keep to your right for Greensboro at Morrisville."

"Greensboro, my foot! Us for points east," announced the fat man, wiping his brow as the motorcycle chugged away. "Phe-e-ew! What's it all about? Been lootin' a bank, you two?"

"Eloping," said Peter. "Keep it under your shirt."

"Gotcha." He eyed the carryall. "All your stuff in there?"

"Yes."

"How about a breath of pure, country air? I'm not so strong for all this public attention."

They kept to side roads until long after dark, bringing up before a restaurant in Tarboro. There the supposed elopers consulted and announced that they didn't care for dinner. "Oh, on me!" cried Mr. Banker. "Mustn't go hungry on your honeymoon."

He ordered profusely. While the steak was cooking, he remarked, he'd just have a look at the car; there was a rattle in the engine that he didn't like. As soon as he had gone, Elspeth said:

"Wonder what the idea is. I never heard a sweeter-running engine for old car. What's more, he's got two sets of license cards. I saw the other one when that inquiring cop—"

But Peter was halfway to the door, after slamming some money on the table and snapping out directions for her to wait, no matter how long he took. Outside, she heard a shout and the rush of a speeding engine. A car without lights sped up the street.

With nothing else to do, Elspeth settled down to leisurely eating. . . .

At nine-thirty, the waiter announced the closing hour as ten, sharp. Beginning to be terrified for Peter and miserable for herself, she ordered more coffee. The bill and tip left her a dollar and fifteen cents.

At nine-fifty, the wreckage of Peter entered the door. Elspeth arose and made a rush upon him, but recoiled.

"Peter! You've been fighting."

"Couldn't help it."

"You've got a black eye."

"That isn't all I've got," he told her.

"No; it isn't. What an *awful*-looking ear!"

"*That* isn't all I've got, either." His grin was bloody, but unbowed.

"Then it must be internal injuries."

"Wrong. It's a car."

"Whose car?"

"Ours now, I expect. I had to come home in something."

"Where's the fat man?"

The grin widened. "Don't know exactly. Neither does he, I reckon. That big-hearted Samaritan, my child, is a road-pirate. He picks people up, plants 'em, and beats it with their luggage. Probably does a little holdup business on the side."

"Tell me what happened, Peter. Go on and eat first."

Between relishing mouthfuls, he unfolded his narrative. "You didn't put me wise a bit too quick. He was moving when I got out but I landed aboard with a flying tackle. Didn't dare grab him for fear we'd crash. He was stepping on it and telling me that when he got me far enough away he was going to beat me up and tie me to a tree. That was an idea! So when he pulled up on some forsaken wood road in a swamp, I beat him up and tied him to a tree."

"Why, Peter! He's twice as big as you."

"I can't help that. It wasn't any time for half measures. It took me an hour to find my way. But here we are."

"I'm glad," she said with a new note in her voice.

"Jumping Jehoshaphat! Is *that* all we've got left?" Aghast, he stared at the sum she put in his hands. "And it's too cold to sleep out tonight. It's an open car, anyhow. Oh, well; our transportation's going to be cheap from now on. What price one more good night's rest? Torney's Haven for Tourists is three miles up the highway. Let's get going."

Torney's provided a cabin for only a dollar. Before turning in, Peter returned to the car, parked a few rods away against a fence, to make a thorough inspection. His companion was in bed on his return.

"I've changed the plates to another set that I found under the seat. Indiana, to match the other set of licenses. It'll be safer in case our friend decides to report the loss, after he gets loose from his tree. There's a nice robe, too. We've come into property. And by the way, Elspeth; you're Mrs. Thaddeus Banker till further notice."

Elspeth pouted. "I'd rather be Mrs. Peter Warne. I'm getting used to that."

"We've got to live up to our new responsibilities." Seated on his cot, he had taken off his shoes, when he started hastily to resume them.

"Where are you going?" she asked plaintively. "Looking for more trouble?"

"Walls of Jericho. I forgot. I'll get the robe out of the car."

"Oh, darn the robe! Why bother? It's pouring, too. Let it go. I don't mind if you don't." All in a perfectly matter-of-fact tone. She added: "You can undress outside. I'm going to sleep."

As soon as he withdrew she got out Corcoran's reply to "Miss Bessie Smith," and read it over again before tearing it into fragments. It ran as follows:

> What's all this about P. W.? Watch out for that bird. Dangerous corner, blind road, and all that sorta thing. At any given moment he might be running a pirate fleet or landing on the throne of the Kingdom of Boopadoopia. Ask him about the bet I stuck him on in college, and then keep your guard up. I'm off for a week on the Keys so you can't get me again until then. Better come back home and be a nice little girl or papa spank. And how!
>
> Cork

The scraps she thrust beneath her pillow and was asleep almost at once. But Peter lay, wakeful, crushing down thoughts that made him furious with himself. At last peace came, and dreams. . . . One of them so poignant, so incredibly dear, that he fought bitterly against its turning to reality.

Yet reality it was; the sense of warmth and softness close upon him; the progress of creeping fingers across his breast, of seeking lips against his throat. His arms drew her down. His mouth found the lips that, for a dizzying moment, clung to his, then trembled aside to whisper:

"No, Peter. I didn't mean—Listen!"

Outside, sounded a light clinking.

"Somebody's stealing the car!"

Elspeth's form, in the lurid pajamas, slid away from Peter like a ghost. He followed to the window. Silent as a shadow the dim bulk of the Banker automobile moved deliberately along under a power not its own. Two other shadows loomed in its rear, propelling it by hand.

"Shall I scream?" whispered the girl.

He put a hand on her mouth. "Wait."

Another of his luminous ideas had fired the brain of Peter Warne. In his role of Thad Banker, he would let the robbers get away, then report the theft to the police and, allowing for reasonable luck, get back his property (or Mr. Banker's) with the full blessing of the authorities.

"I'm going to let 'em get away with it," he murmured. "As soon as they really start, I'll telephone the road patrol."

The dwindling shadow trundled out on the pike, where the engine struck up its song and the car sped southward. Simultaneously Peter made a rush for the camp office. It was all right, he reported, on getting back. He'd been able to get the police at once.

"But suppose they don't catch 'em."

"That'll be just too bad," admitted Peter. He yawned.

"You're sleepy again. You're always sleepy."

"What do you expect at three o'clock in the morning?"

"I'm wide awake," complained Elspeth.

Something had changed within her, made uncertain and uneasy, since she had aroused Peter and found herself for one incendiary moment in his arms. She didn't blame him; he was only half awake at the time. But she had lost confidence in him. Or could it be herself in whom she had lost confidence? In any case, the thought of sharing the same room with him the rest of that night had become too formidable.

"Please go outside again, Peter. I'm going to get dressed. I'm restless."

"Oh, my gosh!" he sighed. "Can't you count some sheep or something?"

"No; I can't." A brilliant idea struck her. "How'd you expect me to sleep when they may be back with the car any minute?"

"And then again, they may not be back till morning."

But Elspeth had a heritage of the immovable Scottish obstinacy. In a voice all prickly little italics she announced that she was *going to get up.* And she was going to walk off her nervousness. It needn't make any difference to Peter. He could go back to bed.

"And let you wander around alone in this blackness? You might not come back."

"What else could I do?"

The forlorn lack of alternative for her struck into his heart. Absolute dependence upon a man of a strange breed in circumstances wholly new. What a situation for a girl like her! And how gallantly, on the whole, she was taking it! How sensible it would be for him to go back to that telephone; call up her father (reverse charges, of course) and tell him the whole thing. *And* get himself thoroughly hated for it.

No; he couldn't throw Elspeth down. Not even for her own good. Carry on. There was nothing else for it, especially now that luck was favoring them. The car, if they got it back, was their safest obtainable method of travel. Her dress was the weak spot and would be more of a danger point after Horace Shapley contributed his evidence to the hunt. Couldn't something be done about that? . . . The dress appeared in the doorway, and Peter went in to array himself for the vigil.

The two state police found the pair waiting at the gate. Apologetically they explained that the thieves had got away into the swamp. Nothing could have suited Peter better, since there would now be no question of his being held as complaining witness. To satisfy the authorities of his ownership was easy. They took his address (fictitious), wished him and his wife good luck, and were off.

"Now we can go back to bed," said Peter.

"Oh, dear! Can't we start on?"

"At this hour? Why, I suppose we could, but—"

"Let's, then." In the turmoil of her spirit she wanted to be quit forever of Torney's Haven for Tourists and its atmosphere of unexpected emotions and disconcerting impulses. Maybe something of this had trickled into Peter's mind, too, for presently he said:

"Don't you know it's dangerous to wake a sound sleeper too suddenly?"

"So I've heard."

"You can't tell what might happen. I mean, a man isn't quite responsible, you know, before he comes quite awake."

So he was apologizing. Very proper.

"Let's forget it."

"Yes," he agreed quietly. "I'll have quite a little to forget."

"So will I," she thought, startled at the realization.

They packed, and chugged out, one cylinder missing. "I hope the old junk-heap holds together till we reach New York," remarked Peter.

"Are we going all the way in this?"

"Unless you can think of a cheaper way."

"But it isn't ours. It's the fat man's."

"I doubt it. Looks to me as if it had been stolen and gypped up with new paint and fake numbers. However, we'll leave it somewhere in Jersey if we get that far, and write to both license numbers to come and get it. How does that set on an empty conscience?"

"Never mind my conscience. That isn't the worst emptiness I'm suffering from. What's in the house for breakfast? It's nearly sunup."

"Potatoes. Pecans." He investigated their scanty store and looked up. "There are only three spuds left."

"Is that all?"

Something careless in her reply made him scan her face sharply. "There ought to be five. There are two missing. You had charge of the larder. Well?"

"I took 'em. You see—"

"Without saying a word about it to me? You must have pinched them out when we were on the island and cooked them for yourself while I was working on the boat," he figured somberly. Part of this was true, but not all of it. The rest she was saving to confound him with. "Do you, by any chance, still think that this is a picnic?"

Now she *wouldn't* tell him! She was indignant and hurt. He'd be sorry! When he came to her with a potato now, she would haughtily decline it—if her rueful stomach didn't get the better of her wrathful fortitude.

In resentment more convincing than her own, he built the wayside fire, boiled the water and inserted one lone potato; the smallest at that. He counted out five pecans, added two more, and handed the lot to her. He then got out his pocketknife, opened it, and prodded the bubbling tuber. Judging it soft enough, he neatly speared it out upon a plate. Elspeth pretended a total lack of interest. She hoped she'd have the resolution to decline her half with hauteur. She didn't get the chance.

Peter split the potato, sprinkled on salt, and ate it all.

With difficulty, Elspeth suppressed a roar of rage. That was the kind of man he was, then! Selfish, greedy, mean, tyrannical, unfair, smug, bad-tempered, uncouth—her stock ran thin. How idiotically she had overestimated him! Rough but noble; that had been her formula for his character. And now look at him, pigging down the last delicious fragments while she was to be content with a handful of nuts. Nuts! She rose in regal resentment, flung her seven pecans into the fire, and stalked back to the car.

Somewhere in the vicinity of Emporia, eighty miles north of their breakfast, he spoke. "No good in sulking, you know."

"I'm *not* sulking." Which closed that opening.

Nevertheless, Elspeth was relieved. An oppressive feeling that maybe his anger would prove more lasting than her own had tainted her satisfaction in being the injured party. One solicitude, too, he exhibited. He kept tucking her up in the robe.

This would have been less reassuring had she understood its genesis. He was afraid her costume might be recognized. He even thought of suggesting that she might effect a trade in some secondhand store. In her present state of childish petulance, however, he judged it useless to suggest this. Some other way must be found.

Some money was still left to them. Elspeth saw her companion shaking his head over it when their gas gave out, happily near a filling station. His worried expression weakened her anger, but she couldn't bring herself to admit she was sorry. Not yet.

"There's a cheap camp seventy miles from here," he said. "But if we sleep there we can't have much of a dinner."

"Potatoes," said the recalcitrant Elspeth. She'd teach him!

They dined at a roadside stand which, in ordinary conditions, she would have considered loathsome. Every odor of it now brought prickly sensations to her palate.

The night presented a problem troubling to her mind. No shared but unpartitioned cabin for her! Last night's experience had been too revelatory. What made things difficult was that she had told him she needed no more walls of Jericho to insure peaceful sleep. Now if she asked him to put up the curtain, what would he think?

Pursuant to his policy of avoiding large cities and the possible interest of traffic cops, Peter had planned their route westward again, giving Richmond a wide berth. They flashed without stop through towns with hospitable restaurants only to pull up at a roadside stand of austere menu, near Sweet Briar.

Never had Elspeth seen the important sum of twenty-five cents laid out so economically as by Peter's method. Baked beans with thick, fat, glorious gollups of pork; a half-loaf of bread, and bitter coffee. To say that her hunger was appeased would be overstatement. But a sense of returned well-being comforted her. She even felt that she could face the morning's potato, if any, with courage. Meantime, there remained the arrangements for the night.

Peter handled that decisively, upon their arrival at the camp. Their cabin was dreary, chill, and stoveless. When he brought in the robe from the car, she hoped for it over her bunk. Not at all; out came his little tool kit; up went the separating cord, and over it was firmly pinned the warm fabric.

With a regrettable though feminine want of logic, Elspeth nursed a grievance; he needn't have been at such pains to raise that wall again without a request from the person most interested. She went to sleep crossly but promptly.

In the morning the robe was tucked snugly about her. How long had that been there? She looked around and made a startling discovery. Her clothes were gone. So was Peter. Also, when she looked out, the car. The wild idea occurred to her that he had stolen her outfit and run away, *à la* Thad Banker. One thing was certain: to rise and wander forth clad in those grotesque pajamas was out of the question. Turning over, she fell asleep again.

Some inner sensation of his nearness awoke her, or perhaps it was, less occultly, his footsteps outside, approaching, pausing. She craned upward to bring her vision level with the window. Peter was standing with his side face toward her, a plump bundle beneath his arm. Her clothes, probably, which he had taken out to clean. How nice of him!

He set down his burden and took off his belt. With a knife he slit the stitches in the leather, carefully prying something from beneath the strips. It was a tight-folded bill.

So he had been holding out on her! Keeping her on a gnat's diet. Letting her go hungry while he gorged himself on boiled potato and salt, and gloated over his reserve fund. Beast! This knowledge, too, she would hold back for his ultimate discomfiture. It was a composed and languid voice which responded to his knock on the door.

"Hello! How are you feeling, Elspeth?"

"Very well, thank you. Where have you been?"

"Act two, scene one of matrimonial crisis," chuckled Peter. "Hubby returns early in the morning. Wife demands explanation. Husband is ready with it: 'You'd be surprised.' "There was a distinct trace of nervousness in his bearing.

"Well, surprise me," returned Elspeth, with hardly concealed hostility. She sat up in bed. "Where are my clothes?"

"That's the point. They're—uh—I—er—well, the fact is, I pawned 'em in Charlottesville."

"You—pawned—my—clothes! Where's the money?" If that was the bill in the belt, she proposed to know it.

"I spent most of it. On other clothes. You said your feet hurt you."

"When we were walking. We don't have to walk any more."

"How do you know? We aren't out of the woods yet. And you don't need such a fancy rig, traveling with me. And we do need the little bit extra I picked up on the trade."

Stern and uncompromising was the glare which she directed upon his bundle. "Let me see."

Her immediate reaction to the dingy, shoddy, nondescript outfit he disclosed was an involuntary yip of distress.

"Don't you like 'em?" he asked.

"They're terrible! They're ghastly!"

"The woman said they were serviceable. Put 'em on. I'll wait outside."

It would have taken a sturdier optimism than Peter's to maintain a sun-kissed countenance in the face of the transformation which he presently witnessed. Hardly could he recognize her in that horrid mis-fit which she was pinning here, adjusting there.

"Hand me the mirror, please."

"Perhaps you'd better not—"

"Will you be so good as to do as I ask?"

"Oh, all *right!*"

She took one long, comprehensive survey and burst into tears.

"Don't, Elspeth," he protested, appalled. "What's the difference? There's no one to see you."

"There's me," she gulped. "And there's you."

"I don't mind." As if he were bearing up courageously under an affliction.

"I'm a *sight*," she wailed. "I'm hideous! Go and get my things back."

"It can't be done."

"I won't go out in these frightful things. I won't. I won't. I *won't!*"

"Who's going to pay the rent if you stay?"

Obtaining no reply to this pertinent inquiry, he sighed and went out. Down the breeze, there presently drifted to Elspeth's nostrils the tang of wood smoke. Her face appeared in the window.

"About those missing potatoes," said she. (How mean she was going to make him feel in a minute!) "Are you interested in knowing what became of them?"

"It doesn't matter. They're gone."

"They're gone where they'll do the most good," she returned with slow impressiveness. "I gave them away."

"Without consulting me?"

"Do I have to consult you about everything I do?"

"We-ell, some people might figure that I had an interest in those potatoes."

"Well, I gave them to a poor old woman who needed them. She was hungry."

"Umph! Feeling sure, I suppose, that your generosity would cost you nothing, as I'd share the remainder with you. Error Number One."

"Peter, I wouldn't have thought anyone could be so des-des-despicable!"

This left him unmoved. "Who was the starving beneficiary? I'll bet it was that old creature with the black bonnet and gold teeth in the bus."

"How did you know?"

"She's the sort you would help. In case you'd like to know, that old hoarder had her bag half full of almond chocolates. I saw her buy 'em at Charleston."

"Hoarder, yourself!" Enraged at the failure of her bombshell, she fell back on her last ammunition. "What did you take out of your belt this morning?"

"Oh, you saw that, did you? Watchful little angel!"

"I'm not! I just happened to see it. A bill. A big one, I'll bet. You had it all the time. And you've starved me and bullied me and made me walk miles and sleep in barns, while you could just as well have—"

"Hired a special train. On ten dollars."

"Ten dollars is a lot of money." (Ideas change.)

"Now, I'll tell you about that ten dollars," said he with cold precision. "It's my backlog. It's the last resort. It's the untouchable. It's the dead line of absolute necessity."

"You needn't touch it on my account." (Just like a nasty-tempered little brat, she told herself.) "Of course, starvation isn't absolute necessity."

"Can you do simple arithmetic?"

"Yes. I'm not quite an idiot, even if you do think so, Peter."

"Try this one, then. We've got something over five hundred miles to go. Gas will average us seventeen cents. This old mudcart of Banker's won't do better than twelve miles on a gallon. Now, can any bright little girl in this class tell me how much over that leaves us to eat, sleep and live on, not counting oil, ferry charge and incidentals?"

"I can't. And I don't want to," retorted Elspeth, very dispirited. A long, dull silence enclosed them like a globe. She shattered it. "Peter!"

"What?"

"D'you know why I hate you?"

"I'll bite," said he, wearily. "Why?"

"Because, darn you! you're always right and I'm always wrong. Peter! Peter, dear! A potato, Peter. Please, Peter; one potato. Just one. The littlest. I know I don't deserve it, but—"

"Oh, what's the *use!*" vociferated Peter, throwing up both hands in abject and glad surrender. And that quarrel drifted on the smoke of their fire down to the limbo of things become insignificant, yet never quite to be forgotten.

Two young people, haggard, gaunt, shabby, bluish with the chill of an April storm, drove their battered car aboard the Fort Lee ferry as the boat pulled out. They were sharing a bag of peanuts with the conscientious exactitude of penury: one to you; one to me. Quarter of the way across, both were asleep. At the halfway distance the whistle blared and they woke up.

"We're nearly there," observed the girl without any special enthusiasm.

"Yes," said the man with still less.

A hiatus of some length. "Why didn't you tell me about blacking Corker's boots?"

"What about it?"

"It was on a bet, wasn't it?"

"Yes. In college. I picked the wrong team. If I'd won, the Corker would have typed my theses for the term. What put you on?"

"A telegram from Cork."

"Oh! The one to Bessie Smith that saved our lives in Raleigh?"

She nodded. "Anyway, I knew all the time you weren't a valet," she asserted.

He cocked a mild, derisive eye at her. "You're not building up any rosy picture of me as a perfect gentleman, are you?"

"No-o. I don't know what you are."

"Don't let it worry you. Go back to sleep."

"You're always telling me to go to sleep," she muttered discontentedly. She rubbed her nose on his shoulder. "Peter."

He sighed and kissed her.

"You needn't be so solemn about it."

"I'm not feeling exactly sprightly."

"Because we're almost home? But we'll be seeing each other soon."

"I thought that headliner of the air was waiting to fly you somewhere."

"Who? Oh-h-h-h, King." She began to laugh. "Isn't that funny! I'd absolutely forgotten about King. He doesn't matter. When am I going to see you?" As he made no reply, she became vaguely alarmed. . . ."You're not going right back?"

"No. I've got that possible contract to look after. Down in Jersey."

"But you'll be in town again. And I'll see you then."

"No."

"Peter! Why not?"

"Self-preservation," he proclaimed oracularly, "is the first law of nature."

"You don't want to see me again?"

"Put it any way you like," came the broad-minded permission, "just so the main point gets across."

"But I think that's absolutely lousy!" Another point occurred to her. "There's no reason why you shouldn't if it's because—well, that business about my being married was a good deal exaggerated. If that makes any difference."

"It does. It makes it worse."

"Oh! . . .You don't seem surprised, though."

"Me? I should say not! I've known from the first that was all bunk."

"Have you, Smarty? How?"

"You tried to put it over that you'd been wearing a wedding ring. But there was no band of white on the tan of your finger."

"Deteckative! I haven't had a bit of luck trying to fool you about anything, have I, Peter? Not even putting across the superior-goddess idea. And now you're the one that's being snooty."

"I'm not. I'm being sensible. See here, Elspeth. It may or may not have been called to your attention that you're a not wholly unat-tractive young person—and that I myself am not yet beyond the age of—"

"Consent," broke in the irrepressible Elspeth.

"—damfoolishness," substituted Peter, with severity. "So," he concluded, with an effect of logic, "we may as well call it a day."

"Not to mention several nights." She turned the brilliance of mirthful eyes upon him. "Wouldn't it be funny if you fell in love with me, Peter?"

"Funny for the spectators. Painful for the bear."

"Then don't mention it, Bear!" Another idea occurred to her. "How much money have you got left?"

"Forty-odd cents."

"Now that you're in New York you can get more, of course."

"Yes? Where?"

"At the bank, I suppose. Where does one get money?"

"That's what I've always wanted to know," he grinned.

"I can get all I want tomorrow. I'll lend you a hundred dollars. Or more if you want it."

"No; thank you."

"But I borrowed yours!" she cried. "At least, you paid for me."

"That's different."

"I don't see how." Of course she did see, and inwardly approved. "But—but I owe you money!" she cried. "I'd forgotten all about that. You'll let me pay that back, of course."

If she expected him to deprecate politely the idea she was swiftly undeceived. "The sooner, the better," said Peter cheerfully.

"I'll bet you've got it all set down in that precious notebook of yours."

"Every cent." He tore out a leaf which he handed to her.

"Where can I send it?"

He gave her an address on a street whose name she had never before heard; Darrow, or Barrow, or some such matter.

In the splendor of the great circular court off Park Avenue, the bedraggled automobile looked impudently out of place. The doorkeeper almost choked with amazement as the luxurious Miss Elspeth Andrews, clad in such garments as had never before affronted those august portals, jumped out, absently responding to his greeting.

"I think your father is expecting you, miss," said he.

"Oh, Lord!" exclaimed Elspeth. "Now, what brought him here?"

Peter could have told her, but didn't. He was looking straight through the windshield. She was looking at him with slightly lifted brows.

"Good-bye, Elspeth," said he huskily.

"Good-bye, Peter. You've been awfully mean to me. I've loved it."

Why, thought Peter as he went on his way, did she have to use that particular word in that special tone at that unhappy moment?

Between Alexander Bruce MacGregor Andrews and his daughter, Elspeth, there existed a lively and irritable affection of precarious status, based upon a fundamental similarity of character and a prevalent lack of mutual understanding. That she should have willfully run away from home and got herself and him on the front pages of the papers, seemed to him an outrage of the first order.

"But it was your smearing the thing all over the air that got us into the papers," pointed out Elspeth, which didn't help much as a contribution to the *entente cordiale*. Both sulked for forty-eight hours.

Meantime, there arrived by special delivery a decidedly humid shoebox addressed in an uncompromisingly straight-up-and-down hand—just exactly the kind one would expect, thought the girl, knowing whose it was at first sight—full of the freshest, most odorous bunch of arbutus she had ever beheld. Something about it unmistakably defined it as having been picked by the sender.

Elspeth searched minutely for a note; there was none. She carried the box to her room and threw three clusters of orchids and a spray of gardenias into the scrapbasket. After that she went to a five-and-ten-cent store, made a purchase at the toy counter, had it boxed, and herself mailed it to the address given her by Peter Warne. The shipment did not include the money she owed him. That detail had escaped her mind.

"Scotty, dear." She greeted her father in the style of their companionable moods. "Do let's be sensible."

Mr. Andrews grunted suspiciously. "Suppose you begin."

"I'm going to. Drink your cocktail first." She settled down on the arm of his chair.

"Now what devilment are you up to?" demanded the apprehensive parent.

"Not a thing. I've decided to tell you about my trip."

Having her narrative all duly mapped out, she ran through it smoothly enough, hoping that he would not notice a few cleverly glossed passages. Disapproval in the paternal expression presently yielded to amused astonishment.

"Nervy kid!" he chuckled. "I'll bet it did you good."

"It didn't do me any harm. And I certainly found out a few things I'd never known before."

"Broadening effect of travel. Who did you say this young man was that looked after you?"

"I'm coming to that. The question is, what are you going to do for him?"

"What does he want?"

"I don't know that he exactly wants anything. But he's terribly poor, Scotty. Why, just think! He had to reckon up each time how much he could afford to spend on a meal!"

"Yes? I'm told there are quite a few people in this country in the same fix," observed Mr. Andrews dryly. "How much'll I make out the check for?"

"That's the trouble. I don't believe he'd take it. He's one of those inde-be-goshdarn-pendent birds. Wouldn't listen to my lending him some money."

"Humph! That probably means he's fallen for your fair young charms. Be funny if he hadn't."

"I'll tell you what would be funnier."

"What?"

"If I'd fallen for him," was the brazen response.

"Poof! You're always imagining you're in love with the newest hero in sight. Remember that young Danish diplo—"

"Yes; I do. What of it? I always get over it, don't I? And I'll get over this. You'd think he was terrible, Dad. He's sure rough. You ought to have seen Little Daughter being bossed around by him and taking it."

"Is that so?" said her father, spacing his words sardonically. "Bossed you, did he? He and who else?"

"Oh, Peter doesn't need any help."

The grin was wiped off the Andrews face. "Who?"

"Peter. That's his name. Peter Warne."

"*What?*"

"Gracious! Don't yell so. Do you know him?"

"I haven't that pleasure as yet. Just let me make sure about this." He went into the adjoining room, whence he emerged with a sheaf of papers. "Peter Warne. So he's poor, is he?"

"Desperately."

"Well, he won't be, after tomorrow."

"Oh, Scotty! How do you know? Is he going to get some money? I'm so glad!"

"Some money is correct. Ten thousand dollars, to be exact."

"From his tar-pine or something process? How did *you* know about it?"

"From me. I don't know anything about—"

"From you?" Her lips parted; her eyes were wide and alarmed. "What for?"

"Information leading to the discovery and return of Elspeth, daughter of—"

"The reward? For me? Peter? I don't believe it. Peter wouldn't do such a thing. Take money for—"

"He has done it. Put in his claim for the reward. Do you want to see the proof?"

"I wouldn't believe it anyway."

Alexander Andrews studied her defiant face with a concern that became graver. This looked serious. Selecting a letter and a telegram from his dossier, he put them into her reluctant hand. At sight of the writing her heart sank. It was unmistakably that of the address on the box of arbutus. The note cited the writer's telegram of the fourteenth ("That's the day after we got off the island," thought Elspeth. "He was selling me out then.") and asked for an appointment.

"He's coming to my office at ten-thirty Thursday morning."

"Are you going to give him the money?"

"It looks as if I'd have to."

"He certainly worked hard enough for it," she said bitterly. "And I expect he needs it."

"I might be able to work a compromise," mused the canny Scot. "Though I'm afraid he's got the material for a bothersome lawsuit. If any of the other claimants"—he indicated the sheaf of letters and telegrams—"had a decent case, we could set off one against the other. The most insistent is a person named Shapley."

"Don't let him have it," said the girl hastily. "I'd rather Peter should get it, though I'd never have believed—Sold down the river!" She forced a laugh. "I brought a price, anyway."

"I've a good mind to give him a fight for it. It would mean more publicity, though."

"Oh, no!" breathed Elspeth.

"Enough's enough, eh? Though it couldn't be worse than what we've had."

"It could. Much worse. If you're going to see Pe—Mr. Warne, I'd better tell you something, Father. I've been traveling as Mrs. Peter Warne."

"*Elspeth!*"

"It isn't what you think. Purely economy—with the accent on the 'pure.' But it wouldn't look pretty in print. Oh, damn!" Her voice broke treacherously. "I thought Peter was so straight."

Her father walked up and down the room several times. He then went over and put his arm around his daughter's shoulders. "It's all right, dawtie. We'll get you out of it. And we'll find a way to keep this fellow's mouth shut. I'm having a detectaphone set up in my office, and if he makes one slip we'll have him by the short hairs for blackmail."

"Peter doesn't make slips," returned his daughter. "It's his specialty not to. Oh, well, let's go in to dinner, Scotty."

Resolutely, she put the arbutus out of her room when she went up to bed that night. But the spicy odor from far springtime woodlands clung about the place like a plea for the absent.

Stern logic of the morning to which she sorrowfully awoke filled in the case against Peter. Nevertheless and notwithstanding, "I don't believe it," said Elspeth's sore heart. "And I won't believe it until—until—"

Severe as were the fittings of Mr. Alexander Bruce MacGregor Andrews' spacious office, they were less so than the glare which apprised Peter Warne, upon his entry, that this spare, square man did not like him and probably never would. That was all right with Peter. He was prepared not to like Mr. Andrews, either. On this propitious basis the two confronted each other.

After a formidable silence which the younger man bore without visible evidence of discomposure, his host barked:

"Sit down."

"Thank you," said Peter. He sat down.

"You have come about the money, I assume."

"Yes."

"Kindly reduce your claim to writing."

"You'll find it there." He handed over a sheet of paper. "Itemized."

"What's this?" Mr. Andrews' surprised eye ran over it.

"Traveling expenses. Elsp—your daughter's."

The father gave the column of figures his analytical attention. "Boat, twenty dollars," he read. "You didn't take my daughter to Cuba, did you?"

"I had to steal a boat to get through the flood. The owner ought to be reimbursed. If you think that's not a fair charge, I'll assume half of it. Everything else is split."

"Humph! My daughter's share of food, lodging and gasoline, excluding the—er—alleged boat, seems to figure up to eighteen dollars and fifty-six cents. Where did you lodge?"

"Wherever we could."

With the paper before him, Mr. Andrews began to hammer his desk. "You have the temerity, the impudence, the effrontery, the—the—anyway, you come here to hold me up for ten thousand dollars and on top of that you try to spring a doctored expense account on me!"

"Doctored!" echoed Peter. "Maybe you think you could do it for less?"

Taken aback, Mr. Andrews ceased his operations on the desk. "We'll pass that for the main point," he grunted. "Upon what do you base your claim for the ten thousand dollars?"

"Nothing," was the placid reply. "I made no claim."

"Your telegram. Your letter—"

"You couldn't have read them. I simply warned you against paying anybody else's claim. You had others, I suppose."

"Others! A couple of hundred!"

"One signed Horace Shapley?"

"I believe so."

"I don't like him," observed Peter, and explained.

"Then your idea," interposed Mr. Andrews, "was to get in first merely to block off this other person. Is that it?"

"Yes."

"And you aren't claiming any part of the reward?"

"No."

"You're crazy," declared the other. "Or maybe I am. What *do* you want?"

Peter gently indicated the expense account. Mr. Andrews went over it again.

"You mean to tell me that you kept my daughter for five days and more on a total of eighteen dollars and fifty-six cents?"

"There are the figures."

Mr. Andrews leaned forward. "Did she kick much?"

Peter's grin was a bit rueful. "There were times when—"

"You'd have liked to sock her. I know. Why didn't you present your bill to her?"

"I did. I reckon she just forgot it."

"She would! . . . Have a cigar." As the young fellow lighted up, his entertainer was writing and entering a check.

"As a matter of correct business, I ought to have Elspeth's O.K. on this bill. However, I'll pass it, including the boat. Receipt here, please." The amount was $1,038.56.

Shaking his head, Peter pushed the check across the desk. "Thank you, but I can't take this, Mr. Andrews."

"Bosh! Elspeth told me you were broke."

"I am . . . No; I'm not, either. I forgot. I've just made a deal on a new process of mine. Anyway, I couldn't take that—that bonus."

"That's funny. If you're no longer broke, I should think you'd be above bringing me a trifling expense account for—er—entertaining my daughter."

"It's a matter of principle," returned Peter firmly.

Mr. Andrews rose and smote his caller on the shoulder. "I begin to see how you made that little spitfire of mine toe the mark. More than I've been able to do for the past ten years. Eighteen dollars and fifty-six cents, huh?" He sank back in his chair and laughed. "See here, my boy; I like you. I like your style. Will you take that money as a present from me?"

"Sorry, sir, but I'd rather not."

The older man stared him down. "Because I'm Elspeth's father, eh? You're in love with her, I suppose."

Peter grew painfully red. "God forbid!" he muttered.

"What do you mean, God forbid?" shouted the magnate. "Better men than you have been in love with her."

"All right, Mr. Andrews," said Peter in desperation. "Then I am, too. I have been from the first. Now, you tell me—you're her father—what's the sense of it with a girl like Elspeth? I'm going back to Florida with a contract for eight thousand a year, to complete my process."

"That's more than I was making at your age."

"It's more than I expect to be making at yours," said Peter with candor. "But how far would that go with her? Look me over, sir. Even if I had a chance with Elspeth, would you advise a fellow like me to try to marry her?"

"No, I wouldn't!" roared the father. "You're too darn good for her."

"Don't talk like a fool," snapped Peter.

"Just for that," reflected Mr. Andrews as his caller withdrew, jamming a substituted check into his pocket, "I'll bet you'll have little enough to say about it when the time comes."

He sent for Elspeth and left her alone with the detectaphone. What that unpoetic cylinder spouted forth rang in her heart like the music of the spheres with the morning and evening stars in the solo parts. So *that* was how Peter felt about it.

Memory obligingly supplied the number on Darrow or Farrow or Barrow or whatever strange street it was. The taxi man whom she hailed earned her admiration by knowing all about it.

Peter said: "Come in," in a spiritless manner. With a totally different vocal effect he added: "What are *you* doing *here?*" and tacked onto that "You oughtn't to be here at all."

"Why not?" Elspeth sat down.

He muttered something wherein the word "proper" seemed to carry the emphasis, and in which the term "landlady" occurred.

"Proper!" jeered his visitor. "You talk to me about propriety after we've been traveling together and sharing the same room for nearly a week!"

"But this is New York," he pointed out.

"And you're packing up to leave it. When?"

"Tonight."

"Without the ten thousand dollar reward?"

"How did you know about that? Your fath—"

"I've just come from his office. You might better have taken the check."

"Don't want it."

"That's silly. What," she inquired reasonably, "have you got to get married on?"

"Eight thousand a ye—I'm not going to get married," he interrupted himself with needless force.

"Not after compromising a young and innocent—"

"I haven't compromised anyone." Sulkily and doggedly.

"Peter! I suppose registering me as your wife all over the map isn't compromising. Did you ever hear of the Mann Act?"

"B-b-b-but—"

"Yes; I know all about that 'but.' It's a great big, important 'but,' but there's another bigger 'but' to be considered. We know what happened and didn't happen on our trip, *but* nobody else would ever believe it in this world. I certainly wouldn't."

"Nor I," he agreed. "Unless," he qualified hastily, "the girl was you."

"Or the man was you."

They laughed with dubious heartiness. When they had done laughing, there seemed to be nothing to follow, logically. Elspeth got up slowly.

"Where are you going?" demanded Peter, in a panic.

"If you don't like me any more"—she put the slightest possible stress on the verb, leaving him to amend it if he chose—"I'm sorry I came."

To this rueful observation, Peter offered no response.

"You did like me once, you know. You as much as admitted it."

Peter swore.

"Did you or did you not tell my father that you would never get over it?"

"It?"

"Well—me."

"Your father," said Peter wrathfully, "is a human sieve."

"No; he isn't. There was a detectaphone listening in on everything you said. I got it all from that."

"In that case," said the now desperate and reckless Peter, "I may as well get it off my chest." And he repeated what he had earlier said about his feelings, with a fervor that wiped the mischief from Elspeth's face.

"Oh-h-h-h!" she murmured, a little dazed. "That's the way you feel."

"No, it isn't. It isn't half of it."

"Where do we go from here?" thought the girl. The atmosphere of sprightly combat and adventure had changed. She was not breathing quite so easily. Her uncertain look fell upon an object at the top of the half-packed carryall. "Oh!" she exclaimed. "You got my present."

"Yes; I got it."

"I hope you liked it." Politely.

"Not particularly."

Her eyes widened. "Why not?"

"Well, I may be oversensitive where you're concerned, but I don't care so much about being called a tinhorn sport, because—well, I don't know, but I suppose it's because I let you pay back the money for our trip," he concluded morosely.

The girl was looking at him with a mixture of contempt, amusement, pity, and something stronger than any of these. "Oh, you boob!" she breathed. "That isn't a tinhorn. That's a trumpet."

"A *trumpet?*"

"The kind What's-his-name blew before the walls of Jericho, if you have to have a diagram. Oh, *Pee*-ter; you're such a dodo!" sighed Elspeth. "What am I ever going to do about you? Would you like to kiss me, Peter?"

"Yes," said Peter. And he did.

"This means," he informed her presently, and dubiously, "our having to live in a Florida swamp—"

"On eighteen dollars and fifty-six cents?"

"On eight thousand a year. That isn't much more, to you. You'll hate it."

"I'll love it. D'you know where I'd like to land on our wedding trip, Peter?"

"Yes. Dake's Two-dollar Cabins; Clean; Comfortable; Reasonable."

"*And* respectable. You're too clever, Peter, darling."

"Because that's exactly what I'd like. Social note: Mr. and Mrs. Peter Warne are stopping in Jaw-jaw on their return trip South."

"Let's go," said Elspeth joyously.

Mrs. Dake, in the wing off the tourist-camp office, yawned herself awake of an early May morning and addressed her husband. "That's a funny couple in Number Seven, Tim. Do you reckon they're respectable?"

"I should worry. They registered all right, didn't they?"

"Uh-huh. Wouldn't take any other cabin but Seven. And wanted an extra blanket. This hot night."

"Well, we could spare it."

"That isn't the only queer thing about 'em. After you was asleep, I looked out and there was the young fellah mopin' around. By and by he went in, and right soon somebody blew a horn. Just as plain as you ever heard. What do you think about that, Tim?"

Mr. Dake yawned. "What they do after they're registered and paid up is their business, not our'n."

Which is the proper and practical attitude for the management of a well-conducted tourist camp.

One Fair Daughter

BY BEN AMES WILLIAMS

en Ames Williams was born in Mississippi and raised in
Ohio, which gave his stories great insight into the mindset of
the people of the South and Midwest. A regular contributor
to *Colliers* and the *Saturday Evening Post,* Williams was also
the author of the Civil War novel, *A House Divided*. In this story, a father's irrational attachment to his daughter stands in the way of her ever
finding happiness with another man. Yet even though loyalties run deep
in the people of the Southern mountains, true love will endure: even in
the face of the harshest opposition.

★   ★   ★   ★   ★

We were fishing the Sheepscot that day, Jim Saladine and Chet and I.
The upper reaches of the river thread a deep valley fifteen miles west of
Fraternity. It is wild country; the farms have one by one been deserted;
you see the decaying farm houses, their windows boarded up, their
yards grown high in weeds. A high ridge bounds this valley on its eastern side, and the roads that drop down this ridge are scoured out by tor-
rents every spring, so that they become mere beds of boulders over
which a light car teeters dangerously. In the bottomlands, thick with
alder and black growth, moose dwell in some numbers; there are deer
along the hardwood ridges. The stream itself, in early summer, when the
spring floods are past, is a pleasant and meandering rivulet, broken by
many small rapids, at the foot of which you come upon deep, dark pools

where trout of a robust growth are like to dwell. There is a great deal of feed in the waters; the trout are not reliable in their diet. I have fished here all the long day with never a strike; have come again a few days later and found appreciative fishes everywhere.

This day we dropped Chet by the mill, whence he would fish down stream through the woods some two miles to the next bridge below. Jim and I made a circuit along the narrow and grass-grown roads, our plan to leave the car at the bridge where Chet would rejoin us, while we fished downstream from there and back up to the car again.

The tortuous road engaged my eyes as I drove; it wound through thick growth in the low lands, then began to climb along the flank of the western slopes, dipping over knolls and rising again like a roller coaster. At the top of one such rise we emerged abruptly from the wood lands and saw a farmhouse on our right and on our left an orchard, sloping down toward the valley which spread below us and away for miles toward Sheepscot Great Pond. As we came out of the woods a movement in the orchard caught my eye, and I saw a large hawk rise heavily and fly away. Where he had been, a huddle of feathers remained.

I said, "That hawk's killed a chicken," and stopped the car.

We got out and went quickly down toward the spot.

The pullet must have been slain a matter of seconds before our coming; blood still trickled from the throat. There was no other wound. I picked it up.

"I'm going to take it up to the house," I told Jim, and he nodded and followed me.

There were other chickens in the barn yard, and a setter barked at us as we approached. Then a woman came out of the kitchen door upon the porch. It is not usual to discover beauty in the women of these remote farms, but she was beautiful. Her dress, of some blue cloth dotted with little white flowers, was fresh and crisp, and it had a white collar that was like a calyx from which rose her lovely throat. Her face was like a warm flower. I saw in her countenance that wistful glorification which may be observed in women whose high task is near. A pace or two short of the steps of the porch I stopped, the pullet dangling in my hand, and pulled off my old felt hat.

She was looking at Saladine, and smiling, and she said, "How-do, Jim!"

He responded, calling her "Nan." After they had exchanged a word or two, he spoke of me, and she greeted me. I held out the pullet and explained how we had found it.

"It's just like its head had been chopped off," Saladine commented.

She smiled in a still way and took it from me and laid it on a chair at her side. I saw that she had a gift for silence.

Jim explained, "We're fishing!"

She nodded, glancing toward the car, from the rear of which our rods protruded.

"Where's the man of the house?" he asked, mildly jocular.

"Up in the wood lot," she explained. "He'd like to see you."

There was in her voice as she spoke a sure and deep affection. I wondered, suddenly, at her age; she might have been any age of woman. She was certainly no longer a girl; was, rather, ripe and ready for fruition. A faint golden bead of fragrance seemed to gild her throat.

"We've got to get along," Jim replied. "You tell him I was here."

Her head dipped in that slow nod again, and we went back to the car and drove away. But even after we had dropped into the woods, the sight of her persisted in my eyes.

"Who is she?" I asked.

"Was Nan Clemons," Jim said slowly. "She lived along the ridge from my house."

"She's Greek," I told him. "Pure, classic beauty. The sort of woman Phidias carved."

"She was always a fine-looking woman," Saladine agreed.

"How old is she?"

He considered. "Must be near thirty-five."

"She's going to have a baby."

"I used to think, whenever I saw her, she was meant for that," he assented gently.

The road engrossed my attention for a while; we emerged at the stream's edge and found the bridge. The trout were waiting. Not till noon, while we ate our lunch in a shaded spot on the edge of the meadow above the Big Rock Pool, did we speak of her again. Then, in response to my questions, Jim told me more about her. Told me the great thing she had done, now fourteen years agone. The warm sun bathed the fresh-cut meadow before us; heat waves flickered above the stubble. Birds, in the noon-day heat, were still. The trout would not be hungry for another hour.

Jim told me that Nan Clemons and her father lived alone for years at her father's farm on the ridge south of Fraternity. Her mother had died when she was a baby; her father's sister kept house for Jonathan Clemons till she, too, died. Nan was then about ten years old, and she must have assumed, about that time, the duties of a housewife. These duties are not a matter of jest, upon a farm. "But the place was always clean as a pin," said Saladine. "And Jonathan was always taken care of good."

It was, Saladine thought, more than the man deserved. Clemons was a small man, physically and in other ways; this daughter of his was inches taller.

"Her mother was a big woman," Saladine explained.

Jonathan and his wife had not been happy together; the little man was irascible, given to bursts of temper which he vented in harsh words. His wife had been a silent sort, humble and still.

"I don't know as he abused her," Saladine told me. "I mean to say, hit her, or anything. I wasn't much more than a boy then. But there've been times since when I've heard him talking to Nan till I felt like paddling him."

This was when Nan was a child, he explained. Saladine himself must have been in the neighborhood of twenty, and that is the age of chivalric thought and deed.

"I felt like paddling him," he repeated.

A definite friendship had grown up between Jim, the young man, and Nan, the child. She had liked to come to his farm and be with him; to follow him about in the fields, or to sit silent and attentive while he manufactured firewood in the shed. Such devotion on the part of a girl child is a first manifestation of that deep-rooted instinct which is one of the great motive forces of the universe, and it was easy to think of this woman I had seen as one in whom those forces operated.

"But she was always a quiet little thing," Jim explained. "Never talking much. I told her stories, some."

They became very close to one another; she gave the young man her confidence, bringing to him her troubles, her hopes, her fears. Saladine said she told him, he thought, everything in her life for years . . .

"That was before she grew up, of course," he confessed. "But we've always been pretty good friends."

This must have been true, for only her confidant could have known as much of her story as Jim repeated to me that day above the Sheepscot.

He drew for me a picture of her father: a small man, alternately choleric and mild.

"He would follow her around," said Jim, without amplifying the statement.

I perceived that Jonathan Clemons, for all his irritability, must have loved this wife who had died; that this love must have transferred itself to his growing daughter. There was in her, even as a child, enough mystery to hold a man's thoughts. Clemons seems to have been a simple person, shallow and easily read; I could imagine that Nan must sometimes have bewildered him by her very silence and her serene calm. "He would follow her around," Jim had told me, and the sentence painted a picture that volumes could not better.

Nan herself told Jim that she did not like her father. Perhaps this was one of those chances of consanguinity which so frequently occur; perhaps the fact that Clemons had not been kind to her mother affected Nan. She always knew that he had been thus unkind. How she knew, it would be hard to tell. Words of neighbors; her father's confessions; the mutual recriminations in which he and the sister who kept house for him sometimes indulged. All that matters is that she did know; that she said as much to Jim.

"It wasn't as though she blamed him," he told me. "It was more like she just took it as a fact that couldn't be got around, and that finished him as far as her loving him was concerned." He added, "Of course, I told her Jonathan was all right."

The picture assumed clarity; details became more vivid. I was able to locate the house in which they had lived, from Jim's description. Small, all the rooms on one floor, the shed and barn trailing out behind, it stood on the eastern slope of the ridge, under the road. A mighty prospect of wooded valley stretched away to the southward, visible from the windows. Down the hill under the house there was a hardwood growth merging gradually into hemlock and spruce and pine toward the river. This river valley is the most beautiful spot about Fraternity, and I imagined Nan sitting by her window with shadowed eyes watching the dusk fall like a deep purple mantle across these slopes. If there were such depths in her as her repose of manner hinted, then she must have found pleasure in watching during such an hour . . . I knew the house; and as Jim spoke, it assumed for me the character of a prison in which this man and his daughter were immured together. The man mystified, confused, and passionately devoted; the daughter aloof, still, full of a passive dislike that never found utterance.

"She didn't rightly hate him," Jim assured me. "Just didn't like old Jonathan, and never would."

Her father was, Jim said, physically demonstrative; he liked to stroke her hair, to kiss her cheek, to hold this daughter of his upon his knee.

"She didn't like it," Jim told me. "Even when she was only about ten years old, she said to me one day that she didn't like it. She said his hands were hairy. He quit it, after a while." When Nan was twelve or thirteen years old, and already almost as tall as he was. "It was after that," Jim explained, "that he got so he was always following her around."

It does not appear that Nan ever rebelled against her father, or ever let him see that she had no kindly feeling for him.

"She took good care of him," Jim assured me. "Kept house fine, and was always pleasant."

A girl in her middle teens, already sure and calm and serene, attending to the tasks life had given her to do with no complaint and no revolt. By the time she was eighteen, she was already mature as a woman.

"I've thought, sometimes, it was queer that I never wanted to marry her myself," Jim said thoughtfully. "Probably she'd have had me. I wa'n't much older, and we were mighty good friends, and she liked me, and I expect old Jonathan wouldn't have had much to say against it. But I never thought about her that way.

"She was the sort you would want to marry, too. I've seen different kinds of women. Pretty women. Some of them you'd like to be friends with; you like to hear them talk, and laugh. And some of them you just want so bad your mouth waters, every time you see them. And then there's the other kind, like Nan. The sort that seem so still and warm and ripe and full . . . She always made me think of a fresh-plowed field, all smoothed out waiting for the sowing of the seeds, and steaming a little in the warm spring sun. Always just had the look of a mother-woman." There was nothing but reverence in his tone. "You saw her today. She was always the same, after she got over being just a girl. Oh, there was men came to see her, and came again; but she was never much for men. Not till Will came along."

Will came along, it appeared, when she was just past twenty years old. Will Jenison. He was five or six years older than Nan. His father owned a farm on the hills beyond Liberty, where Will had grown to manhood. "Kind of a wild boy, he was," Saladine said. He recited some of the things Will had done in his youth. Small matters, arising from an abounding vitality, evidences rather of youth itself and an unformed judgment than any seated defect of character. It was true there had been a girl or two with whom he consorted.

"You know the kind. You know the way folks around here get to talking about a girl. I never knew as there was any harm in them," was Saladine's comment.

But the effect was to give Will Jenison a certain ill repute which made both men and women regard him with a more acute interest. He went to Camden at last, to work there on a ship-building job, handling axe and adze.

"He was always a good hand at working timber," Saladine explained.

Old Jonathan Clemons had some good oak in his woodlot, and the Camden people bought it standing, and set a crew of men to cut the trees. They brought patterns and hewed the oak to shape on the ground where it fell.

"You know the way of it," Saladine reminded me. "You saw them working, down in Chet's woods, two years ago."

I nodded, remembering. I had a clear remembrance of the scene. The hardwood grove, the ground sun-spangled; the snick of axe and grind of saw and crash of falling tree; the steady chick, chick, chick of the adze as the logs were hewed to shape; the piles of huge chips, so perfectly designed for firewood that Chet had only to load and haul them to his shed.

"Will Jenison was one of this crew," Saladine explained. "That's how he came to know Nan."

He had seen her first when he and the other man arrived to begin their work. Old Jonathan showed them how they might drive through the barn and the orchard and so best reach the meadow that ran back to the brow of the hill. Nan stood in the kitchen door watching their arrival. One of the men she already knew, and she greeted him with a faint movement of her head. But Jenison had never seen her before; and at sight of her he smiled with such delight that she remarked him. Their eyes held for a little space, then Nan turned and went indoors. Jenison watched for her reappearance, but she did not come out again.

Within an hour after they had begun work, down the hill, Will nicked his axe on an unsuspected pebble and went up to the house to grind it. There was water in the can by the grindstone, but he tipped this out and so made an excuse to go to the kitchen door for more. Old Jonathan pumped for him. Nan was frying doughnuts in the kitchen, and Will said, "Those smell mighty good." Jonathan was pleased; he had his moods of excessive amiability; and he invited Will to come in and have one. Nan, her cheeks warm from bending above the stove, her brow faintly beaded with moisture, poured out rich milk for him, and Will, talking with Jonathan, ate two of the doughnuts and watched the girl whose skin was white and rich as the milk in his glass. He knew how to be charming, and exerted himself in this wise, but of a sudden she turned and looked at him, and there was something in the depths of her still eyes which vaguely abashed the man and silenced him in turn.

Their next encounter was four days later, a late afternoon when the cows delayed in coming to the barn, and Nan—her father had gone to the village—went down the lane to discover the reason for their delay and drive them in. She found a bar up across the foot of the lane, and wondered at that, till Will rose from behind the wall and faced her. His sudden appearance startled her; she stood still, watching him, and the bold man was abashed and said at last:

"I put the bar up. I'm sorry. It was a fool thing—"

"Why?" she asked.

"I wanted you to come."

"Why?" she repeated with a serene insistence.

"I wanted to see you," he confessed. "I wanted to see you again."

There was never any coquetry in Nan. "You could have come to the house," she told him.

"I know it."

She smiled a little. "It is all right," she told him gently, and let down the bar.

The cows drifted past her and filed along the lane toward the barn, but she did not at once follow them. It was a warm and lovely afternoon; the wind easterly, and cool; the sky filled with scudding white clouds.

Will, usually so ready of tongue, could only say, "The day's fine."

"Yes, it is," she assented.

She turned slowly to look at him; at all of him. Firm lips, decent chin, broad shoulders and slender waist. Beneath the rough fabric of his trousers his thigh muscles swelled; his hands, busy with the small task of filling a pipe, were smooth and strong . . . She liked him. The man, on his part, sensed in her something profound and mysterious and remote; elemental, like a pagan goddess. There was no light thought in his light heart.

"I'll come to the house, next time," he promised her; and after a moment she went away along the lane.

How they drew together, Saladine was able to relate only in general terms. The other men of the crew at work in Jonathan's woods chose to live in the village; Jenison preferred to stay on the ground. He built a small shelter of boughs, walled at the sides, roofed so thickly it would shed any but the most severe rain. He had a small kettle and a frying pan and a pot and a box in which he kept his stores. Sometimes he went to the house in the evening and sat with Jonathan in the kitchen while Nan did the dishes; the two men talked together, but Nan's eyes and Will's met in a continual intercourse.

"I was there, one evening," Saladine explained. "I could see." This was easy to believe, since I knew him to be an observant man, skilled at making deductions. "But Jonathan couldn't see, or didn't see," he added.

Saladine was himself the first to perceive the inevitability of the approaching conflict; he watched for its development, willing to do what might be done on Nan's part. He was fond of the girl, and he liked young Jenison, too.

"He couldn't forget her at all," Saladine told me. "He used to come up to the house at night sometimes, and stay outside, watching her through the kitchen window while she worked. I came on him there once, so. He pretended he'd been just going in, and he went in with me. But there must have been other times."

A curious humility, in such a bold man.

It was inevitable that some old woman in the village should begin to talk about the two young people on the hill; equally inevitable that the gossip should eventually reach old Jonathan's ears. Saladine was in the store one night when Jonathan came stamping in, glaring from man to man.

"Will Jenison here?" he demanded; and Andy Wattles, Bissell's clerk, shook his head.

"Been here?" Jonathan asked.

"Not tonight," Andy replied.

Jonathan stamped out again. Saladine rose and followed him.

"I was curious," he confessed. "And I thought maybe I could help, too. If anything was going to happen. I caught up with Jonathan and asked him what the matter was. He told me, all right, too." He smiled a little at the recollection. "Oh, he was crazy mad!"

Jonathan was hunting for Will Jenison to lay him out, he told Saladine. "The young rip's been dandling around my Nan," he exclaimed. "I don't aim to have it, and I aim to tell him so. I'll shoot him full of holes."

"Nan can take care of herself," Saladine reminded him.

"She don't have to," Jonathan retorted. "Her paw will take care of her. Him they drove out of Liberty; now he's after our girls here—"

There was something hypocritical in this protest which provoked Saladine to reply.

"After only one of them, seemingly."

Jonathan's rage turned on Saladine at that.

"I oughtn't to have said it," Saladine confessed to me. "But I wanted to see him rear up."

He was not disappointed; Jonathan forgot Will in his rage at Saladine. They wrangled together all the way up to the ridge road to Jonathan's house, and Saladine went home sure that Jonathan would not exert himself to seek out Will Jenison that night.

But the old man saw Nan's lover the next day and told him, hotly enough, to keep away from the house thereafter. Will seems to have been reasonable in the matter; he was at first inclined to laugh, until he perceived that Jonathan was deadly serious. Then he argued.

"This ain't the way," he urged. "This way you'll just make me and Nan take to sneaking chances to see each other. We're going to, you know."

"You do and you'll wear bird shot under your hide all your life," old Jonathan promised him.

Will colored with anger, then laughed again. "All right. Have it your way," he retorted, and left the old man simmering in his own bile.

Saladine knew little of what passed between Nan and her lover during the next few days.

"I don't know as they saw each other at all," he confessed. "I talked to Nan one day, and she told me she liked him. That, coming from her, meant—she loved him. But she said she hadn't told him so. Said he hadn't asked her. 'What if he asks you?' I said to her; and she smiled at me, that way you saw, turning her eyes off across the valley like she was dreaming. She was one that could love a man long—"

But chance did involve him in the dénouement. He was able to relate that in some detail. A Sunday afternoon in August. Saladine was at home, in his barnyard, talking with Will Belter. No man loved talking better than Will Belter; his tongue was made for telling tales. Belter would have spoken of Jenison and Nan, but Saladine had a mien which discouraged idle slander, so it was of other matters they talked. By and by Belter perceived a buggy coming along the ridge road, and asked who it was; and Saladine replied:

"Old Jonathan. He went down along, after dinner, to see Dave Hood. He's fixing to sell Dave a cow."

"He'd better stay at home," Belter commented, grinning, but Saladine did not ask why.

When the buggy drew nearer, Jonathan hailed them, and they walked down to the road to talk with him. He was in an amiable mood, full of the good bargain he had made. When he finished the tale, Saladine asked idly, "Nan all right?"

Jonathan nodded with unction. "Yes, she is. Nan's a good girl. I told her not to have anything more to do with Will Jenison, and she never even argued with me."

Will Belter grinned. "Just the same, I shouldn't think you'd want him around."

"He's gone home to Liberty today," Jonathan replied.

Will shook his head. "I saw him coming back through the village, right after dinner," he declared.

Saladine would have stopped the talebearer, but he was too late. He looked at old Jonathan and saw the fury curdling in the man's cheeks. The old man struck at his horse without a word, but Saladine was as quick as he. Quick to catch the buggy and swing in at Jonathan's side.

"I'll go along with you," he explained.

"I'll shoot that young rake-hell," Jonathan swore, and whipped his horse again.

At home, he swung into the barn and looped the reins through a ring and hurried into the house. Came out a moment later with a black countenance, his gun in his hand.

"She ain't here," he told Saladine, chewing the words through his teeth.

Saladine saw his jaw muscles bulge.

"Leave the gun," he said mildly.

"I'll kill him."

"No, you won't," Saladine insisted. "Put it down, and I'll go along with you. There's no sense in shooting a man just because Nan loves him."

"Loves him? She wouldn't love a man like him!"

"Then where's she gone?" Saladine asked.

He laid his hand on the gun, and after a moment's faint struggle Jonathan surrendered it, hurrying through the barn toward the orchard and down the hill. Saladine left the gun on the porch and followed.

Will Jenison had built his little shelter of boughs in the edge of the black growth, near the river. They went that way at a headlong pace. Across the meadow, over the crumbling stone wall, down through the pasture where blueberries grew in low clumps here and there. The hardwood growth, where the men worked during the week, was empty now; they angled across it toward the black growth below, skirted that. So came abruptly to the spot where Jenison had made his home. They came without speech; their footfalls were muffled by the soft turf. Saladine saw the blackened rocks of the rude fireplace, the scoured kettle and frying pan tilted against it; a wooden box in the shade of a low hemlock. The little bough shelter lost itself among the trees; Jonathan was the first to perceive it. He sprang that way, with a triumphant cry. Saladine himself for a moment thought Nan would be there.

"There with her man, snug as two mice between the walls," he murmured, eyes dim with memory. "I thought we'd find her there. I'd have thought no harm of her if she was. Nan wasn't one that could do a wrong thing. Something too big lived in her for that—"

But Nan was not there.

Old Jonathan, finding the shelter empty, was at first bewildered; he turned to Saladine for guidance.

Jim, considering, said: "Belter always tells tales to make trouble. I expect Nan's up at the house right now. In her room asleep, maybe—"

"She wasn't. I looked there," Jonathan told him. "She's here somewhere, Jim."

"We'll look around," Jim agreed, willing to humor the old man.

They climbed toward the hardwood growth again, eyes searching the wood ahead of them.

And so, among the tall oaks, they found the two. Say, rather, encountered them; for Will Jenison and Nan were coming along a wood road toward them, and his arm was about the waist of Nan, who walked by her man's side confidently. They were like two creatures of the wood. The warm sun, piercing the screen of leaves, dappled all the scene with gold; at one moment the two walked in shadow, the next were glorified. At first they did not see Jim and old Jonathan; not till Jonathan cried out and ran toward them. So these four came face to face. The old wood road crossed a low knoll, winding between a great boulder and the trunk of a gigantic beech. Saladine set his back against this beech, watchful and still. And old Jonathan flung himself at Jenison, who caught the little man gently by the arms and held him helpless. In that first madness, Jonathan kicked like a child at the young man's shins, till Nan laid her hand strongly on his shoulder and said,

"Father, be still."

At first, Saladine told me, their talk was only wrangle and accusation on the part of Jonathan, while Will held him watchfully, and Nan kept silent. Then at some foul word Jenison twitched the old man about with an abrupt ferocity, and shook him, and said in a swift command:

"Enough of that! Mind your tongue."

Nan's father was too angry for any logical or reasonable discourse; he passed from first accusation and denunciation to bewailing. "Eh, Nan, I told you to stay away from him," he cried. "Sneaking out so, the minute I'm away."

"I warned you you were driving us to sneaking," Jenison reminded him.

"Driving? Who drove you? Who drove you out of Liberty for the girls you were after all the time?"

Jenison shook his head. "That gets nowhere. True or false, it gets nowhere. A matter between Nan and me."

"There's no matter between Nan and you. She'll have no truck with you."

"We love each other, Nan and me," Jenison said stoutly. "It's not half an hour ago we told each other so. That's something between Nan and me."

"Love?" the old man screamed, his very tone a profanation.

He would have gone on, but Nan abruptly spoke. "Father."

"Eh, what?"

"So much is true. Will loves me, and I him. Why should we not?"

"Because I'll not have it," he told her in a rush of furious words. "Because I'll not have it so. That's why not! Because I'll kill him if it's so. Because I'll lock you up in the house if it's so. That's why, Nan. I'll not let you love a man like him."

"But I do," she reminded him, and her eyes met Jenison's in a deep, slow caress.

"You'll not," he cried. "He'll never have you."

"We're going to get married," Jenison asserted, and Nan's father whirled on him with furious fists.

The issue was joined between them now; as the old man stormed and the young man steadily replied, this issue became a clear-cut thing. Clear that Jonathan would not consent, would never consent to marriage between them; clear on the other hand that Jenison was firmly bent upon it. Nan's attitude was not so clear. Jenison seemed to take it for granted that she would support him, but Saladine, watching her, saw that she had drawn back a little and now leaned against the great boulder, her eyes upon the ground. He saw how the glory which her countenance had worn, when she was fresh from hearing love and confessing it, had slowly faded and given way to grief and pain. He saw now the agonized confusion in her eyes and in her twitching lips, usually so still . . . Some conflict in progress there. He forgot the loud words of the two men in watching this Nan who had always been so dear to him; and in the end, he guessed before she spoke what it was she meant to say.

The question put to her in this hour was one not easy of decision. Jenison, at first faintly inclined to scoff, became serious and steadfast as old Jonathan more and more completely lost all self-control. The contrast between the two men was marked. The hour had matured Will; his boyish carelessness fell away from him; he was sure of himself and of what he meant to do. But Nan's father became intoxicated with his own anger; his voice at times rose to a shout, as though by sheer noise he would beat the other down. He became maudlin and contemptible, while Saladine thought well of Jenison for the way he bore himself. But he was more concerned with watching, reading Nan.

"I guessed what she would decide, guessed it before she decided, maybe," Saladine told me. "But not many women would have done as she did." He smiled faintly. "Of course, if she'd done the other thing, there'd be no story worth telling you here today. There's plenty of girls that run away with the man they love."

But Nan did not run away. The choice must have been a bitter one for her. On the one hand her father, whom she had always disliked, whom she had never more than endured, yet who was, after all, her father, and an old man, and alone . . . And on the other hand this young stalwart, for whom something deep within her cried out longingly, whom with all her womanhood she loved, toward whom her whole soul yearned. Leaning there against the boulder, her body still and motionless, her eyes downcast, she fought the battle through.

"Look at it reasonably, sir," her lover begged her father. "Nan and I are young; we love each other. Say what you will of me, but what does it matter what I've been? It's what I am—and Nan is satisfied with what I am. You fathers have always interfered in such matters, and never helped things yet, at all. You've come here today with ugly words and cursings—bringing a black and shameful scene into an hour that would have been a glory and a beauty all our lives to Nan and me—"

"You'll not dandle me with your fine talk, young man," old Jonathan retorted. He was by this time at fever pitch, his mouth loose and working so that saliva spilled from the corners. "You'll not dandle me, I say. She's my girl, and she'll do my telling."

"But you've no right to tell her, now; father or no. The man she'll marry is her choosing."

Jonathan was driven to flat despotism. "Not her choosing unless I choose," he said with finality. "And I don't choose you."

Jenison's eyes dropped; he seemed considering. And in the pause Jonathan stepped toward his daughter and took her hand and drew her roughly toward him. She came, not resisting, and it was then Saladine knew.

"Come along of me, Nan," old Jonathan said harshly. "Leave this scum of nothing, here."

"I love him," she replied.

"Eh, the fever he's waked will pass in a day," he promised her. "You come along of me."

Jenison lifted his head. "Wait," he commanded. "Just one word, then. I've tried to be reasonable with you, sir. But you won't have it so. All right. Have it this way. We'll be married, with your will or without it. Nan and I!"

He stood very straight, there in the wood, and the sunlight struck across his bare head and his fine countenance. There was a sorrowful triumph in his bearing as he faced old Clemons, a reassuring devotion when his eyes sought Nan's.

But at what he saw there his shoulders faintly drooped; his cheeks turned a little pale with dismay. For Nan, deep eyes tender, yet slowly shook her head.

"No, Will," she told him.

Thus simply was her sacrifice begun.

Saladine said Will did not speak at all after this low word of hers. He said Nan went with her father up the hill, and they could hear old Clemons chuckling as he went, chuckling over Will's humiliation. Saladine stayed with Will, and the young man needed a companion in the bitterness of that hour.

"He wasn't the same after, either," Saladine told me. "It changed him in a day. Never the wild boy he had been, again."

"Did she stick to it?" I asked. "She would, though! I've only seen her today, but I know she would."

He nodded. "Yes, she stuck. Some folks thought she was lucky; that she'd waked up in time. Been saved . . . And some said she'd been foolish to give up Will for that old father of hers. This was after they begun to see that Will was settled down. Oh, they talked to her. She listened, but she was never one to change."

"A tragic thing," I commented. "A woman like her; meant to be wife, and mother. Mother, more even than wife." Abruptly I remembered. "But, Jim, she's married now!"

"Oh, yes," he assented. "Yes. Old Jonathan died about a year ago."

"Whom did she marry?" I asked.

He looked at me in surprise. "Why, I supposed you knew. That was her and Will's farm, back there on the hill."

The meadow before us shimmered in the warm afternoon sun, and the woman came again into the eye of my mind. Fourteen years of waiting, of negation, all that deep beauty in abeyance. I had a moment of bitterness against old Jonathan because of those fourteen years; a warm wonder at the fine and steadfast woman.

Then a trout, with waking appetite, leaped in Big Rock Pool below us. It was time we were afoot again.

The Stove

BY MARJORIE L. C. PICKTHALL

Marjorie L. C. Pickthall was born in England, but eventually made her home in Victoria, British Columbia. She was something of an eccentric, who preferred to spend her time writing in a simple shack deep in the mountains. Her understanding of the remoteness of the Canadian wilderness comes to the fore in this story, where a young woman nurses her wounded brother in a snowbound cabin, awaiting the return of another brother with the doctor. Days pass, and she finds herself obsessed with feeding the large iron stove, which glowers in the center of the cabin like a demanding and eternally hungry beast. When the firewood at last runs out, and the heroine and her brother face freezing to death, she is saved by a mysterious stranger who appears from the dark woods. But is he saint or devil? Her disordered mind cannot tell, but her heart recognizes a kindred spirit.

★   ★   ★   ★   ★

"I'll be back the third day at latest with the doctor. I've left you wood enough for three days and more and you've grub for a month." Garth looked at her anxiously; his strong mouth twitched. Suddenly he leaned forward and brushed her cheek lightly with his yellow beard. "I—hate to leave you, little girl," he said, with a gentleness not common with him, "but I guess it's Derek's only chance."

"Of course you must go. It's Derek's only chance." Dorette faced him steadily. She was pale, slight, sleepy-eyed, but wilderness born and bred, for all that; one guessed a spirit of steel in that fragile sheath. She finished wistfully: "There'll be nothing for me to do—nothing, but—wait."

"Only look after yourself and keep the stove up."

"I'll do it. And you—if you meet Maxime—"

Rage blazed suddenly in her brother's eyes. The barrel of his rifle gleamed blue as he gripped it. "If I meet Maxime," he said, through his teeth, "it's a finish for him or for me!"

He turned about without another word, and swung down the forest trail on his long run to Mandore.

Dorette watched him until he was no more than a dark shadow among the heavy blue shades that hung from spruce to spruce like tangible banners. All life, all sound, all motion seemed to go with him. Mile after mile, she knew, on each side of her was nothing but the same silence, the same stillness, league after league of the desolate fir forest of the North. She went into the cabin and bolted and barred the door behind her, as if the solitude were an enemy which she must keep out.

The cabin was a pleasant place. The walls were sheathed in red cedar, and there were fur rugs on the floor, red curtains at the windows. In the center of the larger of the two rooms into which the cabin was divided stood the great iron stove, in winter the source of their very life.

Its voice filled the cabin with a roar like the forever unsatisfied roaring of the wind and sea—a hungry voice. Dorette swung open the heavy door, wincing from the furnace-glory within, as she flung on more wood. That was her one occupation until Garth came back—feeding the stove.

She went to one of the bunks—like the bunks of a ship—that were built on the wall behind the stove, and looked in.

Derek, her younger brother, lay there without sense or motion, as he had lain ever since the sergeant of police and Garth had carried him in and laid him there. He drowsed between life and death, shot through the body. Now and then he swallowed a little broth, but with no knowledge of the hand that fed him. She dared not touch him. There was nothing she could do for him but keep the cabin warm enough to sustain that flickering lamp of life till the doctor came, for the cold of that country kills like a sword.

Suddenly, clinging to the side of the bunk, she trembled. "If only you could speak to me, Derek," she whispered. "If only I could hear your voice!"

But the only voice was the voice of the great stove.

Her mind painted for her the scene she had not witnessed—the hard men of the mines and the lumber camps, still men with formidable eyes, following Cain's trail from Fort Dismay to Anisette; the end of the trail at a little lonely shack blinded in snow, ringed with watchful men; Derek pleading that Maxime might have "one more chance, boys"; the parley at the door, the shot coming from nowhere; men storming into the shack over Derek's fallen body, and finding it empty; Maxime Dufour escaped again! She saw it all. Heard again Garth's voice in hard-breathed sentences between shut teeth: "But he's not goin' to get away again. He'll have to get food and shelter somewhere; and if it's a thousand miles away, we'll follow and shoot him down like the wolf he is!"

She glanced round, pale and shaken, thinking that still she heard that deep voice of bitter rage. But it was only the undertone of the roaring stove humming its angry song.

She busied herself about such duties as she could find. Twice she fed the stove from the pile of wood on the floor beside it. The fierce heat licked out at her each time, just as a savage beast will strike through the bars of his cage, and each time she shut the door with the sense of prisoning some lion-voiced living thing.

Her work was soon done. Everything in the cabin was tidied and tidied again. She glanced at the clock. Only an hour of the slow time had gone. Garth had only been gone an hour. She turned the clock with its face to the wall, took out a shirt she was making for Garth—red-and-black checked flannel, thick as felt—and stitched resolutely.

Her hearing, accustomed to the sound of the stove, as the ear adjusts itself to the thunder of a waterfall, was acute to catch the faintest noises. She heard the tiny sound of the thread passing through the flannel, the soft thud of snow slipping from the boughs of the forest, the least check and stumble in Derek's shallow breathing. Each time she heard this last, her own heart checked and stumbled in tune with it. She held her own breath till her brother's renewed its weak rhythm.

So the morning passed. In the afternoon, she found a snowshoe that needed re-stringing. Deftly as Montagnais she twisted the gut and wove the net.

It was dark sooner than she could have hoped. She needed no lamp. The stove filled the cabin with its glow. In the dark it became a beautiful and formidable thing, a shape of dull red, with a heart of lambent rose. She glanced at the little windows, sheathed thick with frost-ferns. It would be a cold night. Her thoughts went to Garth, then, with dread, to Maxime Dufour. She dragged her cot from the inner room, set it across the front of the stove, and lay down. The warmth was like a hand pressing on her eyelids.

With the subconscious watchfulness of those who care for the beloved, she was awake five times in the long night to feed the stove. Each time she looked at Derek, and thought, with a pang, that he was deeper sunken among the pillows. His eyes were not quite closed; the silvery line of eyeball reflected the red glow. She would have liked to close them, but her hand shrank from so prophetic an action.

The last time she woke the sun had risen. The gathered crystals on the windows were lit with a glow that paled the stove. Dorette went into the inner room and braided her hair.

That day passed as the first had done. Her brother was weaker. She pleaded with him, passionately tender. "Just a mouthful of soup, Derry. Wake up, Derry dear. Take it for my sake, Derry!" but her voice, which had dimly roused him the day before, could not reach him now. She looked round for something she might do for him.

The diminished heap of logs on the floor showed her work enough. She must bring in a fresh supply from the pile behind the cabin. She ate a hasty breakfast and made herself some coffee. Then, hooded and wrapped against the cold, she opened the door.

She stepped into a world of white, blue, and black; solid, translucent, and motionless as though built from gems. Where the blue sky touched the black trees there seemed to run a setting of gold; where the black trees trailed branches to the snow, was a stain of sapphire shadow. It was fiercely cold. She shut the door behind her, hastily, ran to the snow-buried wood-pile behind the cabin, burdened herself with an armful of small logs, returned, set her load on the threshold, opened the door, and tumbled the wood on the floor. All the morning she worked thus. Her spirits rose; she began to believe that Derek would not die, and soon she might think of Garth's return. The noise of the logs as she flung them on the floor pleased her. It was a change from the one unceasing voice that filled the cabin day and night—the voice of the stove.

The second night she was restless. She dared not sleep at first, for fear she should sleep too well. Wind came up with the electric stars; the great stove sang to a higher, more tremendous note; she could scarcely keep pace with its consuming hunger. The pine knots and bright birch logs fell to ash in a moment. If she slept, she dreamed that the stove was out, and the cold creeping into the cabin in long feathers of frost, that twisted under the door like snakes, until one touched her on the throat and she woke, choking.

Dawn found the sky fleeced with cloud, the cabin warm, and the hurt man yet alive.

Again with the day her heart lightened. Four—five hours from that time, and she might expect Garth with the doctor from the mines at Mandore. She wound the clock, and turned it with its chipped white face to the room, no longer dreading to tell the passage of the hours.

Yet five hours went, and Garth had not come.

She went to the door. Closing it behind her that the cold might not get into the cabin even for a moment, she stared down the trail. It ran in the straight no more than a half-mile; farther than that, she could not see. Yet it was less her eyes than her soul that she thus strained to see beyond the forest.

"Garth! Garth! Garth!"

Who had given that wild cry that rang among the trees? For a moment she wondered, then knew it had come from her own troubled heart.

She must see beyond the first bend of the trail; she must see if, farther than that, the blue-white ribbon between the trees was still empty of her hope.

She built up the fire again, put on coat and hood and snow-shoes, took one glance at Derek, and left the cabin. She sped down the trail. She was panting when she reached the first curve. Almost afraid to look, she saw the long track before her—empty. There was something conscious and deliberate in that emptiness, as if the forest knowingly withheld from her a secret. She dared go no farther. She turned back and fled home.

The clock ticked off another hour—two, three, four. Garth had not come.

Darkness, and he had not come.

Loneliness and suspense were shaking her strong, young nerves. The worst of all was the silence. The voice of the stove became first an annoyance, then a weariness, then an intolerable burden. The voice of its devouring hunger was the very voice of silence, of desolation. She flung the wood in angrily. "If there was only someone to *speak* to," she said, a little wildly— "just someone to give me a word!"

There was no one—then, nor through the endless night, when she feared to sleep, lest, in her dreams, or in reality, that insatiable thing in the stove that kept them alive might escape her, nor with the stormy dawn. Garth did not come.

There was no wood left in the house. Before she did anything else, she wrapped herself and went to the wood-pile.

The wood-pile was heaped against the back of the cabin: it was roofed and sheeted with snow. She pulled at the butt of a log, and the wood came down with a run, mixed, with much snow—such dry snow that the wood was not moistened until she held it in her warm hand. The bitter work was a relief to her. She thrust the soft, dark hair out of her eyes and piled herself such a load that she swayed under it. "But it's something to do for Derek," she said, wistfully. "It's all I can do."

She took in enough for the day. But there was the night.

"Garth will be back by then," she muttered, with cold lips, staring at the stove.

"Garth *must* be back by then." The stove sent a screaming rush of flame up the pipe, as if in mockery. She felt an unreasoning hatred for it, as she went wearily out again to gather enough wood for the night too.

Kneeling beside the wood-pile, she groped with numbed hands. She felt nothing but snow.

She thrust in her arm to the shoulder. She met no resistance but that of the snow.

Her heart beat in shuddering throbs. She brought a long pole and prodded the pile, then swung the pole and levelled it. She found nothing but snow.

"How did it happen?" She heard herself asking this over and over. Easily enough. She or Garth or Derek had been drawing supplies from the other side of the pile, and the snow had slipped from the roof and filled the spaces; hardening, it had stretched a roof over emptiness. The pile, which had been taken for good, hardwood logs, fodder for that roaring hungry heat within, was no more than a heap of snow.

Dorette turned slowly, and went into the cabin.

She stood by Derek's bunk, staring at the wood on the floor. It was enough for the day, but what of the night?

Would Garth return before the night?

She looked about the cabin. There were things there, things that would burn. Her sleepy brown eyes widened. There was war in them as she leaned and kissed Derek's cheek. He did not stir from that deepening sleep of his.

"Sleep on, Derry," she whispered, scarcely knowing what she said, "sleep well, Derry. I'll take care of you, I'll fight for you!"

She took Garth's heavy axe, and began on the chairs.

They were heavy and clumsy things, Garth's pride, since he had made them himself. They would feed the stove well; but they were hard for a girl's arm to chop, even though she struck true as a woodman, and Dorette's hands were scorched from the door of the stove. As she toiled, her eyes ranged the cabin, calculating on this box, that shelf, the table. Her heart beat to every sound. As the wind rose higher, the bitter day was full of sounds. A dozen times she ran to the door, crying, "Garth!" A dozen times she saw nothing but the forest and a driven mist of snow, as fine and dry as dust.

By the earliest dusk she had chopped up everything in the cabin. Each stroke sent a jar of pain to her shoulder from her burned and bruised hands, but she did not feel it. And still the stove roared, insatiable. The dried wood of their furnishings, pine for the most part, burned like straw. The great iron horror must be fed, and she had nothing to feed it.

She took the axe and went out.

The gray forest fronted her in a rustling drive of snow and shadow. There must be a hundred fallen boughs within range of the cabin. She found one, dragged it from the snow, and toiled with it into the house. She twisted it apart, desperately, and there was blood on the rough, broken stuff she thrust into the stove.

She went out again. She was growing more desperate as her strength failed. There was a great branch trailing from a spruce, and she tore and wrenched at it, but it would not yield—it was frozen. She swung her weight upon it, sobbing. She struck with all the force remaining in her, but the axe-blade turned in her weary hands. She felt as though the will in her, passionately strong, should sever the bough as by steel. She did not know she was beaten, until she slipped weakly and fell in the snow and lay there, wailing helplessly and softly as a child.

The bitter snow stung her face like heat—like the heat of the stove. If she stayed there, the stove would be out. She lifted herself to her knees, and saw in the growing dark a man, who stood with a rifle on his arm, looking down at her.

"*Garth!* Oh, Garth!"

But even as the cry left her lips, she knew it was not Garth.

A figure, lithe even under the heavy furs, a face hidden in the cowl he had drawn forward above his fur cap, a certain strange immobility that vaguely chilled her, but surely—help? So swift is thought, that in the transitory seconds before she spoke again her brain had shown her a picture, a memory of a wild-cat which she and Garth had vainly tried to corner in the yard—of the creature's utter immobility until it launched itself and struck.

"The stove! Oh, the stove!"

She thought, as her hands went out to that motionless figure in the shadows, that she had spoken all the desperate appeal that was in her heart. But she only repeated: "Oh, the stove, the stove!"

"What stove?"

"The stove. The stove in our cabin. There's—no more wood for it!"

She waited. Surely he understood. But he remained as he was, motionless, staring down at her.

She looked up at him with a burning appeal. She had forgotten to rise from her knees. She kneeled at his feet in the snow. Her breath came in gasps. "There," she repeated, helplessly, "there—in the cabin— the stove! It's going out!"

Still he waited.

"There's a sick man there—my brother! Oh!" she finished, as he did not stir, "help me, if you're a man!"

"Oh, b'gosh, yes, I'm a man!" She fancied that he was laughing in the shadow of the cowl. "But why should I help you?"

She had no more words. Silently she lifted and held out to him her bleeding hands.

After a long minute he stirred slowly. Without a word he laid his gun crosswise on two fir branches that grew above her reach, easily within his own. He lifted the axe from the snow. She watched him. Four sharp cross-cuts, and the trailing branch fell. He set his foot on it, chopped it quickly into four or five pieces. As each piece rolled free, Dorette snatched it as a starving woman might snatch bread.

"That enough?"

Staggering under her load, she stared at him. "No, no!" she stammered. "It's not enough for the night. For the pity of Heaven, cut me some more!"

She turned away and hurried towards the cabin. Halfway there he overtook her. Without a word he lifted the logs from her arms into his own. She was too spent to thank him. Dumbly she moved at his side, conscious only that strength was here, help was here, that she might yet save Derek.

Entering the cabin, there was no glow, no light at all. With a low sound, Dorette swung open the door of the stove. Nothing was there but a handful of red ash ringed with gray.

With trembling hands she gathered a few splinters and thrust them in; she crouched before the gaunt, iron thing, as though she would hold it in her arms and warm it in her bosom. But the man, who had followed her, thrust her aside curtly enough. She watched him as he shaved a stick into delicate ribbons of wood—watched him as he coaxed them into flame. He tickled the appetite of the sullen, devouring thing in the stove with scraps of resinous bark and little twigs. Presently the fire laid hold on the larger logs, and fed upon them, hissing. He shut the door then, and turned to her.

She had lighted a lamp, and in the light stood looking at him, softly bright. Her eyes were stars of gratitude. She said at once: "My brother's still living."

She gestured towards the bunk. His eyes did not follow the gesture, or move from her pale face, as he said, abruptly: "You stay here with him. I'm goin' to get you in some more wood."

Her eyes flashed suddenly with tears. She said, brokenly: "You're *good*. Oh, you're a good man! While you're—cuttin' the wood, I'll—thank God you came!"

He went out into the night without answering her.

He returned in half an hour, loaded mightily. Sitting on the end of her cot, she smiled at him, falteringly. She had been weeping.

He did not speak to her. Light-footed as a cat, he busied himself about the humming stove, then went forth again.

When he came back the second time, she was asleep.

Her face—very pale, very pure, fragile for one of her life and race—was rosed in the glow of the stove. Her hurt hands were curled within one another, like the hands of a child. Moving in his noiseless way, the man went again, and looked down at her.

His furred cowl had fallen back. His face also caught the light of the stove. Dark, keen, predatory, it was the face less of a man than of some embodied passion of hate or revenge, the face of an Ishmael, the face of Cain. It looked strange now, so little was it shaped or accustomed to the gentleness of expression it momentarily wore, as a breath blurs the gleam of steel. Light and silent as all his movements were, they showed no gentleness. But he seemed gentle when he lifted the end of one of Dorette's dark plaits, which had fallen to the soiled floor, and laid it on the cot beside her just because he hesitated and was clumsy.

The plait of dark, silken hair was warm; his hand lingered over it. He leaned above her, and her breath was warm. That strangely unmoving regard of his was on her face. As if it had called her from her

MARJORIE L. C. PICKTHALL · **213**

dreams, she woke, and lifted to him the clear eyes of a child. "I—did thank God—you came," she whispered, with a child's simplicity. Sleep held her again, almost before she had finished speaking.

The young man drew back, noiselessly lifted the axe, and once more went out.

Sinewy, silent, untiring, he toiled for her all night. And all night she slept.

She had slipped into unconsciousness as a child does, worn out with anxiety and fatigue. She woke a woman, and flushed to her hair, as she realized what she had done.

The man who had helped and guarded her all night, was standing in the doorway. The door was open; there was a frosty freshness in the air, which the roaring stove raised to the warmth of summer. The world outside was a dazzle of sun; silver drops rattled from the eaves; a crow called in the forest. It was the first sun of spring, the year's change. In Dorette's heart was a change also, a quickening, a birth of something new and unknown, that almost brought tears to her eyes. For the first time in her hard life she had rested on another's strength; unconsciously she had found it sweet. That simple heart was in her look as she went to the stranger. She said, softly, "I did not mean to sleep. Why did you let me?"

He said, almost roughly: "You were all tired out."

The tears brimmed over. She did not know if pain or happiness moved her. She went on: "I said—I knew—you were a good man."

"Well," he answered, but not as if he was answering her, "for one night."

His furred hood hid his face. The wakening blush dyed her clear face again, as she said: "Let me see you. Let me see your face."

"Why?"

On the word she faltered, confused. She did not know why. She stammered: "Because of what you have done—of what we owe you."

"We?"

"My brothers and I. Derek's still alive. I almost think he's sleeping better—more natural. When—when Garth comes home, he'll thank you as I'd like to."

She looked up into the shadowed face, wistfully. He had turned from her again, and was gazing down the trail. After a moment, he said: "There's coffee on the back of the stove, and some cornbread. You'd better eat it. I've had some."

She went meekly, shamed that she had slept while her savior served himself. She would have liked to serve him. Something strange and stormy was shaking her; she had no name for it. The food choked her, hungry as she was, but she ate it obediently.

She had scarcely finished, when he called her. She ran and joined him at the door. Something in his voice thrilled her; she saw in him again that strange and threatening immobility of the night before.

He said, swiftly: "You're lookin' for your brother to come back?"

"Yes, yes. Any time."

"With another man?"

"With the doctor. Why?"

He raised his arm and pointed. In the blinding dazzle of sun on snow, she saw two small, dark figures, just rounding the curve of the trail.

Her heart rose and flooded her with a passion of thankfulness. She said, quietly, after a minute: "Yes, yes, it's him and the doctor. Now—now, you'll let him thank you, as you—won't let me."

Her words ended almost in a question, for she saw that, while she had been eating, he had taken his rifle on his arm and put on his snowshoes. Suddenly, she began to tremble a little, aware of something in his silence, his stillness, which vaguely threatened.

He swung upon her suddenly—one would have said, savagely, but that he was laughing. Those two black figures down the trail were sweeping rapidly nearer. All the latent fierceness of the man had flamed into being, at their approach. He laid a hard, slim hand on Dorette's shoulder and turned her, so that, at less than arm's length, she faced him. He said, softly, in the midst of his almost noiseless laughter: "I'll show you how you can thank me."

She looked up at him, her face colorless, her lips parted. In the shadow of the hood his eyes gleamed at her, his face bent nearer. The world fell away from her; there was nothing left in life for a minute but that face, that voice.

She just breathed: "Who are you?"

"You'll know in a minute!" He looked swiftly from her to the two men down the trail. They were coming on fast. He seemed to be measuring his distance from them.

When they were so near that their faces were all but discernible, he caught the girl to him. She was slack in his hold; all her life seemed to be in her dazed eyes; she would have fallen, but that he held her with an arm like a steel bar. And twice and three times he kissed her.

"That's how you can thank me!" He released her laughing still.

She staggered, her hands over her red mouth. With the movement of release he thrust her, rough and swift, within the door of the cabin. A bullet sent a spray of dusty snow over him. She saw, in one reeling instant, Garth on his knee down the trail, rifle leveled for another shot; the other, a laughing shadow, slipping from her hands, from her life, into the shadow of the forest from which he had come.

Another shot, wide of the mark; Garth leaping to his feet again and tearing towards her, followed by the doctor who was to save Derek, and whom he had found at last, thirty miles beyond Mandore. But she had no eyes for them—for a moment, no heart.

Eyes and heart were on that other figure at the edge of the trees, swift, terrible, laughing, calling to her with raised hand:

"Tell him you kissed Maxime Dufour!"

When Garth reached her side, she was on her knees, laughing and sobbing, striving, with her scarred small hands to obliterate his trail in the snow.

Mister Death and the Redheaded Woman

BY HELEN EUSTIS

I n this rip-roaring tall tale, novelist Helen Eustis celebrates the American West. Here, a determined young lady refuses to let her own true love be taken away by the cold hand of Mister Death. She tracks him down on his pale stallion, but is unprepared for her reaction when she pays the forfeit her nemesis demands in return for her lover's life . . . Mister Death, it turns out, has some unexpected depths, possibly enough to turn a girl's red head.

★   ★   ★   ★   ★

Mister Death come aridin' in from the plains on his pale stallion, ashootin' off his pistols, bangety-bang-bang, till you'd 'a' thought some likkered-up Injun was on a spree. Hoo-ee! We was scared, all us little uns, and the grown folks, too, only to them he seemed more familiar.

But he never touched nary a soul that day but Billy-be-damn Bangtry, the one the girls was all crazy for. An' Mister Death no more'n just laid a finger on him, so he didn't die right off, but lay there cold and sweatin', dyin' of a bullet in his belly which was shot off by a drunken cowpoke in a wild euchre game.

Now, many a girl in our town wet the pillow with her tears when she heard how young Billy was like to die, for he was a handsome man and drove all women wild; but the one that cried and carried on

217

the worst was pretty little Maude Applegate with the freckles and the red hair.

Old Injun Mary was anursin' Billy with poultices and healin' herbs, and wouldn't let no other woman near his door, so there wasn't nary a thing Maude Applegate could do for him. But you can't expect a redheaded woman to jest sit around and fret, like you would another color girl, an' Maude was no exception to that rule. Though she cried and carried on for a while, she pretty soon decided something had to be done, so she dried her eyes on her pettishirt, saddled up her daddy's pinto pony and took out across the plains after Mister Death.

Maude Applegate, she rode high and she rode low; she rode through the cow country into the sheep country; through the sheep country into the Injun country; through the Injun country to the far mountains, and there at last she caught up with Mister Death, jest about a mile down the trail from the little ole shack where he lived with his granny, up above the timber line.

When Maude Applegate spied his pale stallion, she was mighty tired and mighty weary; her red hair was all tumbled down her back, and her daddy's pinto wasn't no more'n skin and bone.

But she caught her breath and sang out loud, "Oh, wait up, Mister Death! Wait up for me!"

Mister Death, he pulled up his pale stallion and looked around, surprised-like, for there isn't many that call out to halt him.

"Why, what you want, missy?" he asked Maude Applegate as she rode up alongside. "Jumpin' Jehoshaphat, if you don't look like you rode clean through the brier patch!"

"Oh, Mister Death," Maude panted out, "I rode high and I rode low after you! I rode through cow country into sheep country; through sheep country into Injun country; through Injun country to the far mountains, and all to ask you would you spare Billy-be-damn Bangtry, my own true love!"

At that, Mister Death throwed back his head so's his black sombrero slipped off and hung around his neck by the strings, and he laughed loud.

"Now ain't that cute!" said Mister Death. "Honey, I reckon you're jest about the cutest thing I'm likely to see!"

But Maude Applegate, she'd rode high and she'd rode low, she'd stood thirst and she'd stood hunger, she'd like to killed her daddy's pretty little pinto; furthermore, she was a redheaded woman, and she wasn't goin' to be laughed at so. She took and cussed out Mister Death good. She tole him that where she come from, no gentleman laughed at no lady in her true trouble, and she'd thank him to mind his manners with her, and she'd like to know who brought him up anyhow? Why, she knew dirty nekkid Injun bucks acted better'n him. She'd lay his mammy's aspinnin' in her grave, an' so on.

Well, Mister Death, he sobered down shortly and set up straight in his saddle and listened real still, with only his eyes ablinkin'. When Maude give out of breath, he took out his 'baccy bag, licked a paper an' rolled him a smoke.

"What'll you give me for Billy-be-damn Bangtry?" said he.

But Maude Applegate, she was really wound up. She tossed her red hair like a pony's mane and made a sassy mouth. "I ain't agonna talk business until I've washed my face and had me a bite to eat," said she. "I've rode high and I've rode low—"

"All right, all right!" said Mister Death. "Ride along now, and I'll take you to my cabin, where my ole granny'll take care of you."

So Maude and Mister Death they rode up the slope, Mister Death reinin' in his pale stallion to keep down to the pore tired pinto, until presently they come to a little ole shack with smoke comin' out of the stovepipe. There was Mister Death's granny astandin' in the door, as pleased as Punch to see some company.

"Why, you're right welcome, missy!" she sang out, soon's they were within callin' distance. "The pot's on the stove and the kettle's abilin'. Come right in and rest yourself a while!"

So they pulled up, and Mister Death swung down off his pale stallion, come around by Maude and lifted her right down to the ground, with his two big hands ameetin' around her little waist.

"Oh, ain't she the purty little thing?" his granny kept asayin' all the while, and hobblin' around the dooryard on her crutch like a bird with a broken wing. Then she taken Maude inside and give her warm water, and a ivory comb, and a pretty white silk wrapper from out of her ole brass-bound chest, and when Mister Death come in from seein' to the hosses, there's Maude Applegate asettin' like a redheaded angel, drinkin' tea.

Maude, she perked up soon's she got some vittles inside her, and presently she had Mister Death and his granny laughin' fit to bust with her comical tales of the folks back home.

Soon Mister Death, he set in to yawnin' and gapin'. "I've rode a far piece today," he said to his granny. "I been twice around the world and back, and I think I'll lay my head in your lap and catch forty winks." And shortly he was asnorin'.

Then Death's granny begun to talk low to Maude Applegate, questionin' her all about herself, and where she come from, and why she come. So Maude tole her all about how Billy-be-damn Bangtry, her own true love, lay adyin' of a bullet in his belly, so what could she do but take out after Mister Death to beg him to stay his hand? When Death's granny had heard the whole story, she fetched a great sigh.

"Well," she said, "it's a great pity to me you got your heart set, for you're like the girl I once was, and if I had my way, you're the girl I'd choose for my grandson to marry, for I'm ole and tired and would like to see him settled before I go to my rest. You're young, and you're purty, and you don't stand for no sass, and if my ole eyes don't deceive me, you can do a bit of witchin' too. Now ain't that true?"

"Well," Maude answered her modestly, "jest a little of the plain."

"Like what now?" said Death's granny. "White or black?"

"Little o' both," said Maude. "Witched my little brother into passin' his arithmetic, and I also witched the preacher's wife so she tripped on her shoestring and fell in the horse trough."

Once more Death's granny fetched a sigh. "That's a good start for a young'un," said she. "Don't look to me like a girl like you ought to waste herself on no drunken gamblin' cowhand gets hisself shot up in some fool card game. Howsomever, if you got your heart set, I'll help you. Whenever Death catnaps this way, he shortly begins to talk in his sleep, and when he talks, he'll answer three questions truly, and then wake up. What shall I ask him for you?"

"Ask him," said Maude right away, "what is his price to let off Billy-be-damn Bangtry."

"That's one," said Death's granny. "You got three questions. What else?"

At this, Maude had to think, and presently she said, "Ask him why he took my baby sister from her cradle."

"Very well, chile," said Granny. "And one more."

Then Maude Applegate bent her red head near to the red fire and was still, but at last she said, kinda low and slow, "Ask him what he does when he's lonesome."

To this, Death's granny answered nothing at all, and so they set in quiet until shortly Death begun to mumble in his sleep. Then his granny took aholt of a lock of his coal-black hair and tweaked it, gentle-like.

"Yes?" Death said, but without wakin' up. "Yes?"

"Tell me, son," Death's granny said, bendin' over his ear. "What will you take to let off Billy-be-damn Bangtry?"

At this, Death twitched and turned in his sleep. "Oh, granny," he said, "she's such a pretty girl! If it was some, I'd make it an eye. An' if it was others, I'd make it ten years o' life. But for her, I'll make it that she must ride with me two times around the world and give me a kiss on the lips."

At this, Maude drawed a great deep breath and leaned back in her chair.

"Well, son," said granny, "here's another question she asks of you. Why did you take her baby sister from the cradle?"

Then Death twisted and turned in his sleep again. "She was sick," he said. "She was full of pain. I took her so she need never cry no more."

At this, Maude bowed her head and hid her cheek in her hand.

"Well, son," said Death's granny, "an' here's the last. What is it you do when you're lonesome?"

At this, Death give a regular heave and a great groan, and turned his face from the light of the fire. For a long time he whispered and mumbled, and finally he said real low, "I peep through the windows at how the human bein's sleep in each other's arms."

And with this last, he woke up with a jerk, give a mighty yawn, sayin', "My stars, I must of dropped off!"

Now Mister Death and his granny was cheerful folks in spite o' his profession, and that evenin' they gave Maude Applegate such a high ole time that she was almost glad she come. Death's granny, she tole some mighty edifyin' stories about her young days, and furthermore, she got out a jug of her blackberry wine, and Death, he played such merry tunes on his fiddle that Maude Applegate got right out of her chair, picked up her skirts and danced. It was late that night when Death's granny showed Maude to the little trundle bed all made up fresh beside her own four-poster.

In the mornin', Death's granny had Maude's own dress all mended and pressed for her, and a fine breakfast of coffee and ham and grits to stay their stomachs for their long trip, and when Mister Death brought round his pale stallion, all saddled and bridled to go, the tears was standin' in his granny's eyes as she kissed Maude Applegate good-by.

"Good-by," Maude said. "I thank you for your fine hospitality, and if it wasn't for Billy-be-damn Bangtry, my own true love, I'd be right sorry to go."

Mister Death, he lifted Maude up to his big stallion and leaped astride; then away they rode, right up the snowy mountaintop into the sky, and Maude Applegate was surprised to find herself warm and comfortable, ridin' pillion with her arms wrapped around Mister Death's waist.

Then didn't they have a ride! Mister Death, he rode his pale stallion up the mountains of the storm to the pastures of the sky, where the little clouds was grazin' beside their big fat white mammies, and the big black daddy clouds kept watch around the edge. And he rode right up in the fields where the stars grow, and let Maude Applegate pluck a few to wear in her red hair. He rode past the moon, and when Maude Applegate reached out and touched it, it was cold as snow, and slippery too. They couldn't go too near the sun, Mister Death said, lest they might get burned.

But Mister Death, he had his business to tend to, so pretty soon they set out across the wide ocean on their way to twice around the world. Mister Death, he wrapped Maude in his cloak of invisibility, and he took her to all sorts of houses in all sorts of climes—houses where Chinee folks lived, and Rooshian, and Japanee, and African, and folks that never spoke a word of English since the day they was born. He showed her castles and dirty little huts the like of which she never seen in all the state of Texas; he showed her kings and princes and poor folks and all, and maybe she didn't just open her eyes! But in one respect she noticed they was all alike: when Mister Death come, the living couldn't see him, and wept and wailed, but the folks that was dyin' rose up to greet him, and smiled at him on their way, like they knew him for a friend. She was right glad to see that everybody didn't take him for such a bad fellow after all. While they rode, Mister Death, he tole Maude Applegate many a pretty tale about his far travels, and it was plain to see he was a man knew more'n likker and women and ridin' herd.

And when they was on their last lap around and on their way home, Mister Death, he rode out over the ocean and showed Maude Applegate where the whales played—she saw 'em just as plain, aplowin' through the clear green water like a herd of buffalo on a grassy plain. And he rode over the North Pole, for her to see the polar bears, which was all white but for their noses, and he showed her the crocodiles of Egypt driftin' down the Nile, and the tigers of India, too, and every strange creature with his mate. And at last Maude Applegate couldn't help feeling sorry for Mister Death, that he was the only one who had to be alone in all the whole wide world.

But at last they was lopin' back over the plain toward our town; they seen the smoke arisin' from the stovepipes and chimleys into the pale blue sky; they rode right down the main street past Tarbell's Emporium, past the Wells Fargo office, and reined up before the Blue Bird Saloon.

"Why, what you pullin' up here for?" Maude Applegate asked of Mister Death, feelin' surprised, but Mister Death only answered, "Ne'mind; you'll see," and swung down out of the saddle.

Then he reached up and lifted Maude down from off his pale stallion, and he wrapped her once more in his cloak of invisibility, and he said to her, "Now fer the rest of the bargain."

So Maude stood there with her eyes shut, kinda stiff, and steelin' herself for his kiss, but nothin' happened at all, so she opened 'em again, and Mister Death said to her, "No, Maude, the bargain was that you was to kiss me."

So Maude, she was obliged to ask Mister Death to lean down his head, which he did, and she was obliged to reach up and put her mouth on his. Now maybe she thought it would be cold, and maybe she thought it would be fearful to kiss Mister Death—I don't know, I'm sure—but it surely come as a great surprise to her when she found her two arms around his neck without her knowin' how they got there, and her own two lips on his, and the truth of the matter is, it was Mister Death stepped away the first, and tole her, soft and low, "Run along now, Maude. Billy-be-damn Bangtry, your own true love, is settin' right in there in the Blue Bird Saloon."

Then Mister Death unwrapped her from his cloak of invisibility, so's she couldn't see him no more—only hear his spurs jinglin' as he walked away—and Maude Applegate was left standin' by herself before the Blue Bird Saloon, where, inside the window, she could see Billy-be-damn Bangtry, her own true love, settin' at a table drinkin' whisky with a bunch of fly young women of a kind doesn't mind settin' in saloons. Oh, then Maude Applegate's bosom was so full of a thousand feelin's she thought she would bust, and she didn't know whether what she wanted most was to wrench up the hitchin' rail, bust into the Blue Bird Saloon and lambaste her own true love, or whether she'd simply like to melt of shame and sink through the ground. Then she noticed that her daddy's pinto, all groomed and saddled, was tied up by the Blue Bird door. She was jest about decided to mount him and gallop off home before anybody seen her, when Billy-be-damn Bangtry caught a sight of her through the window, and come pushin' out the swingin' doors, swaggerin' and hitchin' his pants like he'd never been half dead in his life.

"Why," he sings out, "if it ain't little Maude Applegate waitin' for me outside the Blue Bird Saloon! Where you been, honey? Heared you was away."

Maude Applegate, she felt the red comin' up in her face. She snapped back at him, "Heared you was mighty sick."

"Mighty sick," Billy said, shakin' his head. "Mighty sick and like to die, but ole Injun Mary, she doctored me good as new with her poultices and herbs!"

Now this was the last straw to Maude Applegate. She'd rode high and she'd rode low; she'd rode through cow country to sheep country; through sheep country to Injun country; through Injun country to the far mountains, all to stay the hand of Mister Death from takin' Billy-be-damn Bangtry, her own true love; she'd rode twice around the world and back and give a kiss on the lips to a strange man, and all to save a feller which turned out to be this horse-smellin', whisky-breathin', tobaccer-chewin', loose-livin', gamblin', no-good cow hand standin' here lookin' at her like she was a ripe peach an' all he had to do was shake the tree. Maude Applegate was so mad she could of cried, but she didn't do no such of a thing, since she was a redheaded woman, and besides, somethin' better come to her mind.

Just then she seen ole Pap Tarbell lean outen the upstairs winder of Tarbell's Emporium, and Maude, she took and witched a spell. When Pap let fly with his tobaccer juice, Maude, she witched it straight into Billy-be-damn Bangtry's eye. And while he was still standin' there acursin' and aswearin' in such language as no lady cares to hear, Maude unhitched her daddy's little pinto pony and leaped astride. She dug in her heels and set the dust aflyin' as she galloped down the street out of town. She rode through cow country into sheep country, through sheep country into Injun country, through Injun country to the far mountains, until she caught sight of Mister Death on his pale stallion.

Then she sung out, "Oh, wait up, Mister Death! Wait up for me!"

And when Mister Death heard her he turned and rode back down the trail—though he is one who turns back for no man—and he snatched her off her little pinto and onto his pale stallion, he held her close and he kissed her good and pretty soon he said, "I guess granny'll be mighty proud to see you."

And Maude Applegate said to him, "Jest don't let me hear no talk about peepin' through folks' windows never no more."

Now Maude Applegate she lived long and happy with Mister Death, and from all I hear, she's with him yet. Fact is, she took to helpin' him with his work, and when we was little uns, and cross at bedtime, and startin' to cry, our mammies'd tell us, "Hush, now, honey, close your eyes, and pretty soon Maude Applegate'll sit by your bed and sing you a lullaby."

And she used to too. Heard her myself.

The Coming of Pan

BY JAMES STEPHENS

Dublin-born James Stephens was a self-educated poet, fiction writer, and radio lecturer. His 1912 work, *The Crock of Gold,* combined a love of Irish folklore with his own brand of sly humor, and spread his reputation as a writer throughout Europe and North America. This short story reveals the effect on a beautiful young woman of the unexpected appearance of a displaced Greek deity in her father's fields. Both sexual awakening and youthful curiosity draw the heroine from her familiar pastures into the realm of otherworldly love.

★ ★ ★ ★ ★

Meehawl MacMurrachu had good reason to be perplexed. He was the father of one child only, and she was the most beautiful girl in the whole world. The pity of it was that no one at all knew she was beautiful, and she did not even know it herself. At times when she bathed in the eddy of a mountain stream and saw her reflection looking up from the placid water she thought that she looked very nice, and then a great sadness would come upon her, for what is the use of looking nice if there is nobody to see one's beauty? Beauty, also, is usefulness. The arts as well as the crafts, the graces equally with the utilities must stand up in the market place and be judged by the gombeen men.

The only house near to her father's was that occupied by Bessie Hannigan. The other few houses were scattered widely with long, quiet miles of hill and bog between them, so that she had hardly seen more than a couple of men beside her father since she was born. She helped her father and mother in all the small businesses of their house, and every day also she drove their three cows and two goats to pasture on the mountain slopes. Here through the sunny days the years had passed in a slow, warm thoughtlessness wherein, without thinking, many thoughts had entered into her mind and many pictures hung for a moment like birds in the thin air. At first, and for a long time, she had been happy enough; there were many things in which a child might be interested: the spacious heavens which never wore the same beauty on any day; the innumerable little creatures living among the grasses or in the heather; the steep swing of a bird down from the mountain to the infinite plains below; the little flowers which were so contented each in its peaceful place; the bees gathering food for their houses, and the stout beetles who are always losing their way in the dusk. These things, and many others, interested her. The three cows after they had grazed for a long time would come and lie by her side and look at her as they chewed their cud and the goats would prance from the bracken to push their heads against her breast because they loved her.

Indeed, everything in her quiet world loved this girl: but very slowly there was growing in her consciousness an unrest, a disquietude to which she had hitherto been a stranger. Sometimes an infinite weariness oppressed her to the earth. A thought was born in her mind and it had no name. It was growing and could not be expressed. She had no words wherewith to meet it, to exorcise or greet this stranger who, more and more insistently and pleadingly, tapped upon her doors and begged to be spoken to, admitted and caressed and nourished. A thought is a real thing and words are only its raiment, but a thought is as shy as a virgin; unless it is fittingly appareled we may not look on its shadowy nakedness: it will fly from us and only return again in the darkness crying in a thin, childish voice which we may not comprehend until, with aching mind, listening and divining, we at last fashion for it those symbols which are its protection and its banner. So she could not understand the touch that came to her from afar and yet how intimately, the whisper so aloof and yet so thrillingly personal. The standard of either language or experience was not hers; she could listen but not think, she could feel but not know, her eyes looked forward and did not see, her hands groped in the sunlight and felt nothing. It was like the edge of a little wind which stirred her tresses but could not lift them, or the first white peep of the dawn which is neither light nor darkness. But she listened, not with her ears, but with her blood. The fingers of her soul stretched out to clasp a stranger's hand, and her disquietude was quickened through with an eagerness which was neither physical nor mental, for neither her body nor her mind was definitely interested. Some dim region between these grew alarmed and watched and waited and did not sleep or grow weary at all.

One morning she lay among the long, warm grasses. She watched a bird who soared and sang for a little time, and then it sped swiftly away down the steep air and out of sight in the blue distance. Even when it was gone the song seemed to ring in her ears. It seemed to linger with her as a faint, sweet echo, coming fitfully, with little pauses as though a wind disturbed it, and careless, distant eddies. After a few moments she knew it was not a bird. No bird's song had that consecutive melody, for their themes are as careless as their wings. She sat up and looked about her, but there was nothing in sight: the mountains sloped gently above her and away to the clear sky; around her the scattered clumps of heather were drowsing in the sunlight; far below she could see her father's house, a little, gray patch near some trees—and then the music stopped and left her wondering.

She could not find her goats anywhere, although for a long time she searched. They came to her at last of their own accord from behind a fold in the hills and they were more wildly excited than she had ever seen them before. Even the cows forsook their solemnity and broke into awkward gambols around her. As she walked home that evening a strange elation taught her feet to dance. Hither and thither she flitted in front of the beasts and behind them. Her feet tripped to a wayward measure. There was a tune in her ears and she danced to it, throwing her arms out and above her head and swaying and bending as she went. The full freedom of her body was hers now: the lightness and poise and certainty of her limbs delighted her, and the strength that did not tire delighted her also. The evening was full of peace and quietude, the mellow, dusky sunlight made a path for her feet, and everywhere through the wide fields birds were flashing and singing, and she sang with them a song that had no words and wanted none.

The following day she heard the music again, faint and thin, wonderfully sweet and as wild as the song of a bird, but it was a melody which no bird would adhere to. A theme was repeated again and again. In the middle of trills, grace notes, runs and catches it recurred with a strange, almost holy, solemnity. A hushing, slender melody full of austerity and aloofness. There was something in it to set her heart beating. She yearned to it with her ears and her lips. Was it joy, menace, carelessness? She did not know, but this she did know, that however terrible it was personal to her. It was her unborn thought strangely audible and felt rather than understood.

On that day she did not see anybody either. She drove her charges home in the evening listlessly and the beasts also were very quiet.

When the music came again she made no effort to discover where it came from. She only listened, and when the tune was ended she saw a figure rise from the fold of a little hill. The sunlight was gleaming from his arms and shoulders, but the rest of his body was hidden by the bracken, and he did not look at her as he went away playing softly on a double pipe.

The next day he did look at her. He stood waist-deep in greenery fronting her squarely. She had never seen so strange a face before. Her eyes almost died on him as she gazed, and he returned her look for a long minute with an intent, expressionless regard. His hair was a cluster of brown curls, his nose was little and straight, and his wide mouth drooped sadly at the corners. His eyes were wide and most mournful and his forehead was very broad and white. His sad eyes and mouth almost made her weep.

When he turned away he smiled at her, and it was as though the sun had shone suddenly in a dark place banishing all sadness and gloom. Then he went mincingly away. As he went he lifted the slender double reed to his lips and blew a few careless notes.

The next day he fronted her as before, looking down to her eyes from a short distance. He played for only a few moments, and fitfully, and then he came to her. When he left the bracken the girl suddenly clapped her hands against her eyes affrighted. There was something different, terrible about him. The upper part of his body was beautiful, but the lower part. . . . She dared not look at him again. She would have risen and fled away, but she feared he might pursue her, and the thought of such a chase and the inevitable capture froze her blood. The thought of anything behind us is always terrible. The sound of pursuing feet is worse than the murder from which we fly.—So she sat still and waited, but nothing happened. At last, desperately, she dropped her hands. He was sitting on the ground a few paces from her. He was not looking at her, but far away sidewards across the spreading hill. His legs were crossed; they were shaggy and hoofed like the legs of a goat: but she would not look at these because of his wonderful, sad, grotesque face. Gaiety is good to look upon and an innocent face is delightful to our souls, but no woman can resist sadness or weakness, and ugliness she dare not resist. Her nature leaps to be the comforter. It is her reason. It exalts her to an ecstasy wherein nothing but the sacrifice of herself has any proportion. Men are not fathers by instinct but by chance, but women are mothers beyond thought, beyond instinct which is the father of thought. Motherliness, pity, self-sacrifice—these are the charges of her primal cell, and not even the discovery that men are comedians, liars, and egotists will wean her from this. As she looked at the pathos of his face she repudiated the hideousness of his body. The beast which is in all men is glossed by women; it is his childishness, the destructive energy inseparable from youth and high spirits, and it is always forgiven by women, often forgotten, sometimes, and not rarely, cherished and fostered.

After a few moments of this silence he placed the reed to his lips and played a plaintive little air, and then he spoke to her in a strange voice, coming like a wind from distant places.

"What is your name, shepherd girl?" said he.

"Caitilin, Ingin Ni Murrachu," she whispered.

"Daughter of Murrachu," said he, "I have come from a far place where there are high hills. The men and maidens who follow their flocks in that place know me and love me, for I am the Master of the Shepherds. They sing and dance and are glad when I come to them in the sunlight; but in this country no people have done any reverence to me. The shepherds fly away when they hear my pipes in the pastures; the maidens scream in fear when I dance to them in the meadows. I am very lonely in this strange country. You also, although you danced to the music of my pipes, have covered your face against me and made no reverence."

"I will do whatever you say if it is right," said she.

"You must not do anything because it is right, but because it is your wish. Right is a word and Wrong is a word, but the sun shines in the morning and the dew falls in the dusk without thinking of these words which have no meaning. The bee flies to the flower and the seed goes abroad and is happy. Is that right, shepherd girl?—it is wrong also. I come to you because the bee goes to the flower—it is wrong! If I did not come to you to whom would I go? There is no right and no wrong, but only the will of the gods."

"I am afraid of you," said the girl.

"You fear me because my legs are shaggy like the legs of a goat. Look at them well, O Maiden, and know that they are indeed the legs of a beast and then you will not be afraid any more. Do you not love beasts? Surely you should love them for they yearn to you humbly or fiercely, craving your hand upon their heads as I do. If I were not fashioned thus I would not come to you because I would not need you. Man is a god and a brute. He aspires to the stars with his head, but his feet are contented in the grasses of the field, and when he forsakes the brute upon which he stands then there will be no more men and no more women and the immortal gods will blow this world away like smoke."

"I don't know what you want me to do," said the girl.

"I want you to want me. I want you to forget right and wrong; to be as happy as the beasts, as careless as the flowers and the birds. To live to the depths of your nature as well as to the heights. Truly there are stars in the heights and they will be a garland for your forehead. But the depths are equal to the heights. Wondrous deep are the depths, very fertile is the lowest deep. There are stars there also, brighter than the stars on high. The name of the heights is Wisdom and the name of the depths is Love. How shall they come together and be fruitful if you do not plunge deeply and fearlessly? Wisdom is the spirit and the wings of the spirit, Love is the shaggy beast that goes down. Gallantly he dives, below thought, beyond Wisdom, to rise again as high above these as he had first descended. Wisdom is righteous and clean, but Love is unclean and holy. I sing of the beast and the descent: the great unclean purging itself in fire: the thought that is not born in the measure or the ice or the head, but in the feet and the hot blood and the pulse of fury. The Crown of Life is not lodged in the sun: the wise gods have buried it deeply where the thoughtful will not find it, nor the good: but the Gay Ones, the Adventurous Ones, the Careless Plungers, they will bring it to the wise and astonish them. All things are seen in the light—How shall we value that which is easy to see? But the precious things which are hidden, they will be more precious for our search: they will be beautiful with our sorrow: they will be noble because of our desire for them. Come away with me, shepherd girl, through the fields and we will be careless and happy, and we will leave thought to find us when it can, for that is the duty of thought and it is more anxious to discover us than we are to be found."

So Caitilin Ni Murrachu arose and went with him through the fields, and she did not go with him because of love, nor because his words had been understood by her, but only because he was naked and unashamed.

The Sudden Wings

T H O M A S   B U R N E T T   S W A N N

Fantasy author Thomas Burnett Swann wrote compellingly of an ancient world peopled with Minotaurs, Minikins, and other creatures of the distant fabled past. A number of his short stories, such as "Where Is the Bird of Fire" and "The Manor of Roses," were nominated for Hugo Awards. In this tale, a brother and sister journeying to Petra, the towering city carved into a sandstone mountain, meet up with Eros, the Roman god of love. Equally intrigued by the siblings, the young god gives them a gift that is synonymous with our modern interpretation of romantic love: the ability to soar.

★   ★   ★   ★   ★

DRAGONFLY

'Gaius and Phoebe!' Mark called, pointing towards the coast of Greece. Above their heads a scarlet sail groaned in the wind and hurried them south toward Rhodes, Cyprus, and Gaza on their way to Petra, the rock-built capital of the Nabataeans. The voyage was long, the coastline dull, and Mark had spent the morning asleep in the sun or playing a lyre to his sister Phoebe, while their uncle, Gaius, chatted with the sailors about the respective merits of Roman and Asiatic women. Towards noon Mark had laid aside the lyre and strolled to the side of the ship in time to see a remarkable sight.

'Look,' he called, his red, wind-blown hair a riot of curls. A short blue tunic outlined the young manliness of his body.

Phoebe came at once, but Gaius took his time, and Mark heard him call to his companions, 'But Etruscan women—they are the deep ones. Their slanted eyes hold secrets older than Babylon.' Casually he walked to Mark's side.

'You look as if you had seen a god,' he said, his lean tanned face seeming to say. 'What you have to show me had better be good.' Slender and straight as a battering ram, with eyes like onyx, he seemed more brother than uncle. Ten years ago, at the age of twenty, he had taken part with Titus (now emperor) in the sack of Jerusalem, and he always carried himself with martial erectness.

'In a sense I have,' Mark said. On a rocky headland, where the waves beat a mist of spray, a curious creature had paused to watch the vessel.

'A centaur,' cried Mark, an antiquarian at twenty. There was no race, he knew, more ancient than the centaurs, who had roamed the Greek mainland when the Cretans first waded ashore from their ships with purple sails. The centaur drummed a hoof on the rocks and his flanks glittered in the sun. His bearded face looked as old as the rocks, as mottled and brown, but somehow gentle.

'Hellooooo,' Mark called, his voice almost lost in the forward plunge of the ship. Tentatively the centaur raised an arm and returned the greeting. Even as they watched, a woman, nude except for her riotous blue hair, emerged from the cliffs and joined him on the headland.

'His nymph,' Mark whispered. 'The centaurs have no women of their own. She may be an Oread.' She placed her arm around his shoulder and stared after the ship. The whiteness of her body formed an eerie contrast to the blue of her hair. She looked as if she had spent her life in a stream or a tree, avoiding the sun. There was no friendliness in her eyes for the voyagers. Doubtless she remembered the centaurs slain by Greek and Roman warriors. At last she took her lord by the hand and led him away from the sea. They did not look back at the ship.

Mark felt a sharp loneliness as they disappeared; he hated the old cruelties which had made the nymph distrustful and wanted to shout to her: 'Wait, I won't hurt you!' Once as a child he had caught sight of a satyr on the slopes of Vesuvius and felt the same loss when it eluded him. Before Romulus, the entire Mediterranean world had abounded in satyrs and centaurs; Tritons had played in the sea-pools, and even the air, it was said, had throbbed with sudden wings as boys and girls had tumbled through the clouds. But now, thanks to the depredations of man, such creatures were almost extinct. Mark's eyes misted.

'Tears for a centaur,' Gaius reproached him, 'but never for a maiden. Twenty years old and heartfree still. You have set a bad example for your sister. She thinks she must remain single to look after you. And so she follows you into the further corners of the world.' Impulsively he hugged them against his chest; his crisp linen tunic was fragrant with bitter almonds, an essence much prized by Roman gentlemen. 'Children, children. You will find no mates among the rocks and scorpions.'

Mark laughed. 'There are always the Arabs.'

'With camel urine in their hair,' sniffed Phoebe.

Then they noticed that one of the sailors had joined them and was staring where the centaur and nymph had disappeared. The sailor looked perplexed and frightened. His calloused hands tightened on the gunwales.

'The Old Ones,' he muttered. 'It is a bad sign.'

'A bad sign?' asked Mark. 'How could they harm us?'

'Not those. Others.'

'You think we will meet others?'

'Aye, *you* will. At Petra. The Boy with Wings, the Dragonfly. His face is as young as your own, his heart, as old as evil. I have never seen him myself—never been beyond Gaza, nor want to go.'

Mark's interest mounted. A boy with wings, a creature more fabulous than centaurs. 'You make him sound dangerous.'

'The natives think so. They have offered a hundred camels to anyone who captures him.'

'Is he dangerous to Romans?'

'That I can't say. To your sister, I should think. She will draw him down like honey on idols. And you—your hair is the very colour of his wings. He may grow jealous.' He reached out and gripped Mark by the shoulder. 'Beware of him, boy. Beware of him! They say—'

'Decimus,' came an angry cry from the stern, 'man the rudder oar!' The sailor broke off and hurried to his post.

Phoebe's eyes were round as honey cakes.

Mark took her hand. 'Frightened?' At nineteen she made him think of kittens and lambs and baby dolphins, of eiderdown and pink rose buds, of all things soft, vulnerable, and delicious. But she was more than soft and girlish; she was adolescence becoming womanhood. Even a voluminous stola could not conceal the delectable undulations of her body. A ripe fig, the young men of Rome had said, hoping in vain to pluck her.

She shivered and squeezed his hand. 'Not with you.'

Gaius laughed. 'You are babies, both of you. As pink and smooth as children, and as inexperienced. Look at Mark. Not the shadow of a beard! What does he know of Dragonflies or of cities in the desert, where the tribesmen sacrifice boys to the god Dusares? You ought to have married Romans, both of you, and stayed at home.'

'What is there left in Rome,' Mark wanted to know, 'with you away?' What was left in Italy, for that matter? Two years ago there had been a villa in Pompeii, devoted parents and friends beloved since childhood. Then came the rain of fire, the shaken earth, the frantic flight to the sea with Phoebe and the cat he had rescued from the burning temple of Venus, and finally escape in a fishing bark. They had sailed to Rome to live with their uncle Gaius. When the new emperor Titus, his general in the attack on Jerusalem, had sent him as unofficial emissary to prepare for a possible Roman occupation of Petra, they had asked to go with him.

Gaius returned to his conversation with the sailors and Mark and Phoebe strolled together around the deck of the ship. Mark looked at her with adoration. Her jonquil-yellow hair, curled on top, was drawn into a fillet behind her head. The fullness of her lips in another woman would have seemed a pout; in Phoebe it was girlhood grown voluptuous, and her blue enormous eyes were those of a maiden who, a little shocked by the licentiousness of Rome, had chosen to observe with wonder rather than participate.

Venus Cat, large, yellow, and, since Pompeii, almost tailless, trotted between them. Discriminating, he ignored most humans, but brother and sister he followed with a doglike constancy.

They paused beneath a bronze image of Portumnus, the harbour god for whom the ship was named.

'I should have married you to one of my friends in Rome,' Mark said mischievously, knowing that the subject annoyed her. 'That would have satisfied Gaius.'

'To a dandy in a silken toga, with myrrh in his curls? Who divides his time between the games and the baths? You would have done better to marry my friend, Cornelia.'

'A sweet thing, Cornelia. Her eyes reminded me of a ewe's. I always expected her to bleat.'

'You see,' she said, 'we both think up reasons not to marry.' It was not uncommon for maidens to wed at twelve and boys at fourteen; Mark and Phoebe, then, had long been marriageable.

Venus Cat mewed peremptorily, a signal for attention. He placed his shoulders on the deck and lifted his stub of a tail to indicate that he wished to be stroked where the tail joined the body.

'But are we enough, the three of us and Venus Cat? We have shut out so much since Pompeii.'

'The more we admit, the more we can lose,' Phoebe said with finality. He knew that she was remembering their villa ignited by lava and their parents trapped in the flames. They had both suffered nightmares for two years. 'We are admitting Petra. Surely that is enough.'

'It is Petrans we need, not Petra.' But he was no more eager than Phoebe to make room in his heart for the hurtful ties of friendship and love.

'There is always the Dragonfly,' she said lightly.

'He sounds unsociable, but I want to see him.' He yawned. 'But we still have a long journey and I am feeling drowsy.'

The wind sighed in the tall square sail and the painted emblem, a shewolf suckling the twins, trembled as if to spring from the canvas. The little ship surged forward at five or more knots. Phoebe remained on deck while Mark retreated to the wicker cabin under the curving neck of the stern. Ensconcing Venus Cat beside him on the couch, he tried to sleep. Usually sleep came soon and, except for nightmares, he slept long and soundly whatever the hour. But a winged boy danced in his brain. He rose, opened a chest of citrus wood, and took a small bronze image in his hand—Vaticanus, god of the Vatican Hill where Gaius owned his villa and where Mark and Phoebe had lived with him for two years; Mark's household god. In the immemorial attitude of prayer, he raised his arms and prayed:

'God of the hill, be with us on our journey, if you can. And the dragonfly boy—may we find him friendly.'

At the entrance to the Sik or ravine leading to Petra stood the Grand Portal, a fifty foot decorative arch with statues and niches. Beyond the portal precipitous walls overtowered the Romans and their guides with brown and yellow sandstone and made a twilight of morning. A paved road ran beside a dry river bed. Glens broke away to the side, brimming with olive and fig trees. His mouth was dry and dusty, and Mark would have paused to pick some figs, but the Arab guides, reeking with sweat and the camel urine with which they oiled their hair, hurried him forward and furtively peered at the sky. Even Venus Cat was shooed from the alluring byways which plunged among the vegetation. The Arabs seemed little acquainted with cats and avoided him as if he were a scorpion, but they did not hesitate, when he turned aside, to drive him into the path.

'They expect the Dragonfly,' Gaius whispered. 'They are speaking Aramaic, which I learned at the siege of Jerusalem. One of them said they must sacrifice to Dusares, because the Dragonfly has been seen in the area lately.'

'What will they sacrifice?' Phoebe whispered.

'A boy, most likely. With unblemished skin and the rosy innocence of youth.'

Phoebe looked horrified and tugged at Mark's tunic. 'Gaius, you are describing Mark.'

Gaius laughed. 'A Roman citizen should be safe enough. The Nabataean king, Rabel II, is said to be eager to conciliate the Romans—

even to consolidate with them. That, of course, is why I am here. He is still very young—younger that Mark—and thought to be weary of his mother's domination.'

A shadow broke the ribbon of sunlight at their feet. They looked up. A bird-like creature wheeled above their heads.

The Arabs stopped and peered at the sky. They spoke rapidly. Diaphanous wings glinted in the sunlight. Mark stood very still; his heart-beat quickened. The Dragonfly sank into the gorge. His features materialized in the fitful light: firm but slender limbs, hair as red as Mark's but wild with a hundred winds, and—half again as tall as the body—pointed wings which opened and closed with the slow, deliberate strokes of anemones under the sea. He descended in lilting curves, like milk weed settling in a breeze. The Arabs had fled to the empty river bed, where they crouched among the boulders and hurled stones at the invader. He began to laugh, a deep laugh, musical yet chilling, that echoed down the gorge and set bulbuls springing from olive trees. Now he was almost within reach of the stones. He poised just above them, beating his wings to hold his position.

Mark waved his arms in a frantic warning. 'Go back,' he shouted. 'They will hurt you!' He imagined the delicate wings broken by rocks, the creature falling into the hands of the natives who would sacrifice him in their ghastly rituals. 'Go back!'

The Dragonfly laughed. He caught a rising stone and dropped it on his attackers. The Arabs who were bombarding him scrambled for cover. He looked at Mark and Phoebe and waved his hand.

'Red Hair and Yellow Hair,' he called. 'You with your golden cat. Welcome—and be my friends.' He fanned them with the rush of wings, and Mark looked directly into his face—high slender cheekbones, eyes as green and unfathomable as the sea beyond the Pillars of Hercules. A young face, a boy's face, but with eyes is old as—what had the sailor said?—evil. They stared after him as he beat his way up the gorge and vanished over the edge.

The Arabs emerged from the watercourse and resumed their journey. With every few steps they peered anxiously at the sky, muttered to each other, and glared at Mark as if he had summoned the creature with Roman magic.

Mark, Phoebe, and Gaius walked in silence, peering hopefully at the top of the gorge, now three hundred feet above their path. Even Gaius, the practical warrior, seemed shaken by the encounter. It was Phoebe who finally spoke.

'He was beautiful,' she said. 'Like a king. Like a—'

'God whose image we saw in Rome,' interrupted Mark.

'I am trying to think which one. But he looks so lonely. The Arabs hate him. Who can he find for a friend?'

'The birds,' said Phoebe. 'Would you be lonely with wings?'

'I would want my sister and uncle to have them too. Vultures make poor company. I should think the extent of their conversation would be directions for finding the latest carcass.'

'I suppose you are right. *We* shall have to become his friends.'

'You will do nothing of the kind,' snapped Gaius. 'For all we know he is deadly—not a boy at all, but a demon with a boy's face. Like the sirens who sang to Ulysses.'

They looked at him in surprise.

'Listen to me, my innocents. We will learn more about him in Petra. The Arabs may have good reason for fearing him.'

The gorge flared suddenly into a glen where, directly in their path, a temple loomed from the living rock, its red façade rising in columns, pediments, and, on the second level a rounded tower. The side walls were the unhewn rock itself. It was like a great poppy, flowering from the desert by some divine horticulture, a poppy on the scale of the giant hero Moses who, in local legend, was said to have channelled the Sik with a blow of his magic rod.

'It must be the Khazneh,' Gaius said. 'The Arabs call it the Treasury of Pharaoh, but it is really a temple to Isis.'

An image of the goddess stood in the open tower and smiled benignantly down on the petty humans who sought entrance to her valley. The Arabs greeted her with salaams and cries of praise. But Mark suspected that it was not Isis who controlled the valley.

'It might be called the temple of the Dragonfly,' he whispered to Phoebe.

She squeezed his hand. 'We will find him again?'

'Tomorrow,' said Mark. But a vague uneasiness gripped him. Her enthusiasm seemed excessive. What was she feeling? He had often encouraged her to fall in love. But a boy with wings—

He chided himself. Phoebe in love? Ridiculous. She was only curious like himself. Tomorrow they would satisfy their curiosity and the matter would end. Suddenly he remembered the god who had looked like the Dragonfly. His image stood in the Forum—Mors, the lord of death.

MOON-GIRL

Mark and Gaius had gone to a banquet in the palace, but Phoebe, a woman and therefore uninvited, remained in the house reserved for them by the king—an extraordinary house cut into the side of a mountain. Room after room plunged into the dark rock, the walls hung with tapestries which smouldered in the light of tall candelabra. But the rock-hewn walls were cold and damp in spite of the hangings, and Phoebe, bathed and scented by an Arab slave girl, had stretched on a couch and drawn a coverlet around her shoulders. A lamp was left burning, a crouching lion which seemed to spit fire from its jaws. She had hated the dark since Pompeii; besides, there were scorpions in Petra.

She fell asleep at once, with Venus Cat beside her. The old dream returned. It was autumn, and a great fire had broken from the mouth of Vesuvius. Giant shapes seemed to dance in the fire and fling it in streamers down the slopes. A heat wave gripped the city and the parched inhabitants gasped in the shade while stones and ashes possessed the sky. The sun vanished as if eclipsed, the ground shuddered and split—

Phoebe cried out and opened her eyes. The dream was gone but another had taken its place. The Dragonfly leaned above her, his wings as tall as the roof, and said, 'Yellow Hair.'

She sat up.

'I am glad you are finally awake,' he continued, 'I thought I was going to have to shake you. I have been here for a long time.'

It was not a dream; he sat beside her on the couch. She uttered a little cry and he looked at her with wide, serious eyes.

'Have you been on my couch all the time?' she asked.

He pointed to a chair with a curving back. 'The cathedra was hard. There was no room for my wings. Besides, I have been watching you sleep.'

The coverlet had fallen to the floor. She was wearing a lavender tunic, less than knee length, with a silken sash. A highly indecorous garment for any pursuit except sleeping. She drew a pillow over her knees.

'I have been watching the rise and fall of your bosom,' he continued without a smile. 'It is a pretty thing to watch—up and down, up and down, like a little swelling sea. It has made me want to kiss you.'

Phoebe stiffened and took Venus Cat in her arms. 'I must call my brother. He wanted to see you again.'

'He has not returned. I have already looked for him.' He reached up and touched her hair which, free of its fillet, had spilled in a saffron chaos over the couch.

'Yellow Hair,' he said. 'A pretty name. But you must have another.'

'Phoebe.' I am alone with the Dragonfly, she thought. I am dressed for sleeping, not company, and he has said that he wishes to kiss me. If I cry out, a slave will come at once. But wonder wrestled with fear, and she did not call. It was like those assignations her friends had told her about in Rome, when a young man came to their bedchambers, evading the watchful eye of parents and slaves, and made indelicate advances, which might or might not be encouraged. I will talk to him and learn his intentions, she told herself. Then perhaps I shall scream for a slave.

'Phoebe, the Moon,' he said. 'Not silver nor white, but a harvest moon, round and warm and golden. My name is Eros.'

'Eros. Love?'

'For you. And Red Hair. Tell me about him.'

She spoke quickly. It was always a pleasure to speak of Mark. 'He pretends not to care about things. He sleeps a great deal and laughs easily. He jokes and teases. He will tell you that he possesses no real ability. But he is a fine poet, and a brave and honourable man. When Pompeii was burning he carried me safely to a boat and went back into the city to rescue some children who were trapped in a temple.'

'His hair is red like mine. I want him to be my friend. Will he love me?'

'He wanted to see you again.'

'Will you love me too?'

She hesitated, uncertain how he meant the word. 'I am very fond of you.'

'Will you come with me?'

'Where?'

'To my home in the mountain.'

'Tomorrow, with Mark.'

His eyes darkened. 'You don't love me then.'

'It is too soon.'

'Soon? Is love the sum of minutes or days? No, it is a pine torch kindled in a second. I saw you in my valley and I loved you instantly.' His face was even younger than Mark's, and his artless, literal speech was that of a child. But his eyes were old. To look into them was to tumble down stairways of malachite with fireflies whirling around her.

He leaned forward and kissed her. She felt the brush of his wings, like butterflies, and wondered how anything so soft and tenuous could lift him from the ground. His breath was as sweet as nard, and she thought of the herbs and flowers he must gather from the mountaintops to season his delicate foods.

'Do you know now if you love me?'

'I am not sure.'

'Have you had many lovers?'

'No,' she said sharply.

'Not even one? A slave perhaps who caught your eye in the marketplace, or a young friend of your brother?'

'Not even one.'

'I have heard that Roman women take husbands at twelve and lovers not later than fifteen. Sometimes I eavesdrop on caravans, and the great Roman ladies, the wives of consuls and governors—bound to join their husbands—do not always sleep alone.'

'I have neither a husband nor a lover, and I am a mature woman of nineteen.'

'Ah,' he said, 'That is why you are not sure if you love me. You have had no practice. I am glad. I will teach you how to love. But first we will talk.'

'Why do you never smile?' she asked him. She too could talk with the directness of a child. She felt as if he were a new playmate and she must get to know him as quickly as possible, without the polite evasions of adult society.

'Because there is nothing to smile about. I guess I have forgotten how.'

'Yet I heard you laugh this morning.'

'With scorn, not joy. Scorn for those dirty Nabataeans who were throwing rocks at me. It is joy I have forgotten.'

'You are lonely,' she said, 'and no wonder. How long have you been in Petra?'

'Before the Edomites, before the Kenites and Horites even, the valley belonged to my people. There were hundreds of us, and we slept in the caves and beat the air with our wings. But the Kenites were thousands, and they drove us to the cliffs and one by one the others died or were killed.'

She touched his wing in a gesture of sympathy and felt it shudder. 'All those centuries you have had no friends?'

'There have been a few,' he said. 'Once there was a Nabataean boy, I taught him to chisel animals out of the rocks—gazelle and jackal and coney with the face of a pig and the hands of a child. But they sacrificed him to Dusares. I found him at the Place of Sacrifice with a knife in his heart. That was a hundred years ago. He was the last.'

'A hundred years without a friend!' She would befriend him, she would love him. Too long she had held herself aloof in her brother's love. But Mark would be the last to begrudge her the Dragonfly. 'I will come to your mountain now, if you like. You must show it to Mark tomorrow.'

'Of course. You have said he will be my friend.' He handed her a cloak. 'Wrap yourself in your palla. The sky is cold.'

Her sandals made no sound on the carpeted floors, and Eros, barefoot, walked as quietly as a lizard. Venus Cat padded after them, puzzled by this tall winged boy who had come in the hush of night. In the vestibule at the entrance, the guard was sleeping, his head on his knees.

'He was easy to put to sleep,' said Eros. 'You ought to be better guarded. Someone might carry you away.'

She did not ask him what power he had used on the guard. It was a night of spells.

White broom flowers, so thick around their feet that neither stems nor leaves were visible, carpeted the roadside and a honied fragrance permeated the air. Phoebe stared at the rock-cut front of the house, a dusky purple in the light of torches which burned between the four entrances and cast the columns into a fitful dancing. Briefly she regretted the loss of this solid mansion, with its slaves and friendly torches and Venus Cat, and fought down an urge to wake the guard. Eros saw her shiver and drew the palla closely around her shoulders.

He lifted her in his arms and sprang into the air. The valley wheeled below them, the tall hills jutting toward the sky, their faces pitted with caves whose entrances were broken with columns and whose accesses were flights of stairs chiselled in the rock. He breathed heavily with his burden. Phoebe dared not question him; she lay like a cast-off cloak in his arms and scarcely dared to open her eyes.

But fear yielded to amazement. His slender, powerful arms assured her that he would not falter. His breath came regularly now. He pointed out hills and buildings. In the heart of the valley, a palace, a temple, a market place with stalls and a covered walkway crouched by a river like animals beside a water course. The temple and palace were elephants, the stalls, zebras, and the walkway, the curving length of a serpent. They crossed the Wady Moussa, the river which divided the town, and circled the rock Al Habi, where a thousand pigeons slept in the honeycombed façade of the Columbarium.

The torchlight of the city dwindled, the fragrance of white broom became the freshness of nearby rains, of closeness to the clouds, and Phoebe's heart expanded with the wonder of her flight. The stars burned as brightly as the torches they had left in the city. Were they going to the moon, that fretted amber palace? A fitting home for the Dragonfly. What were his wings but starlight materialized, his hair, a tangle of moonbeams?

Behind them the fires of the city blinked into darkness. Night is a raven, she thought, and his black hushed wings have seized us. But the Dragonfly will defend me—what darkness can shake his flight?

They approached the face of a great cliff, whose craggy expanse seemed to offer no entrance. But soon a small cavern loomed in their path. He settled on a ledge and led her into the blackness which, as they advanced, lessened and opened into a large chamber with lamps like swans. Carpets woven of rushes were strewn on the floor, while the walls held frescos where the birds of the land frolicked in poppies and oleanders—with white breasts and red patches on their tails. A couch stood at the rear, beside it a marble table like a truncated Doric column.

'My house,' he said proudly.

'You painted the walls yourself?'

'Yes, and gathered the furnishings from caravans. Some of them are very old—older than the Romans even.' He showed her a gaming board whose squares of shell were inlaid with lapis-lazuli and red limestone. 'That is from Ur. Once a Chaldean princess passed through this land. I came to her caravan at night and played with her. She would not come back with me, as you have, but she gave me the board. In return I gave her an Egyptian emerald as large as a pigeon's egg.'

She felt the desolation of a life in which his only friends were the travellers of the desert, shadows who paused and passed, leaving him all the lonelier for their momentary presence. She wanted to take him in her arms and be to him more than the Chaldean princess who had left behind her the hard, inadequate comfort of a gaming board.

She shivered. 'The flight has made me ill.'

'It is not the flight,' he said. 'You are afraid of me. Why? Surely I am not a monster. I have looked at myself in the mountain streams and seen a boy like your brother.'

She stared at his skin in the lamplight, reddish like the cliffs of Petra, and wondered if the wind had beaten the red of the rocks into his pores until he became the desert, as beautiful and unknowable. 'Your beauty troubles me,' she said at last.

He helped her to the couch. From a glass flagon he filled an amber goblet and placed it in her hand. 'Drink,' he said. 'It will make you at ease with me.'

She drank the liquid, part wine, part honey, with a curious tartness she did not recognize.

'You understand that I am going to kiss you,' he said. 'But I will wait until you have rested.'

She said nothing. Nausea pressed at her throat. His hair burned with rose and amber, and the light in its tangles made her dizzy.

'I—I am rested,' she said.

He kissed her and cupped her face between his hands. Still he did not smile. 'Phoebe, the moon,' he said. 'But the moon is pale tonight. What shall I do to kindle its yellow fires?'

'You are the moon, not I.'

'No, I am Eros, who calls to the moon. Do you love me, moongirl, Phoebe?'

'Yes.' She did not hedge her words; she did not debate the multiple meanings of love. 'Yes.'

'Come.' He rose and held out his hand to her.

'Eros, must we fly again so soon?'

'The moon must learn how to fly,' he said. 'Was there ever a moon who looked up instead of down? The heavens should be your home.'

Again they stood on the ledge, with the cliff falling sheer below them, black and terrible. Her sandals dislodged a stone; its scraping descent faded into silence.

He let go of her.

'Take my hand,' she cried. 'I am afraid by myself.'

'I am here to give you strength,' he said, and he was smiling for the first time. 'You must do what I say. Do you trust me, moon-girl?'

'Yes.'

He touched her cheek and his strength sustained her. Yes, she could face the night again in his arms. But he did not take her in his arms.

He stepped back and said: 'Jump.'

EROS AND MORS

The banquet was small, intimate, and very Roman. Nine guests—the king, two Nabataean advisers, and six Romans including Gaius and Mark—reclined on couches in a semicircle around a table with feet like a camel's. A suckling pig revolved on a portable spit, and young Arab slaves, as noiseless as jackals, served the dates, cucumbers, melons, cheeses, kids boiled in milk, and locusts on skewers from the kitchen. Conversation soon turned to the benefits of union with Rome. The king and his ministers listened with enthusiasm as Gaius, august in his white toga, enumerated the advantages of the Pax Romana. Petra, said Gaius, harassed by an endless succession of wars, could secure her borders through alliance with Rome, and further, share in the benefits of Latin civilization—the roads, the aqueducts, the arts and games.

'A personable young man, the king,' Gaius said to Mark later in the evening, as they left the palace and headed for their villa. 'If he has his way, Petra will be the next Roman colony.'

'But his mother, Shaquilath, opposes annexation?'

'Bitterly. Till a year ago she ruled as regent, and her power is still formidable. She wishes to preserve the independence of her people at any price. I have not met the woman, but she is said to believe that the only good Roman is one whose bones have been picked by the vultures.'

The square, flat-roofed palace, with its façade of obelisks in half-relief, faded behind them and they entered a garden of scattered paths and summer houses roofed with the boughs of palm trees. A river barred their way, and oleanders rioted along its banks, their deep green leaves black in the moonlight. A frightened coney vanished on soundless hooves. They paused beside a bridge, talking of the banquet, the king, the implacable Shaquilath. Mark grew thirsty.

'Is the river water good?' he asked.

'All the water in Petra is good,' Gaius said. 'That is why so many armies have fought for the place.'

Mark stooped and filled his hands with water. He tasted it gingerly. Yes, it was clear and cold. He began to drink. He heard a footstep but, anticipating Gaius, did not turn his head. An object struck his temple and pain exploded into blackness.

He awoke shivering. He was nude; his feet and hands were bound and the rough thongs cut into his flesh. He seemed to be lying on a stone platform a little longer than himself and approached by shallow steps. The stone was jagged beneath his back. Cymbals clashed and tambourines jangled. Torches lurched in the darkness, as if their bearers were drunk. Figures leaped through the air, and he saw that they were nude like himself, their brown limbs glittering in the light of a moon so bright that it made him blink. They whistled and clapped their hands, but paid him little attention. He remembered the young men sacrificed to Dusares and hoped that he would continue to be ignored.

'You are awake,' said a woman's voice in uncertain Latin.

'It is well. I would talk with you.' She was the tallest woman he had ever seen, a giantess with arms that bulged like a Spartan's beneath her thin silk robe. Everything about her was massive and masculine except her voice, which was strangely soft.

Mark was frightened but he was also angry. 'I am a citizen of Rome,' he cried. 'This very night I have dined with the king. Release me at once.'

A tinkle of laughter greeted his command. 'I know you have dined with my son. My men had you under surveillance the entire evening.'

This, then, was Shaquilath. Surely the queen would not be a party to human sacrifice, however she hated the Romans.

'What do you intend to do with me?'

'Send you to Dusares, what else?'

'The Romans will send *you* an army.'

'Better an army than smooth-tongued ambassadors. The entrance to this valley is almost impregnable. But Roman ambassadors speak with silver tongues and my son listens. Why do you think I chose you for the sacrifice? To end this traitorous talk of annexation by Rome. The Romans will hardly negotiate with a country which has murdered—as they see it—one of their citizens. They will either ignore us or attack us. For either we shall be ready.' She looked at him appraisingly; nude and bound, he felt like a side of beef in the marketplace. 'You are beautiful enough for any god. When beauty is joined to political expediency—' She leaned very close to him. Her breath smelled of wine and olive oil.

'You are little older than my son. A boy like him, stubborn and foolish, but I could have loved you.' She touched his cheek with the fingertips; her bony fingers were surprisingly gentle. 'You are almost too beautiful to give to the god. I wish I could afford the luxury of saving you.'

The dance had become a bacchanalia; indeed, Mark recalled, the Arabs identified Dusares with the Greek Bacchus. Clouds had covered the moon, and the whirling figures, vivid by moonlight, looked now as shadowy and terrible as shades of the Underworld, dancing beside the Styx. He remembered a line which Gaius had read to him from a holy book of the Jews: how King David had 'danced before the Lord with all his might'. But the lord of the Arabs was not the lord of the Jews; this dance held a sinister difference. He breathed a prayer to his household god, Vaticanus:

'God of the Roman hill, be with me on this alien hill!'

The queen bent and kissed him on the cheek. 'Understand it is not that I wish you ill.' She turned and addressed the crowd in Aramaic. The dancing ceased, the dancers watched her with rapt attention, or rather they watched the knife in her upraised hand. Mark shuddered, no longer with cold, and thought of Phoebe. Beloved sister, I must die and leave you in a strange land, with Gaius and Venus Cat your only friends. I will come to you if I can, as a shade, and watch over your sleep and your journeys, but when were the dead a comfort to the living?

He closed his eyes and whispered her name.

The arms which lifted him were quick and firm. He opened his eyes.

'Lie still,' said the Dragonfly, as he sprang from the altar. He dipped towards the ground and struggled above the heads of the astonished watchers before they could gather their wits. With the moon behind clouds, they had missed his approach, but now they cried out in rage and hurled insults in Aramaic whose meaning even Mark could guess.

With his heavy burden, the Dragonfly laboured like a galley in the Straits of Messina. He must surely sink, Mark thought. To increase their danger, the crowd had begun to throw stones, and the Dragonfly must dodge the sharp-edged missiles as well as keep to the air. At last they glided over the rim of the cliff and sank into darkness and safety.

They found shelter on a ledge midway down the side of the cliff and obscured from the Arabs by an overhanging rock; the sounds of their outraged pursuers came to them muffled as if by fathoms of water. The Dragonfly gasped; his strength was gone. But he lost no time in unbinding Mark and massaging his wrists and ankles.

It was hard for Mark to speak. What could he say? The Dragonfly's risk had been enormous. 'They would have killed you if they could.'

'Yes, the god would have gorged himself,' said the Dragonfly. 'Two victims instead of one. Now they will seize some poor Arab boy who came to watch the sacrifice.'

'There was every chance you would be caught. Yet you ran the risk for a stranger.'

'Stranger? We met in the Sik, did we not? I welcomed you. Could I let you die? My name, by the way, is Eros.'

'And mine is Mark.'

'I know.'

'But how did you learn of my danger?'

'I came to look for you in your house, and you had not returned. I had come earlier, and your sister had told me of the banquet. I flew to the palace, which was now dark. I retraced your route and found Gaius unconscious in the garden. When he revived and told me what had happened, I guessed where you were and came to the Place of Sacrifice. He was going to bring soldiers from the king, but I knew it would be too late by the time they had climbed the cliff. I crouched out of sight on this very ledge until the moon went behind a cloud and the people had hypnotized themselves with dancing and words.'

'You say you talked to Phoebe in the villa?'

'And took her to my mountain. She is waiting for you.'

'Can you take me there now?'

'I am not able to lift you so high. Phoebe was lighter.'

'To the villa then?'

'Perhaps. But rest now. It is too soon. We have things to talk about.'

'You have done me a great service,' said Mark, with a depth of feeling rare for him since Pompeii. His heart went out to this bold, miraculous being who had saved his life. He grasped his hand and Eros returned the pressure.

'Yes, I have helped you,' said Eros. 'Therefore I love you the more. But what have you done for me?'

Startled, Mark asked, 'What could I have done?'

'Nothing—yet.'

'Will there be something?'

'Soon. First we must talk. Phoebe loves me. She had hidden her heart in a little silver casket, but I found the key. There are hearts like agate in sunken galleys, and brave is the man who dives to recover them. There are hearts like an eagle's nest, on the tallest windy cliff. Where is your heart, Mark?'

'It is yours in friendship.'

'You do not know what I am going to ask of you.'

'Ask it then.'

'First you must serve me in little ways. See, I am hurt.' He held out his arm and disclosed a wound below the elbow. A flying stone had struck him. He tore a strip from his tunic.

'Bind my wound and thus draw close to me. A man loves where he lessens pain.'

Mark bound the wound, tenderly as if he were binding a child, and loved him. I have found a friend, he thought. In this wild land of rocks and tombs, the heart I lost in Pompeii has stirred, a little, and let me love. Phoebe will love him as I do. We will make him one with us; he will bring us his hurts and his loneliness.

'Have you other wounds?' he asked.

'Yes. They are not of the body.'

'Of the heart then. Loneliness perhaps?'

'Till tonight I was utterly alone. Like an ibex on a dark hill, with wolves in the valley. Half of me hungers still. For the love of a brother for brother, the clasp of hands; the field where comrades battle a common foe. Man's love for a woman has moods like the moon-drawn tide. It ebbs and flows, colours with the hour and the shape of the clouds. Man's love for his brother is constant. The clear hard burning of a diamond. Will you call me brother?'

'Yes, my brother.'

'And trust me?'

'You have saved my life.'

From a pouch hung at his side he drew a small vial. 'Drink,' he said. 'It will make you strong.'

Mark drank. The liquid was sweet with honey and bitter with a herb he did not recognize. It burned his throat and pulsed in his veins like lava.

'Now,' Eros said, 'you must jump from the ledge.'

'Jump?' he cried. 'I would die on the rocks! I have no wings like you.'

'I will give you wings. First you must trust me. Phoebe jumped.'

He looked at the Dragonfly with growing horror. 'From this cliff?'

'A taller one.'

'And—?'

'She fell on the rocks. I came to her and held out my hand and drew her beside me. Her body was whole, because she had trusted me. From her shoulders sprouted wings like my own. She said: "You must find Mark and give him wings."'

'I must see her at once!'

'After you have jumped. You should trust me without proof, as she did.'

Mark shook his head vehemently. 'I want to see her now.'

'I have spoken to you as a friend and brother. Your answer is no?'

'Until I have seen my sister.'

'Mark, Mark, what is love without trust? You have disappointed me. Come, I will take you back to your villa. Then I will send Phoebe to you. But you have lost her. She has chosen to remain with me.'

The Dragonfly rose to his feet and drew Mark beside him on the narrow ledge. 'I have loved you,' he said.

And Mark loved him. Dark, sweet currents flooded the tide pools of his body, those sun-parched pits of broken shell; a swift renewing tide freighted with sea grapes and the purple murex. Did he tell the truth, after all, this creature who seemed too beautiful to lie? This boy with amber in his hair and moonlight in his wings?

But the sirens, beautiful and sweet-tongued, had lured Ulysses. No, Mark dared not trust him.

A shadow sank from the moon. 'Mark, I have found you!'

'Phoebe,' he cried, 'it is true then. He has given you wings.'

'And you,' she said. 'You shall have them too. Trust him.'

'It is too late,' said the Dragonfly sadly.

'It is *not* too late,' Mark cried, and jumped.

He opened his eyes and found them standing above him, their faces anguished. They expected to find me dead, he thought, and truly I am dying. The pain is like a crucifixion, with a hundred nails piercing my body.

Eros knelt. 'Can you take my hand?' he asked doubtfully. Mark strained towards him, wrenching his body into a fury of pain. But the fingers of the Dragonfly eased him and somehow he struggled to his feet.

'Mark,' cried Phoebe. 'Your shoulders—they are sprouting wings!'

Eros examined them, marvelling. 'It will be a long time,' he said, 'before they are grown. You were not yet ready. But you were less unready than I feared.'

'You told me that love was a pine torch,' said Phoebe to Eros, 'kindled in a second. There is another kind, I think. A field set afire by the slow accumulating rays of a summer sun. Sudden wings or slow— either is love.'

Permissions Acknowledgments

Helen Eustis, "Mister Death and the Redheaded Woman" (originally titled "The Rider on the Pale Horse") from *The Saturday Evening Post* (February 11, 1950). Reprinted with the permission of The Curtis Publishing Company.

Thomas Burnett Swann, "The Sudden Wings" from *Science Fantasy* (October 1962). Copyright © 1962 by Thomas Burnett Swann. Reprinted with the permission of the Estate of Margaret Gaines Swann.